The Cas

The Case of Jason Mitchell

Report of the Independent Panel of Inquiry

Louis Blom-Cooper
Adrian Grounds
Pat Guinan
Anne Parker
Michael Taylor

Duckworth

First published in the UK in 1996 by
Gerald Duckworth & Co. Ltd.
The Old Piano Factory
48 Hoxton Square, London N1 6PB

© 1996 by Suffolk Health Authority

A catalogue record for this book
is available from the British Library

ISBN 0 7156 2723 6

Typeset by Ray Davies
Printed in Great Britain by
Redwood Books Ltd, Trowbridge

Contents

Preface

An ounce of foresight is better than a pound of hindsight.
Franklin D. Roosevelt, Speech in 1934,
Public Papers and Addresses

On accepting the invitation from Suffolk Health Authority to inquire into the care and treatment accorded to Jason Mitchell, leading up to the triple killings of December 1994, and in embarking upon the task of conducting the inquiry in accordance with the detailed terms of reference (see Annex 1) we asked ourselves: what is the task of a public inquiry and, in particular, what was our role and function under the guidance from the Department of Health for *Inquiries After Homicide*, contained in NHS Executive Guidance HSG (94)27 of 10 May 1994.

The foremost task of a public inquiry is akin to the role of an historian, namely, to reconstruct events of the past and to understand how and why they happened. Yet, as a reviewer in the *Times Literary Supplement* once observed:

> Writing history is an oddly schizoid activity. It involves imposing upon the past, but also stripping away from it, layers of retrospective interpretation. It aims to reconstruct 'what actually happened', but it goes about this in apparently contradictory ways: by allowing preoccupation with the present to determine what we find relevant from the past, so that history becomes a device for explaining how we got to where we are; but also by rejecting such 'presentism' on grounds that those who made history can hardly have had our concerns uppermost in their minds when they did so. To say that the past affects the present but that the present affects only our perception of the past is to point out an obvious asymmetry. But the corollary principle, that time, so far as we know, flows only in one direction ... has not impressed itself upon historians as one might think. (John Lewis Gaddis, 'A time of confrontation and confusion', *TLS*, 8 May 1987)

Nor, despite the recognition of the seductive appeal of hindsight (to which we allude below), has the principle impinged sufficiently upon those who conduct public inquiries. Accordingly we have addressed some of the problems that intrinsically afflict public inquiries after homicide as envisaged by the NHS Executive Guidance.

While the NHS Executive Guidance is silent on the point, Suffolk Health Authority assumed – as indeed we ourselves did – that our chairman was to chair the panel as *primus inter pares* and was not to act as the sole judge with panel members functioning only in support as advisers. The practice adopted was for the sponsoring authority to identify, in consultation with the chairman-designate, the range of expertise needed and to select suitable persons from the disciplines indicated. Since the prime consideration will always be the quality of care and treatment which the patient was receiving at the time of the homicidal event, it would be inevitable that a psychiatrist (probably of consultant status and perhaps preferably with forensic qualifications) would be appointed. A third member would frequently be drawn from the field of community care services. While a panel of three should be the norm, there will be cases where the issues raised suggest panel members drawn from other disciplines. In our case the issue relating to diagnostic assessment (including psychological testing and behavioural treatment) called for a clinical psychologist with forensic experience. A discrete issue relating to the responsibility of police forces to trace patients absent from hospital without leave indicated additionally the value of police experience. Hence the nature of the composition of our panel of five members.

Our *modus operandi* was for each member to participate fully in every facet of the inquiry process, with the chairman having the additional task only of orchestrating the formal proceedings. All of us collectively identified the issues to be explored and the questions that needed answering. To that end we determined the scope of the documentation and the list of witnesses whom we recognised would need to be heard in addition to their written statements. Each one of us put questions directly to the witness, but only after the witness had been questioned either by his/her own legal representative or by counsel to the Inquiry. We record our unalloyed admiration for, and gratitude to Oliver Thorold who marshalled all our concerns and, with consummate ease, asked, probingly but never hostilely, the questions we had rehearsed with him. He often had his own penetrating line of questions. Our own questioning was thus rendered shorter and more pointed. We add our thanks to those who appeared as advocates. Mr John Taylor, of Hempsons, solicitor for Dr Goddard, and Mr Howard Weston, of Mills &

Reeves, solicitor for the East Suffolk Local Health Services NHS Trust, were extremely helpful in assisting the process of the Inquiry with commendable economy of words. Other lawyers with minor parts likewise helped the Inquiry.

We have all had a hand in drafting the report. We have considered the drafts of the various chapters in plenary sessions, and we have agreed to everything said in the report. Our report is unanimous.

We were acutely aware that not only among practising professionals and medical defence unions, but also in professional circles, there has been for some time now a feeling that public inquiries are doing more harm than good. There is no doubt that whatever usefully comes out of the report of a public inquiry can potentially be outweighed by the adverse effect that inquiries have on those under potential criticism. Often they have to wait anxiously for months to learn about any damage to their professional careers, over and above the unpleasant experience of having to give evidence, perhaps in public. During the plethora of child abuse inquiries in the 1980s the social work profession was forthright in its dislike of public inquiries which often led to its members being pilloried in the media. There is no doubt that those who had been responsible for the care and treatment of a mental health patient, Jason Mitchell, may likewise have found themselves attacked in the press (often even before the Inquiry began its task) feeding off the inquiry processes which are primarily, but not exclusively, focused on individuals' blameworthiness. Too little, if any attention is devoted, it is asserted, to the context in which carers and treaters function. As a result, public inquiries often are focused on blameworthiness and rarely look at issues that go beyond the allotting or allocating of blame and pointing to individual criticism.

There is the constant cry, moreover, that inquiries all too readily slip into the habit of 'hindsight-bias'. The point is justly made that the significance of past events under present scrutiny, when viewed through that unreliable diagnostic instrument, 'the retrospectivescope', is far removed from the hectic, demanding and fleeting moments as they were experienced at work in the psychiatric setting of a hospital. Dr Ray Goddard was right to remind us that clinical work is not like an Inquiry. There is not the time or the resources to get the detail on an individual that our Inquiry had before it. Any hour from the daily pattern of life, moreover, will seem odd if moved across months and studied at a different intensity to the way in which it was actually lived. As the Third Priest comments in T.S. Eliot's *Murder in the Cathedral*:

> ... one moment
> weighs like another. Only in retrospection, selection,
> we say, that was the day. The critical moment.

Our Inquiry has not been fixed upon a single date or a single event; it did not alight on one single moment of time. It isolated a slice of time (or rather discrete slices of time) covering the overall period from February 1990 until December 1994, during which a number of agencies, professional persons, hospital staff and social services, played their respective parts in either the management of Jason Mitchell's case and/or in his care and treatment. The Inquiry surveyed a spectrum of that time and related it back to the *mise-en-scène*, relevant to the systems and the fallible human beings that inhabit, and function within them. Our report, and the recommendations that flow from it, will inevitably have been influenced by retrospection of the events within the spectrum of time. But we think it is too facile to call into question such findings, simply by alleging 'hindsight-bias'. Of course, we cannot escape the fact that in making our judgments about past conduct or events, we have been conditioned by the present and the instant knowledge the present brings. No one could shut out of mind the horrendous homicides of December 1994. In judging now the quality of diagnostic assessment in, say, May 1993 or August 1994 (two occasions when assessments were necessarily to be made about Jason Mitchell's psychopathology) we have endeavoured to exclude (or at least to put on one side) the knowledge now available to us which, by definition, could not have been known to the diagnosticians of those earlier days. In recognising the danger of substituting today's views of events for the operative factors of yesteryear, we have kept in the forefront of our deliberations the task of judging the extent or the degree to which the actors of the time span should have had the foresight of things to come. Foresight, after all, is the tool employed by the law in testing whether any person can be successfully sued for civil wrongdoing. Too readily foresight, with its supplementary focus on questions of practice and procedure, is treated as if it were an exercise in impermissible hindsight. In the practice of psychiatry the exercise of foresight equates with the process of risk assessment. Judgment about foreseeability must not be deflected by bald assertions of hindsight-bias.

The public debate over the ability of public inquiries, including the thorny topic of 'hindsight-bias' in judging past assessments by professionals, led us to conclude that the time was ripe for some considered study of inquiries, at least those now mandated by the Department of Health on Health Authorities and Local Authority Social Services Departments. Following the precedent of the Ashworth Hospital Inquiry of 1991-2 and the Robinson Inquiry of 1994, we asked Dr Jill Peay, of the Law Department of Brunel University, if she would organise a day seminar at which an invited audience could consider the range of aspects of public inquiries that are currently being discussed. Dr Peay arranged a highly successful seminar under the title *Inquiries after Homicide: exposition, expiation or ...* on 3 November 1995. The fruits of that excellent seminar are to be found in a volume published simultaneously with this report. We are confident in saying that the contributions will greatly inform policy-makers who, sooner or later, will have to sort out the country's haphazard way of handling public scandals or disasters. The fact that we were able to mount the seminar on public inquiries was due entirely to the readiness with which Mr Nicholas Ridley, Mrs Joanna Spicer, and Mr David White of Suffolk Health Authority responded to our suggestion. Indeed their enthusiasm infused the enterprise. It reflected the approach of softening the intellectual discomfort of a public inquiry, by engaging in a bout of healthy self-criticism.

Throughout the Inquiry, they lent their unswerving support to our methods of proceeding, while retaining scrupulously their distance from any of our deliberations. When we encountered initially some hindrance from outside agencies in gathering documents, Mrs Spicer readily promoted our request to Ministers for statutory powers, which in the event we did not need to pursue. All the agencies, both statutory and voluntary, did in fact exhibit a willingness and readiness to supply all their relevant documentation; they were simply cautious in handing over material without the consent of the individuals protected by confidentiality.

Our greatest good fortune was to have instantly to hand – even before the formal announcement of the Inquiry on 22 May 1995 – a secretarial team from Suffolk Health Authority, led, indefatigably and with a cheerfulness that overcame the heavy demands we made, by Mr Brian Morden. The support which we had from Mr Mike Daniels, Mrs Liz Farrow and Mrs Dot Tessier was truly impressive. Our working relationship with all four of them became one of the happiest aspects of the Inquiry. It also greatly facilitated the smooth operation of the hearings and the preparation of our report.

The translation of our draft early chapters was expertly handled in the first instance by our Chairman's fortunate circumstance of an office in Belfast, thus providing optimum security for our embryonic report. Mr Trevor French and Mrs Kate Challis manfully and womanfully respectively grappled with the early drafts. Our gratitude to them is boundless. The completion of the task of translation of scripts to final report was performed in the offices of Bates, Wells & Braithwaite, a distinguished firm of solicitors, to whom we turned for help. We are grateful to Mr John Trotter and his staff for rendering this service, as well as for having conducted a large number of interviews of witnesses during the summer of 1995 in the Suffolk area.

Finally but most importantly, we wish to convey our respects to the direct victims of those terrible events just before Christmas in Bramford, near Ipswich. Our huge regard for the manner in which the three children of the late Mr and Mrs Wilson acquitted themselves is unstinted. Between them they attended every session of the public hearings, at which they conducted themselves with a dignity that evoked admiration. They never displayed any sense of vindictiveness or revenge. Mr Christopher Wilson on behalf of himself and his two sisters made an oral statement to the Inquiry which we gladly reproduce in Annex 2.

The voices of the Mitchell family, for understandable reasons, have not been heard in the same way as those of the Wilsons. But the Mitchell family too have suffered severely through their bereavement. Mr Mitchell's four other children have lost the father who brought them up single-handedly in their early years and with whom they continued to have a close and affectionate relationship. One of his daughters remarked that in the task of bringing the children up, 'he did a brilliant job'. Because of the publicity surrounding the killings, the family, on the advice of the police, had a private cremation service unknown to friends and acquaintances of Mr Mitchell, who would have wished to pay their respects. His ashes were returned to his original home in Scotland where his immediate relatives held a memorial service. His own family include his sister and his elderly parents who are both in their 80s and who were too frail to attend their son's funeral in Suffolk.

Mr Mitchell's sons and daughters coped with their bereavement on their own, and received no contact or support from the Trust or Health Authority until approached by the Secretary to the Inquiry. They did receive advice from the police. They have had no professional help in their awesome personal task of trying to understand what one of their own has done and what it may imply for themselves and their children. As one of the family told us, in addition to the death of their father, they also suffered a second loss, namely that of a younger brother who had done something they could not comprehend and who was now indefinitely detained.

Chronology of Events

July 23, 1970   Jason John Mitchell (JM) born in Ipswich to Robert and Brenda Mitchell. JM is the youngest of five children.

Spring 1971   JM's mother left the family home. JM thereafter brought up by father.

Dec. 6, 1978   JM attending Bramford Primary School caught shoplifting for a second time. Following representations to the Education Department JM subsequently placed in a specialist school, the Parkside Unit, Ipswich. Subsequent history of truancy, anti-social behaviour and clashes with authority. Left in May 1986.

1984

May 20   JM cautioned by Ipswich Police for criminal damage.

June 27   JM cautioned by Ipswich Police for going equipped to steal.

Sept. 19   JM cautioned by Ipswich Police for tampering with a vehicle.

1986

April 23   JM appeared at Ipswich Juvenile Court:

Theft from shop (x 3)	– 24 hours attendance centre
Taking vehicle w/o consent	– 18 hours attendance centre (conc)
Driving under age	– 18 hours attendance centre (conc)
No insurance	– Fined £25, lic. endorsed.

Oct. 25   JM appeared at Ipswich Juvenile Court:

Driving under age	– 18 hours attendance centre (conc)
Burglary, value £6.50	– 12 months Supervision Order
Driving while disqualified	– Fined £20
No insurance	– Fined £20
Careless driving	– Fined £20. To pay at £1 per week.

1987

Feb. 25   JM appeared at Ipswich Juvenile Court for failing to pay fines. He was ordered to pay a total of £56 at £4 per fortnight.

Oct. 22   JM appeared at Ipswich Magistrates' Court charged with robbery and burglary (x 3). The robbery was from a wine shop when JM took £117 from the till threatening the young pregnant shop assistant with a screwdriver. He was remanded in custody to Norwich Prison.

1988

Jan. 9   JM seen while on remand alone in cell behaving very strangely. Reported by PO McPhee.

Feb. 19   JM appeared at Ipswich Crown Court and sentenced to a total of 2 years' youth custody for robbery and other offences.

Feb. 24   JM transferred to Hollesley Bay YOI.

Mar. 24   Dr Berry, visiting consultant psychiatrist reports to the Governor that JM 'is not ill' following staff reports that JM 'is not all there'. JM subsequently placed almost continuously on Rule 46.

May 31	JM transferred to Feltham YOI, Bittern Unit.
July 27	On advice of locum MO, Dr Dexter, JM seen by visiting consultant psychiatrist, Dr Latif who saw JM on 30 further occasions during next 7 months. JM describes auditory hallucinations. Dr Latif did not consider that JM suffered from any mental illness.

1989

Mar. 14	JM returned to Hollesley Bay YOI.
Mar. 22	JM threatened to hang himself in cell. Subsequently reported bullying and assaults by other inmates.
May 12	JM released to Richmond Fellowship hostel in Cambridge.
July 27	JM threatened member of staff with knife.
Aug. 21	JM left the Richmond Fellowship for Church Army Hostel. Thereafter he is thought to have returned to Ipswich.

1990

Feb. 8	JM attacked the cleaner at St Barnabas Church, Epsom. Charged with attempted murder and other offences. Remanded in custody to Feltham YOI.
April 4	JM transferred under section 36, Mental Health Act 1983 to West Park Hospital, having been diagnosed by the Senior MO and assessed by Dr Penrose from West Park, as suffering from a treatable mental illness.
Sept. 10	JM appears at the Central Criminal Court and pleads guilty to common assault and possession of offensive weapons (two knives). Made subject of a Hospital Order and Restriction Order unlimited in time under sections 37 & 41, Mental Health Act 1983, and returned to West Park Hospital. RMO is Professor Merry.

1991

Feb. (date unknown)	Jackie Leaver, Occupational Therapy Technical Instructor, prepared a lengthy report which contained details of JM's homicidal thoughts and fantasies.
Mar. 25	JM applies to Mental Health Review Tribunal (MHRT) for discharge as a restricted patient.
April 29	Dr Crellin, Professor Merry's senior registrar, recommended conditional discharge.
June 7	Dr Lintner, independent psychiatrist, recommended discharge, subject to suitable accommodation.
Sept. 3	MHRT ordered that JM be conditionally discharged but this to be deferred until arrangements made for hostel residence, acceptance of medication and submission to out-patient monitoring. Recommendations also made regarding reduction and then cessation of medication, move to open ward and unescorted leave.
Oct. 27	Dr Yeldham became JM's RMO.

1992

April 1   Dr Yeldham informed the clerk to the MHRT that 'the situation for Jason is now different ... he has a continuing mental illness ... we must all adopt a graduated process'.

Dec. 29   Dr Yeldham informed the Home Office that she considered 'it essential that psychiatric supervision continues ... rehabilitation could best be carried out in Jason's home area ... now that his psychiatric condition is reasonably stable'.

1993

Mar. 17   Dr Goddard met JM briefly at St Audry's Hospital, Melton, Woodbridge, and subsequently wrote to Dr Yeldham agreeing to have JM transferred to his care as a restricted patient.

April 6   MHRT endorsed the previous Tribunal decision and the transfer of JM to St Clement's Hospital, Ipswich 'in order to facilitate his conditional discharge'.

May 5   JM transferred to St Clement's Hospital (Easton House).

Dec. 29   JM absconded, returning later the same day.

1994

Feb. 17   JM absconded, subsequently arrested on 4.3.94 by Cheshire Police near Warrington and returned to Easton House.

Mar. 12   JM absconded, apparently staying at home with his father, before returning voluntarily on 22.3.94.

May 18   JM placed in MIND shared accommodation at Larkhill Way, Felixstowe.

Aug. 18   JM conditionally discharged from Hospital Order with restrictions.

Nov. 8   Following disruptive behaviour, JM is received back in to Easton House as an informal patient.

Dec. 9   JM left and failed to return.

Dec. 20   JM arrested for murder.

Part A

Triple Homicide

I. The Story of the Killings:
The External Evidence

Every agency has gone into great detail to explain its role of the care
and control of Jason Mitchell and its aspirations for him. We must
not forget that he is now locked away for at least 10 years. He is also
a victim; and I say to you that possibly you have all failed him.

Extract from the statement made to the Inquiry
by the children of Arthur and Shirley Wilson

Around 7 o'clock on Friday evening, 9 December 1994, Jason
Mitchell, aged 24, walked out of Easton House, a challenging
behaviour unit at St Clement's Hospital, Ipswich. He failed to come
back that night, or at all; the missing patient's procedure was
promptly activated by the night staff at Easton House. At that time
he was in fact merely resident in Easton House while social services
arranged suitable accommodation, following the breakdown of his
placement in supervised shared accommodation in Felixstowe, run
by East Suffolk MIND. Jason Mitchell had been a restricted patient
under a deferred conditional discharge in Easton House from May
1993 until August 1994 when the conditional discharge was confirmed by a Mental Health Review Tribunal on his taking up the
accommodation in Felixstowe. On 8 November 1994 his RMO, Dr
Ray Goddard, had authorised Jason Mitchell's return, pending new
arrangements. But this was not for any clinical reasons, it was a
kind of respite care. Dr Goddard wrote to C3 Division of the Home
Office stating that Jason Mitchell was occupying a valuable bed in
a rehabilitation unit for social reasons only. On 8 November 1994,
when he had returned to the Unit, he displayed behaviour which
was familiar to staff at Easton House. The contemporary nursing
notes reflect his 'usual arrogant self-centred attitude', his 'coming
and going as he pleases', and 'treating the place like a hotel'. Jason
Mitchell had a marked ability to cause dissension in the ward,
without becoming involved in the ensuing disturbance. During that
period he made no attempt to endear himself to others, unless it
was for his own ends. Dr Goddard told us that when Jason Mitchell
came back from Felixstowe at the beginning of November his
behaviour at first was 'cranky and irritable'.

In late November and early December he apparently underwent a mild behavioural transformation. During the first week of December 1994 Jason Mitchell had been 'a model patient' in the unit at Easton House. He was helpful and pleasant, generally displaying good humour. When a member of the nursing staff mentioned his own plans for a family Christmas Jason Mitchell was quick to point out that he had never had a 'family Christmas'.

On 9 December Jason Mitchell's behaviour continued to be pleasant and unusually helpful. On the day of his departure he had put up the Christmas decorations in the unit. His behaviour then was in marked contrast to his previous attitude to staff and other patients. Shortly after 7 pm he approached the Staff Nurse, Andy Palmer, and asked permission to go out for a while. Jason Mitchell was smartly dressed, and the nurse commented on his appearance. When he left Easton House on that evening he was free to go out so long as he returned, according to 'house rules', by 9.15 pm.

Jason Mitchell went straight from the hospital to the family home at 11 Acton Road, Bramford, a village on the north-western outskirts of Ipswich. It was there that he had been brought up by his father Robert (his mother having left the family home when Jason Mitchell, the youngest of five children, was less than one year old) and where he stayed sporadically in later years between periods of detention beginning in 1986 when he was 16. Although Jason Mitchell has talked occasionally since the killings of harbouring a desire to kill his father, there is no evidence that the relationship latterly showed any signs of acrimony.

Jason Mitchell spent the ensuing weekend with his father, only leaving the house on Sunday 11 December in the early evening to buy some tobacco at the village shop. During that short excursion he frightened two teenage girls when he chased them briefly. To reach the 'Happy Shopper', Jason Mitchell would have turned left from Acton Road into Bramford's main thoroughfare, The Street, and almost immediately passed No. 112, an attractive detached two-bedroomed bungalow occupied by Arthur and Shirley Wilson. Both aged 65, the devoted couple were looking forward to an active retirement. He had been the Station Manager at Ipswich Railway Station, she a librarian. They were well known in the local community, not least as strong supporters of the church next door to their home. It is not thought that they knew Jason Mitchell, or he them.

The Wilsons had been in Bramford only since 1985, during which time Jason Mitchell was mainly away in various institutions.

On Jason Mitchell's own subsequent admission, on Saturday 10 December, he tried to break into the Wilsons' bungalow through a rear window, but was unsuccessful and abandoned the attempt, returning to his father's home. Jason Mitchell spent the whole of the time between his leaving hospital on 9/10 December and his arrest on 20 December in or around the village of Bramford, mostly at his father's house at 11 Acton Road. If he had thought that he was bound to be found by the police – his previous absences would have put him wise to the consequences of being absent without leave from hospital – he took no evasive action. It is almost as if at one level he wanted to be traced and returned to hospital. Despite the calls that police had made to 11 Acton Road on previous occasions, when Jason Mitchell had been reported to them as missing, this time there were no enquiries made by the police at the house where he stayed for four days (see Chapter XVII).

Jason Mitchell stayed indoors on Monday 12 December, until around noon, when he told his father that he intended to return to Easton House. Robert Mitchell gave his son, who by now had no money, a couple of Red Band cigarettes. Jason Mitchell left the house but remained in the vicinity, eventually gaining entry to the Wilson's home during the afternoon, while Arthur Wilson washed his car in the driveway. Jason Mitchell concealed himself in a bedroom, emerging later, after Shirley Wilson had returned home, to confront the couple at knife point. The Wilsons were tied up and put in separate rooms. Shortly afterwards he strangled them.

Jason Mitchell spent some time in the house, eating some food and smoking one of the Red Band cigarettes. He stole £25 but other monies in the house were left untouched. At about 5.15 pm he ran from the bungalow and made his way to the Bosmere Guest House in Norwich Road, Ipswich, paying £15 cash for a room for one night. Whatever may be the explanation for these two apparently senseless killings, they were certainly not the result of a bungled burglary. No burglar would conceivably have hung around the scene of his crime, awaiting the householders' return home and, after killing them, dallying for one moment.

By 5.45 am on Tuesday 13 December he had left the guest house and made his way to Bramford where a number of people saw him, principally in the area of Paper Mill Lane, close to the village shop. Two witnesses separately describe him as smiling unnaturally.

From the evening of 12 December there had been concern for the safety of the Wilsons, and this grew. At 1.35 am on Wednesday 14 December police officers forced entry to 112 The Street and found the bodies of Shirley and Arthur Wilson. The murder enquiry began.

During the morning of 14 December, while considerable police activity was centred on the Wilsons' bungalow, Jason Mitchell was seen nearby by a number of people, again in the Paper Mill Lane area, about half a mile from the Wilsons' home. When news of the killings spread, a witness volunteered to the police that she had seen Jason Mitchell in Bramford on the previous day (13 December) 'with a silly smirk on his face'. This was the first mention of Jason Mitchell in the murder enquiry. Another witness saw him loitering near her home as she left. When she returned, the house had been burgled and £60 cash stolen.

At around noon Jason Mitchell returned to the Bosmere Guest House in Ipswich and paid for a room for one night, having first tried unsuccessfully to stay at another guest house nearby.

On the following day police officers paid their first call at 11 Acton Road since Jason Mitchell had been reported as missing. The callers were members of the murder enquiry team. Robert Mitchell gave them a statement with details of Jason Mitchell's stay at the house from 9-12 December, mentioning the Red Band cigarettes which he had given to his son. By that time the forensic examination at 112 The Street had revealed the Red Band cigarette stub left by Jason Mitchell. It was known that the Wilsons were non-smokers. The link was thus significant.

While police enquiries continued on 15 December Jason Mitchell was seen throughout the day by staff in the Bosmere Guest House behaving restlessly. He paid a further £15 for another night's lodging, and it is believed that he stayed there. But again he left early in the morning without having breakfast.

On Friday 16 December Jason Mitchell was seen close to the centre of Ipswich by a nurse who telephoned Easton House. Staff there informed the police about one hour later. By now he was regarded as somebody whom the murder team detectives wished to 'implicate or eliminate' from their enquiry, but he still was not traced. At this stage only hospital staff and police officers knew that this tall and heavily tattooed young man was sought for interview in a murder enquiry.

Jason Michell now returned to 11 Acton Road to stay with his father. Robert Mitchell had apparently told the murder enquiry officers who interviewed him on 15 December that he would contact them if and when Jason Mitchell returned. Whatever his true intentions, he did not do so. He was seen with Jason Mitchell near his home on Saturday 17 December at about 2.30 pm, about a hundred yards from the police major incident caravan parked around the corner opposite the Wilsons' bungalow.

Late on Saturday 17, or early on Sunday 18 December Jason Mitchell called his father upstairs on the pretext of helping him to make the bed and, taking him unawares, strangled him with a tie. After talking to the body, he left it lying on the bed. Jason Mitchell spent the next two days almost wholly in the house, leaving it only briefly at about 5.30 pm on 19 December. He then proceeded to dismember his father's body, leaving the torso on the bed but hiding the arms, legs and head in sports bags in the loft.

What the police had found during an exhaustive forensic examination of the Wilsons' bungalow were numerous fingerprint impressions. Some that were found on 14 December defied identification until they had been chemically treated on more than one occasion, finally being suitable for photographic comparison on 19 December. These and others which had been found on 17 December were submitted to the Suffolk Police Headquarters Fingerprint Bureau on 20 December. They were rapidly identified as having been made by Jason Mitchell.

At 5.30 pm on 20 December police officers from the murder enquiry team paid their second call at 11 Acton Road, Bramford. The house was in darkness and there was no reply to repeated knocking. They forced their way in and found Jason Mitchell sitting quietly on a sofa in the living room looking vacant and disoriented. Almost immediately he told the police that he had strangled his father and cut up the body. After the officers had found the dismembered torso in an upstairs bedroom, Jason Mitchell was handcuffed and taken to Ipswich Police Station. He appeared entirely calm and self-possessed. In killing his father, Jason Mitchell – if what he has said to others can be believed – had found the resolution to do what he had in mind ever since he was a boy of six.

II. An Overview of Responsibility

> It must be true that whenever a sensational murder is committed there are people who – though they are, quite properly, of no interest to law enforcers, attorneys, or newspaper reporters – weep, lie sleepless, and realise at last that their lives have been changed by a crime in which they played no part.
>
> Vina Delmar, American playwright,
> *The Becker Scandal*, 1968

When sentencing Jason Mitchell to three terms of life imprisonment for manslaughter on the grounds of diminished responsibility, Mr Justice Blofeld expressed himself forcefully on the public responsibility for the three deaths, over and beyond the criminal responsibility of Jason Mitchell. On what he had been told during the short hearing at Ipswich Crown Court on 7 July 1995 – inevitably the information conveyed was partial and limited in scope – the judge found it difficult to see what reasons there could have been for releasing Jason Mitchell back into the community. In welcoming the setting up of the Inquiry, the judge said:

> It seems to me that the whole circumstances since his sentencing at the Central Criminal Court in 1990 need to be fully investigated. On the face of it this man should not have been released .... It may be that that tribunal [meaning the independent panel of inquiry] will find reasons why he should have been released. On what has been opened to this court, I am bound to say it is difficult to see what those reasons can be but I hope that ... a full and detailed report will be made, not only of what took place under the auspices of the Suffolk Health Authority at Easton House, but also the earlier period, including his detention in West Park Hospital, Epsom.

It is no overstatement to conclude from that judicial utterance, however cautiously the language was chosen and couched, that the finger of blame was being pointed at either, or both, Jason Mitchell's RMO, Dr Ray Goddard, or the two Mental Health Review Tribunals which had authorised Jason Mitchell's conditional discharge. The media coverage of that day's court proceedings indicated as much.

The *East Anglian Daily Times* of 8 July 1995 headlined the lead story on its front page, in bold lettering, with a sentence from a letter written by Dr Goddard (pictured prominently) in August 1994 to Jason Mitchell's general practitioner, stating that 'he is a pleasant young man with no real malice'. (Dr Goddard explained this unfortunate phrase as an attempt to strike a balance in conveying the kind of patient Jason Mitchell was.) An editorial, under the heading 'Tragedy that must never happen again', said:

> Searching questions need to be asked. One year after Mitchell was committed to Epsom's West Park Hospital under section 41 of the Mental Health Act, a tribunal decided without reference to the courts, that he no longer posed a threat to public safety .... In words which may come to haunt his consultant psychiatrist, Ray Goddard, [the headlined words were repeated] .... Dr Goddard will continue in his duties.

The editorial concluded:

> Quite how experts proved so blind to the true nature of Mitchell's psychotic state must urgently be answered. Such a tragedy must never be allowed to happen again.

The national press was altogether more sensational in its treatment of the hearing before Mr Justice Blofeld on 7 July 1995. The front page of the *Daily Mail* for Saturday, 8 July 1995, reproduced on page 10, was, by tabloid standards, comparatively restrained.

We have conducted an exhaustive examination of the extensive documentary material, and heard much oral evidence. In this short chapter we endeavour to provide a conspectus of complex issues. Any assertion we have made will, we hope, find its substantiation in what follows in the rest of our report.

We called as an independent psychiatric witness, Dr Jeremy Christie Brown of the Maudsley Hospital, who gave us an expert opinion on the diagnostic assessments of Jason Mitchell's mental state; and we have observed the failings in the procedures of the two tribunals. In the result we are convinced that neither of the identified, provisional pointers of blame by Mr Justice Blofeld is warranted. No one who had been responsible for the care and treatment of Jason Mitchell during the period of his hospitalisation either at West Park Hospital, Epsom (from April 1990 to May 1993) or at St Clement's Hospital, Ipswich (May 1993 – December 1994) could be blamed for the inexplicable and unpredictable homicides. Nor does any blame attach to those responsible for Jason Mitchell's

Doctor's amazing verdict on psychopath

SUCH A NICE TRIPLE KILLER

A DEVASTATED family demanded to know yesterday why a paranoid schizophrenic was released into the community to commit three sickening killings.

Despite a record of violence which included attacking an elderly church cleaner with a baseball bat, Jason Mitchell was described by the consultant psychiatrist who sanctioned his release as 'a pleasant young man with no real malice'.

The diagnosis was to prove horrifically wrong. Weeks after being allowed to move into a hostel, Mitchell strangled pensioners Arthur and Shirley Wilson before killing and then dismembering his

By MICHAEL SEAMARK

father Bob. The crazed killer told police that he wanted to eat his victims but decided they were too old. Detectives claimed that Mitchell appeared to be living out a fantasy based on the serial killer Hannibal Lecter in the film The Silence of the Lambs.

Yesterday, a judge rejected defence claims that Mitchell should be sent back to a mental hospital. At Ipswich Crown Court, Mr Justice Blofeld sentenced the heavily-tattooed killer to three concurrent life sentences and ruled that he should serve a minimum of ten years before any decision to free him was considered.

'Seldom has such an appalling outline of terrible events been opened before a court,' said the judge. 'You are potentially an extremely dangerous young man.' Mr and Mrs Wilson's distraught

Turn to Page 7, Col. 1

INSIDE: Weather 2, Femail 34-35, Books 36-37, Motoring 44-45, Gardening 46, placement in the summer and autumn of 1994 in the shared accommodation provided by East Suffolk MIND, or the breakdown of that placement. Culpability for three violent and unnatural deaths rests solely with Jason Mitchell, although even his criminality was diminished by reason of his substantially impaired mental state, such as to result in a verdict of manslaughter.

The state of Jason Mitchell's mental health was at all relevant times problematical and elusive to the various psychiatrists who assessed him. For those psychiatrists at West Park Hospital, Epsom, who saw him following the criminal event of February 1990 – Drs Penrose, Pugh and Yeldham – Jason Mitchell suffered from schizophrenia, although that diagnosis did not wholly exclude exacerbation of his mental ill-health by reliance on illicit drugs. Even granted the speedy recovery which led to his early deferred conditional discharge in September 1991, the diagnosis of schizophrenia remained. This view is strengthened now in the light of the contents of the medical records relating to Jason Mitchell's period of Youth Custody, mislaid by the Prison Service since May 1989 and recovered only in October 1995. The records suggesting incipient schizophrenia, discernible in 1988-89, were out of sight and mind of all subsequent clinicians and other professionals responsible for Jason Mitchell's case. The loss of the records of that period gives rise to a major concern about the flow of important information between the penal and mental health systems. They contained valuable material about Jason Mitchell's mental health and, had they been available, they would have formed part of any subsequent report on Jason Mitchell as he passed through prison after-care, criminal justice and the mental health system.

The diagnosis of schizophrenia, as Dr Goddard inherited it from West Park, was substantially rejected as a result of an over-valued appraisal of the evidence of sustained illicit drug-taking by Jason Mitchell. Given the firm diagnosis by the West Park psychiatrists and Jason Mitchell's history of offending, Dr Goddard could usefully have turned for a second opinion to the forensic psychiatric services at the Norvic Clinic in Norwich. (Dr Ward from the Norvic Clinic regularly conducted a monthly clinic at St Clement's). It is a theme of this report that those engaged in general psychiatry need constantly, when dealing with difficult-to-manage patients, particularly restricted patients, to seek advice and assistance from the forensic psychiatric services, although we recognise the scarcity of that resource at present.

All but one of the doctors who saw Jason Mitchell *after* the killings of December 1994 – Drs Ball, Bowden, Ward and Wilson – were in favour of a diagnosis of schizophrenia. Dr Bowden asserted that the mental illness had probably been present for ten years. The exception was Dr Ray Goddard, Jason Mitchell's RMO at St Clement's Hospital for the whole of his stay, from May 1993 – December 1994. Dr Goddard rejected the diagnosis of schizophrenia in favour of drug-induced psychosis and a personality disorder. Dr Goddard's diagnosis was considered by Dr Jeremy Christie Brown not to be unreasonable, although he too tended to opt for a diagnosis of schizophrenia. Given the more complete picture of the symptomatology which we have uncovered, we think that Jason Mitchell had been suffering from schizophrenia since at least as far back as 1988. The evaluation of Jason Mitchell's care and treatment does not rest on psychiatric diagnosis alone. Of equal importance are the issues of management of his care, the professional support he received, the assessment of risk, the aftercare arrangements which were made on his discharge into the community and the policy and resource context in which the services were delivered.

Jason Mitchell's transition from being a restricted patient to freedom in the community was, by common experience, astonishingly rapid. Within a year of the imposition of a restriction order at the Central Criminal Court in September 1990 Jason Mitchell was given a deferred conditional discharge by a Mental Health Review Tribunal. Whether that would have been the result, had the psychiatrists and the tribunal known of the previous history of psychotic symptoms, must be conjectural. Once, however, the conditional discharge was ordered – deferred only pending the provision of suitable accommodation outside hospital – Jason Mitchell was firmly set on the road to freedom. The transfer to Ipswich in May 1993 was prompted by the desire to provide that freedom in Jason Mitchell's home environs. Whatever the different psychiatric diagnosis concluded by Dr Goddard and his team, it could not properly have deflected them from their duty to promote Jason Mitchell's move back into the community, even if they might have wished – which they did not – to delay that move. Given Jason Mitchell's legal entitlement to his discharge, the leitmotif of his care and treatment at Easton House, from May 1993 to August 1994, was rehabilitative. It was no one's fault that the search for suitable accommodation was so protracted. For them Jason

Mitchell came to Easton House on the verge of recovering his liberty and there was no clinical reason to change course. When Jason Mitchell was admitted back to Easton House in November 1994 he 'occupied a bed in a specialist unit at the moment almost purely for social reasons'.

Our terms of reference specifically call for an examination of the adequacy and appropriateness of inter-agency arrangements and collaboration among the relevant agencies in East Suffolk. We have carried out that examination in the context of existing resources and systems. Given the constraints on contemporary mental health services we asked ourselves, if the outcome of the killings in December 1994 was unpredictable (as we firmly conclude), did all those responsible for his care and treatment take appropriate action? To the question: were the killings preventable, we must say it is unanswerable in any meaningful sense. It is possible, however, to provide answers to the questions related to possible outcomes in terms of management choices, both clinical and administrative.

The management of Jason Mitchell's case was limited in two respects. First, the scope and nature of the therapeutic regime limited the clinical approach to Jason Mitchell's care, both within the hospital and in the after-care arrangements.

Secondly, there was generally an unrealistic or over-optimistic view of Jason Mitchell's chances of being capable of survival in the community, given his persistently poor social relationships and the prospect of resort to illicit drugs. (Miss Jane Barnett, social worker, and Ms Erica Smiter, formerly Head Occupational Therapist, St Clement's Hospital, Suffolk, deserve to be singled out as expressing a healthy pessimism about Jason Mitchell's chances of survival in the community unless he received substantial support.)

The five aspects of risk assessment which might have produced different results are:

(1) The evaluation of the criminal event of February 1990 by the criminal justice system was defective in not identifying the kind of specialist services that met Jason Mitchell's needs. A proper assessment of the criminal event indicated a referral and possible admission to a Special Hospital, in the absence in the Surrey area of a Regional Secure Unit (see Chapter VII).

(2) Key data relating to the criminal event of February 1990 were under-rated in their significance for the purpose of risk assessment and case management (see Chapter VIII).

(3) A contribution came in the form of a document detailing Jason Mitchell's innermost thoughts from an unqualified member of staff who was on the 'periphery' of the multi-disciplinary team. The report by Mrs Jackie Leaver, an Occupational Therapy Technical Instructor at West Park Hospital, was dealt with dismissively by clinicians and other staff (see Chapter IV).

(4) Important options for assessing the mental health of Jason Mitchell were never pursued. There was, for example, no substantial psychological input into the handling of Jason Mitchell's case; in particular there was an absence of any psychological/psychodynamic approach to understanding his emotional and personality development; and little attention was paid to family dynamics and relationships. There was no monitoring of Jason Mitchell's inner life. Indeed, there was a deliberate avoidance of his subjective mental state (see Chapter IV).

(5) Had there been a concerted effort to elicit from Jason Mitchell himself the homicidal intentions which he had fleetingly communicated to some people at odd occasions, there would have been a perceived need for clinical evaluation. Had such evaluation then taken place, the homicidal intentions would have influenced the assessment of risk of future violent behaviour.

Everyone at Easton House from whom we have heard has expressed his or her inability to understand the motivation for the killings. Others who cared for and treated Jason Mitchell for his schizophrenic illness in 1990 have also been dumbfounded by the events of December 1994. Asked by us whether she now considered the killings understandable, Dr Denise Yeldham (Jason Mitchell's RMO from September 1990 to May 1993) said:

> When I first heard about it I thought, 'I am not sure that this fits at all,' and I thought about it a bit more and I thought, 'Maybe I can see a bit of the fit.' And I guess as I have got used to the idea I have come to accept it more so that on the surface you could see, well, yes, there were, there were feelings perhaps in the fantasies, there were one or two things. There were times when he didn't appear to be concerned about the consequences of his action. So you start to put bits together. But there is no way that I can make a pattern and say, 'This is something I would have expected this man to do.' I mean it just isn't.

Whatever else may be said about the confusing picture presented to the clinicians diagnosing Jason Mitchell's mental condition – and we expatiate at length on diagnosis in Part B of this report – two responsible consultant psychiatrists, both familiar with their patient exhibiting psychotic symptoms at different stages of the patient's time in hospital, may in any event reasonably come to different – even diametrically opposite – diagnoses. In their search for symptoms of schizophrenia or drug-induced psychosis, there were, arguably, pointers in both directions, even if the care and treatment of Jason Mitchell did depend simply on a psychiatric diagnosis – which it did not.

None of what we have said should be taken as affecting our view that there could have been improvements in the management of Jason Mitchell's case, within the hospital setting, the community placement, the operation of the missing patients procedure, the tribunal system and the Home Office in respect of restricted patients and the flow of inter-agency information. Any service provider can improve the value and quality of service and seek to address limitations in its clinical approach. We have, therefore, highlighted a number of aspects of Jason Mitchell's care and treatment as he passed through the mental health system which are deserving of study, review and perhaps change.

We repeat; as circumstanced, the killings could not have been predicted. There was, furthermore, no causal link between any act or omission by any one person or organisation and the deaths on 12 and 17 December 1994. The deficiencies and defects which we have uncovered do not significantly detract from our overall view that the quality of services delivered, both at West Park Hospital and at St Clement's Hospital, to Jason Mitchell, and the documentation that supported those services, were much better than each of us, in our different capacities within the mental health system, has experienced in other comparable institutions. Any reader of the copious records – in many instances commendably thorough – will readily appreciate why no claim of any significant lack of resources was volunteered by those who gave evidence save for an expressed wish, so far unavailing, to appoint a clinical psychologist. What is detectable from a study of the case is a notable omission from the services provided of a more expansive use of alternative therapeutic regimes. In our view the good level of investment in mental health services in the Suffolk area could and should be rebalanced to develop a more specialised range of services including both residential provision and psychotherapeutic services for people like Jason Mitchell. In the clinical context, with some exceptions here and there, no concerted exploration in depth and in an appropriate setting of privacy of Jason Mitchell's fragmented and damaging childhood was ever undertaken. More seriously, Jason Mitchell's inner life was left unexplored by all the clinicians. Dr Goddard deliberately chose not to adopt the path of a psycho-dynamic approach. In his view, a personality disorder is solely a physiological phenomenon: in this, we think, he is mistaken.

Part B

Psychopathology of Jason Mitchell

III. Diagnostic Assessments

If we forgo the making of a diagnosis, we also forgo all application of the extensive knowledge which has been accumulated in the past. This would be sheer folly; we cannot wilfully ignore what is known. If we refrain from diagnosis we shall be left in the individual case without the help of general concepts. The wise physician never neglects the individual peculiarities of his patient; but he will first see how far he can be fitted into general patterns, and he will not mistake a quality which is characteristic of the group, such as thought disorder or auditory hallucination, as either without significance or as something to be interpreted by the life-history of that one patient alone.

Meyer-Gross, Slater and Roth,
Clinical Psychiatry (3rd ed., 1969) pp. 4-5.

West Park Hospital

When Jason Mitchell was first admitted to psychiatric hospital, at West Park, Surrey, on 4 April 1990, it was thought most likely that he was suffering from schizophrenia. At that time he was aged 19.

His background history was as follows. He was a young man who was born in Ipswich, the youngest of five children. His mother left the family home when he was less than one year old and he was brought up single-handedly by his father. At secondary school Jason Mitchell had been disruptive, rebellious and, because of his disturbed behaviour, he had been transferred to a special school which he left at the age of 16 with no qualifications. He took a job in a chicken factory for a few days and from then on was unemployed. He lived an isolated, itinerant existence without establishing any close relationships. As a young teenager he commenced abusing drugs, including cannabis, amphetamines and latterly LSD. He began committing criminal offences at the age of 13, and by the age of 16 had convictions for theft and burglary. In February 1988, at the age of 17, he was sentenced to two years' youth custody following conviction for offences of burglary, theft, and robbery when he threatened a young pregnant female shop assistant with a screwdriver and stole cash from the till. During that sentence, at Feltham Young Offenders Institution, he had contact with a visiting consultant psychiatrist (see Chapter VI) but no details of this were available to the clinicians at West Park Hospital. After leaving prison in April 1989 Jason Mitchell lived at The Richmond Fellowship in Cambridge, a placement arranged by his probation officer. He moved to another hostel, subsequently returning to stay with his father in Ipswich until January 1990. According to his account he went to Amsterdam for a short period and then returned to London, homeless. From there he took a train to Epsom and sheltered in St Barnabas Church where, on 8 February 1990, he assaulted the elderly caretaker (See Chapter VII).

The first full psychiatric report, prepared by Dr Kate Pugh, locum senior registrar (10 August 1990), summarised the history of his symptoms of psychiatric illness as follows:

Jason Mitchell has been experiencing strange experiences for six years according to his report. He started off 'just feeling different, having changes in my mind and paranoia, then going on to hear voices, and that's about it'. He changed from liking things to disliking things in an abnormally intense way, e.g. television programmes would take on emotional significance 'same way you would feel as if you was in love with somebody'. He began to misinterpret ordinary events as being persecutory, e.g. 'I believe that there were groups of people who flash their car headlights in my face and believe people on the streets to be talking about me'. He had delusions of reference, also about television, e.g. during comedy shows he thought the jokes were at his expense and the audience were laughing at him. About five years ago he started to hear voices that came from outside his head, usually when alone or when watching TV. They sounded like people mimicking the voice of his father and brother, and they talked of things he had done in the past. He would look for these people and search the house for microphones, videos and heat sensitive lights, which he believed must be hidden there to explain his experience. He explained the voices' knowledge of him by thinking that he had been the victim of an experiment from his birth, and believed he had lost all his privacy. Occasionally it was like hearing a conversation, occasionally the voices spoke to him, usually critical. He experienced it as somebody nagging continually. He believed that the voices could influence him as they constantly commented on his actions, however, he did not feel controlled by alien forces.

Jason Mitchell then experienced the voice saying 'you should kill the vicar, this is the time that you should kill that man'. He slept and the next morning the caretaker came and he decided that he must kill the caretaker with the vicar in order not to get caught. His belief was that the vicar was responsible for his distress. He had a lump of wood to assault the caretaker and he asked the caretaker if he would lie down on the ground so that he could knock him out with the minimum of damage, the caretaker ran away and Jason Mitchell waited for the police to arrive. He believed that the voices had tricked him into this situation.

The medical notes on admission also record Jason Mitchell saying:

I tried to kill someone – I don't know him – just a vicar – he was doing something to me. I hear voices – they can control me – they make me feel pretty depressed.

He [the vicar] was one of the ones who was the leader of all the voices – I was told by another voice – I was going to use a knife to kill him – victimised – I can't live my life, kill, I want to.

A later note (19 August 1990) records that he had bought the knives with the aim of killing someone to relieve himself of his symptoms.

Dr Pugh's report noted that Jason Mitchell described voices which referred to him both in the second person and third person; the voices commented on his actions and were critical, and they also conversed between themselves. He had some difficulty in quoting what the voices said, but gave as examples hearing the voice of an ex-psychiatrist saying, 'I guarantee you will hear less,' and a critical voice talking of his haircut saying, 'It's not very well done.' (The significance of the first example given by Jason Mitchell became clear only much later when information was discovered about the episode of psychiatric illness which Jason Mitchell had suffered a year earlier in prison, and for which he was treated by many sessions of psychiatric advice and counselling.) Jason Mitchell's mood state was inappropriate, in that he responded in a very bland manner to questions about his illness and offences, and he lacked anxiety. Dr Pugh concluded that Jason Mitchell's mental illness was likely to be paranoid schizophrenia. The consultant initially responsible for Jason Mitchell's care, Dr Standish-Barry, also concluded in a separate report to Jason Mitchell's solicitors (7 September 1990) that he felt there was little doubt that Jason Mitchell was suffering from paranoid schizophrenia.

On several occasions in West Park Hospital Jason Mitchell appeared to have a relapse in his psychotic symptoms when he stopped taking anti-psychotic medication. He was initially treated with such medication in oral form (Droperidol) and by long-acting intramuscular injections (Depixol). His psychotic symptoms improved. After six weeks he no longer had delusions of reference associated with the TV, and after another month he reported no hallucinations. At about this time he started refusing to take

further medication, and his behaviour was generally unco-operative. About six weeks later, in mid-August 1990, he was experiencing the TV talking about him again, and auditory hallucinations of
male voices giving a running commentary and talking 'gibberish'.
It was also noted, however, that there were no objective manifestations in his behaviour to indicate psychotic symptoms. He agreed
to restart taking anti-psychotic medication, the dose of which was
gradually increased, and after two months his abnormal experiences ceased.

During the next year, while he continued on anti-psychotic
medication, there were incidents of troublesome behaviour. He was
rebellious, absconded, went out drinking and on one occasion was
suspected of getting illicit drugs from another patient. He began to
give a more detailed history of illicit drug-taking, including use of
hallucinogens in 1989. In June 1991, there was a reduction in the
dose of his depot anti-psychotic medication, after which he was said
to have become 'increasingly unrealistic ... slightly arrogant, possibly grandiose ... somewhat provocative. His recent consumption
of alcohol increased this facet of his behaviour.' In September 1991
in response to a recommendation from the Mental Health Review
Tribunal (see Chapter IX) he moved to an open ward where his
behaviour became more troublesome and disturbed, with threatening behaviour to staff, absconding, playing loud music at night and
allegedly striking another patient. Dr Yeldham's report of 18
February 1993 summarised his condition and ensuing events as
follows:

> ... he became increasingly hostile and there were various angry and
> rebellious interchanges with staff and other patients. There were
> recurrent disagreements about possible explanations for what nurs-
> ing staff saw as occasionally bizarre or inexplicable behaviour. There
> were no clear psychotic phenomena but a marked deterioration in
> relationships with both staff and patients, which was recognised by
> Jason Mitchell. The situation eventually became uncontainable and
> at the end of October 1991, Jason Mitchell was transferred back to
> Drummond Ward.
>   In November 1991 I took over supervision of Jason Mitchell's care
> and we agreed that it would be [a] reasonable use of his return to
> Drummond to try reducing his medication with a view to cessation
> in line with tribunal recommendations. At this point Mr Mitchell
> objected to continuing medication, feeling that he was not ill, had
> not been ill, and did not require it. He complained of some side
> effects, notably akathesia. Mr Mitchell felt his difficulties on Elgar
> Ward had been largely due to other people's attitudes towards him,

although acknowledging that his own responses played a part, but he did not feel that any contribution was made by illness, or that he was in any way relapsing.

In the following three months, Mr Mitchell's behaviour was initially erratic; it was difficult to assess this, since there was associated cannabis use, but by the end of January there was marked consistent deterioration, e.g. he neglected himself, was often up at night, (sometimes painting or pre-occupied with religious/philosophical subjects). He was often unable/unwilling to communicate verbally, was suspicious and at times appeared to be hallucinating. There was also some evidence of thought disorder. Depot phenothiazines in the form of Depixol were recommended at the beginning of February [1992].

(The clinical records had described Jason Mitchell at the end of January 1992 as walking oddly, neglecting his hygiene, eating poorly and losing weight and talking strangely again. He was hostile and defensive, probably thought disordered and possibly hallucinated. He was thought to be experiencing psychotic phenomena which he was reluctant to reveal.)

Dr Yeldham's report of 18 February 1993 continued:

By mid March 1992, Mr Mitchell's mental state had improved considerably, he was more open and friendly, able and willing to sustain conversations, and at his request commenced work in the horticultural department, as a step towards rehabilitation. However, this was not a stable situation and in early May he was unpredictably irritable, at times aggressive, and somewhat disinhibited. His depot was changed to Haldol and in June he was again improved, although there continued to be occasional evidence of thought disorder and paranoid experiences/beliefs. This appeared to play a part in his decision to stop working in the horticultural department. In August occasional use of cannabis and alcohol disturbed the stability of his mental state, and between August and December it became apparent that without the depot medication Mr Mitchell finds it very difficult to maintain relationships, direction and purpose in life.

Without sufficient appropriate medication Mr Mitchell becomes irritable and his communicative abilities are markedly impaired. He becomes religiously or philosophically preoccupied, at times to the exclusion of necessary day to day activity, and is by turns grandiose or apathetic. There have at times [during 1992] been evidence of frank psychosis with thought disorder and paranoia. He has appeared to respond to hallucinations, but has always recently denied anything other than loud noises.

Dr Yeldham concluded that Jason Mitchell suffered from schizophrenia, and that there was evidence that withdrawal of medication had precipitated a relapse in early 1992. Reductions in the
dosage of medication had also resulted in increased irritability,
preoccupations and difficulty in sustaining a course of action. Dr
Yeldham noted that the depot medication:

> appears to protect Mr Mitchell from relapse during periods of change
> or challenge by other stresses. This is entirely consistent with a
> diagnosis of schizophrenia which is responsive to anti-psychotic
> medication.

It was clear, however, that Jason Mitchell's case was one of
considerable diagnostic difficulty. He was known to have a history
of illicit drug-taking, there was concern that illicit drugs could
adversely affect his mental state, and a note made at West Park
Hospital at the time of Jason Mitchell's transfer to St Clement's
stated:

> ... aware of risks from further drug taking ... young man with
> rebellious streak, diagnosis likely paranoid schizophrenia – I'm not
> sure of the relevance of the drug taking – most likely a precipitant
> rather than causal ....

The diagnostic importance of illicit drug-taking had been difficult
to evaluate. The notes showed that Dr Yeldham considered that
cannabis did worsen Jason Mitchell's mental state. In September
1992 she also told Jason Mitchell that she was convinced he was
dependent on hallucinogenic drugs.

When giving oral evidence to the Inquiry, Dr Yeldham confirmed
that there had been diagnostic uncertainties in Jason Mitchell's
case, and her relative weighting in favour of a diagnosis of schizophrenia, rather than a drug-induced psychosis, was expressed as
follows:

> I think it would be nearer 60/40 or 65/35.

Easton House – St Clement's Hospital

Jason Mitchell was transferred from West Park to St Clement's
Hospital, Ipswich, on 4 May 1993. His prescription of regular
anti-psychotic medication initially continued. During his first few
months at St Clement's, Jason Mitchell appeared well and the

diagnostic question was reviewed. A report by Dr M. Mohammed, SHO to Dr Goddard, dated 14 December 1993, noted:

> During his stay on Easton Ward in St Clement's Hospital, Jason Mitchell did not display any psychotic features and his mental state seemed to be quite stable. He soon gained the confidence of most of the staff members and was granted ground parole which he used quite sensibly and did not give the staff any concerns. He continued to make progress and enjoyed and followed his OT programme. Around early August this year [1993] it was queried whether the psychosis Jason Mitchell suffered from initially could have been drug induced and was there really any schizophrenia. It was strongly thought by the medical and nursing staff that Jason Mitchell should be given a chance without medication to see if the psychosis returned. In view of the above, the Haldol injection was reduced and then gradually discontinued. ... Jason Mitchell was reviewed on a weekly basis to make sure that his mental state remained stable. Since then, to date, Jason Mitchell has not shown any signs for concern. His mood has stayed euthymic, he has not shown any features of psychosis or thought disorder.

During the time that he was responsible for Jason Mitchell's care at St Clement's Hospital, Dr Goddard came to the view that drug-induced psychosis was the more likely diagnosis than schizophrenia. This conclusion was reached after a long period of observation, and a further prolonged trial off medication. Dr Goddard described how Jason Mitchell's mental state seemed normal on admission. He presented himself in an open, friendly and confident manner and established good rapport. Initially, he was closely observed and maintained on medication for three months. In July 1993 there was an occasion when he was seen inhaling solvents. When asked about the voices he was said to have experienced in the past, Jason Mitchell's statements about them varied, and he would claim variously that the voices were an invention to excuse criminal behaviour, that they were real and were helped by medication, that they were caused by medication, or that they were an effect of ingesting illegal drugs.

The uncertainty about whether Jason Mitchell had an underlying schizophrenic illness, or whether his symptoms were drug-induced, was discussed by the staff and with Jason Mitchell at a case conference on 4 August 1993; the decision was made to take him off his medication and keep him under observation and away from illicit drugs, so that the relative importance of these factors could be ascertained.

During the following weeks Jason Mitchell's condition was regularly reviewed. His mood remained normal and he showed no features of psychosis or disordered thinking. His behaviour and manner varied from being pleasant and sociable to irritable, argumentative and unco-operative. He could swing from being pleasant and sociable to aggressive and hostile. He absented himself from the ward on a few occasions, was found to have consumed alcohol and was suspected of taking illicit drugs.

On 29 December 1993 he absconded again for a few hours and Dr Goddard was concerned that his sullen, rude and unpleasant manner could prelude a recurrence of psychotic illness. But, after assessing Jason Mitchell in interview, he found no clear evidence of mental illness, and decided that medication should continue to be withheld. Possible explanations for the deterioration in Jason Mitchell's behaviour were framed in terms of his personality characteristics, his anxieties about returning to life outside hospital, and the adverse effects of substance misuse.

On 12 January 1994, Jason Mitchell reported that he heard voices and had done so since he had been at St Clement's Hospital, but they did not bother him. His behaviour and manner, however, were noted to be generally pleasant and settled, and the fact that there did not appear to be manifestations in his behaviour to corroborate his accounts of experiencing voices led to the decision that, once again, there was insufficient evidence to justify resumption of anti-psychotic medication.

In his written statement to the Inquiry, Dr Goddard explained the reasoning behind the decision as follows:

'Convincing' evidence of the return of psychotic symptoms was considered to require more than passing reference to hallucinatory voices and the occasional silly remark. My team has been very well trained and has great experience over many years in assessing both objective evidence of psychotic behaviour and reported symptoms. All staff of all disciplines were aware that they were particularly to watch out for signs of positive symptoms of psychosis such as observed responses to hallucinatory disturbances (e.g. muttering to himself, looking about in a distracted and incomprehensible fashion), together with other signs such as poor concentration, incoherence of speech, thought blocking, perplexity, etc., which might indicate psychotic thought disorder. They were also required to ask direct questions as part of the mental state examination to illicit subjective symptoms of psychosis. They were aware that Jason Mitchell had a considerable knowledge of psychiatry, had many books on the subject, and had given conflicting reports of previous apparent psychotic symptoms. In particular, full mental state examinations were required to be made by the junior medical staff working for me and were complemented by my own observations.

The nursing note of 12 January 1994 was duly noted, but weighted against the paucity of similar reports over the previous six months and the absence of corroborative reports from other team members. It was decided not to act hastily on this information but to gather more evidence over a longer period of time before taking action. The medical note of 22 January 1994 was likewise duly noted, but again weight was attached to the experience and skill of the interviewer and Jason Mitchell's propensity to play games.

The contemporaneous medical and nursing notes described Jason Mitchell as sullen, angry, rude and unpleasant, following his return to the ward on 29 December 1993. On 11 January 1994 he was said to be smiling and laughing inappropriately, and at the case conference on 12 January 1994 the notes record that he was admitting to hearing voices, but said they were worse on medication. He exhibited mannerisms, inappropriate laughing and his behaviour was chaotic and agitated. There was also reference to 'deterioration of personality'. During the following two days he was noted to be verbally abusive and, on 18 January 1994, said still to be hearing voices. Four days later there were further references to his affect being inappropriate and voices continuing. On 5 March his mood was said to be flat, his activity increased and his thinking concrete. During March 1994 he was generally again described as rude, aggressive and, on 11 March, he was threatening to another patient and spitting. By early April his behaviour appeared generally to have improved.

As described below, the view of an independent general psychiatrist, Dr Christie Brown, who had been commissioned by the Inquiry to report on the diagnostic and treatment issues in Jason Mitchell's case, was that the records were suggestive of quite a marked deterioration in manner and behaviour at this period, which would better fit with a diagnosis of schizophrenia, although the apparent improvement in his condition, which occurred without resumption of medication, would fit with the variability of a drug-inducted state. Dr Christie Brown also noted that the lack of the subtle long-term impairments of emotional expression and personality, which are often seen in chronic schizophrenic illnesses, might also have weighed in favour of drug-induced symptomatology rather than an underlying schizophrenic disorder.

Jason Mitchell absconded from the ward on two more occasions.

On 17 February 1994, he was away for sixteen days and on 12 March 1994 for ten days. The police and Home Office were informed. His behaviour was described as normal, pleasant and co-operative when he returned on the second occasion. During the following months no indications of psychotic symptomatology were evident to the Easton House staff. The overall diagnostic view of the team, by the end of Jason Mitchell's period of detention, was summarised by Dr Goddard, writing to Jason Mitchell's prospective general practitioner in Felixstowe on 24 August 1994:

> Over the course of time Jason Mitchell was found to be a bright, alert, intelligent young man, with a keen sense of humour, and given one or two aberrations, a willingness to conform and comply with the treatment regime.
> The clinical team became increasingly of the opinion that while Jason Mitchell had been displaying clearly psychotic symptoms, this was almost certainly drug induced, and there was no underlying fundamental psychotic illness. As a result Jason was weaned off medication and became medication free in September 1993, and remains so to date.
> There can be little doubt that Jason Mitchell has a wilful, unpredictable personality, and is inclined to act without regard for consequences, and this has not been helped by his less than stable upbringing and socialization process. He presents as immature and impulsive but willing to learn, and has settled in to a more structured and stable lifestyle quite well.

In the medical notes Dr Goddard had recorded (17 August 1994):

> Jason Mitchell is feeling well and remains free of any psychotic symptomatology. He now claims (convincingly) that all references to voices and being controlled were fabricated in recent years in order to gain care in hospital. He does, however, acknowledge that in the past he has had these experiences under the influence of illicit drugs ....

When difficulties arose at the MIND hostel in Larkhill Way, Felixstowe, after Jason Mitchell's discharge from Easton House, he was readmitted informally to Easton House on 8 November 1994. His mental state was reassessed and a urine drug screen was arranged and was negative. The medical and nursing observations recorded no abnormalities indicating psychotic illness. Although initially unpleasant and unco-operative on re-admission, Jason Mitchell's behaviour became more settled. This continued to be the case up until the time of his final departure from the ward on 9 December 1994.

Dr Christie Brown

As noted above, the Inquiry decided to commission an independent report from an experienced general psychiatrist who could review the available clinical records and report on the issues of diagnosis, and the standards of clinical assessment and management to be reasonably expected in the case. Dr J.R.W. Christie Brown, Consultant Psychiatrist at the Maudsley Hospital, London, carried out this task in a most thorough and painstaking way, and his report and oral evidence were of great assistance.

In approaching the question of whether Jason Mitchell suffered from schizophrenia or a drug-induced psychosis, Dr Christie Brown noted that consideration must first be given to how the term 'drug-induced psychosis' is conventionally used. The psychiatric effects of illicit drugs fall broadly into three categories. The first and most common effect is to produce intoxication. With drugs, like cannabis, taken in large quantity, and hallucinogenic drugs, intoxication can produce an acute psychotic illness, and intoxication can be expected to end when the drug is cleared from the body. Secondly, in some cases, particularly following heavier or more prolonged drug use, a psychotic disorder may continue for a longer period after the use of the drug has ended. This kind of illness may also be called a drug-induced psychosis. Thirdly, there is a view that the use of drugs may in some cases provoke a psychotic illness, which then persists for much longer after drug use ceases. In these cases it might be thought that the drugs trigger the illness, or are one causal factor, among others, which set an illness going. The term drug-induced psychosis, however, becomes more tenuous, and may be less applicable in this third category of cases. It is in this area that there is most controversy.

Dr Christie Brown further noted that cannabis, in particular, may relate to psychiatric illness in a number of different ways. First, acute cannabis intoxication can present as a brief psychotic illness. Secondly, many authorities believe that, particularly after heavy use, cannabis may produce a psychosis persisting for longer than acute intoxication, with characteristics of schizophrenia. Thirdly, some studies have reported an association between heavy cannabis use and the later development of schizophrenia, and there is also good evidence that cannabis use may worsen the symptoms of an established schizophrenic illness.

The research findings in this field therefore present a complex and uncertain picture.

In Jason Mitchell's case there were clearly difficulties in deciding what role drugs played in his psychotic illness. Acute intoxication was not the issue. As Dr Christie Brown noted:

> There was doubt as to whether he should be thought of as having a drug-induced psychotic disorder which could be expected to resolve without medication if he abstained from drug use; a 'residual and late onset psychotic disorder' perhaps provoked by drugs but continuing independently; or an independent schizophrenic illness possibly made worse by drugs.

Dr Christie Brown's view, with which we agree, is that it was both reasonable and right for Dr Goddard and his colleagues to consider the diagnosis of drug-induced psychosis after Jason Mitchell had been transferred to their care. Jason Mitchell was a young man whose illness had developed in a setting of drug abuse, and his behaviour had been difficult and troublesome, both when he had been on and off anti-psychotic medication. It would be wrong and undesirable for a patient to remain on long term anti-psychotic medication when it was not necessary, and therefore a further trial off medication was not unreasonable.

In conclusion, on the basis of his detailed review of the records from West Park and St Clement's Hospitals, Dr Christie Brown reported that in his view schizophrenia was the 'best fit' diagnosis, but he also stated clearly that this was not a straightforward case and the diagnosis was not clear cut. A diagnosis of drug-induced psychosis was not unreasonable.

Oral evidence

In giving oral evidence Dr Christie Brown told the Inquiry that he thought the most compelling evidence favouring a diagnosis of schizophrenia, rather than drug-induced psychosis, was that when medication was withdrawn Jason Mitchell developed symptoms strongly suggestive of schizophrenia. The features he displayed were not simply disruptive, aggressive, difficult behaviour, but there were suggestions of thought disorder and complaints of auditory hallucinations.

Dr Yeldham, in her oral evidence to the Inquiry, distinguished between the features in Jason Mitchell's behaviour which she saw as an expression of his prevailing personality, and other forms of a behaviour which appeared to be indicative of psychotic illness. She described him in personality as an angry young man, inclined to rebel against authority, disliking rules and not placing a high value on other people's property. His ability or willingness to talk about what he was feeling and experiencing was also variable. Distinct from those features, however, she described another set of behaviours which came gradually to dominate the picture when Jason Mitchell was off medication:

> What I eventually came to see as signs of deterioration were a neglect of [his] appearance. He would neglect his hygiene, he would avoid bathing and further than that he would wear clothing that either he did not care about or he did not assemble with the same kind of care that he usually did.
>
> ... He would become much more disruptive in terms of his sleeping pattern. He might sleep very little for the whole night and he would not necessarily make up in sleep the next day. And the activities he engaged in whilst he was up at night would be different – one might say the normal activities might be television or music, albeit too loud or disturbing to other people ... when he was ill he might be doing things like drawing or carrying on some kind of conversation or even at times sitting in the dark, sitting and staring at a blank television screen, and when interrupted or asked about that afterwards, he sometimes said that he was meditating but more often would not explain it at all.
>
> ... There was a general change in the way he communicated .... When he deteriorated off medication he withdrew much more into himself and he neglected those relationships [with staff] and he did not talk with them or did not talk in a way that they could understand and would sit for many hours in different positions.
>
> ... He was actually in general pleasanter and more accessible when well, and when ill it was even more difficult to get him to talk and he was more irritable and he was not able – there was occasional evidence of thought disorder – that it was much harder to actually hold a conversation with him ... he could be a very warm, caring individual, which perhaps one would not necessarily expect to see from somebody who was recovering from a schizophrenic illness.

Similarly, Dr Yeldham summarised the features that became evident in early 1992 after Jason Mitchell's medication was stopped as follows:

Changes in his ability to communicate; his tendency to withdraw from friends; preoccupation with religious matters; he had taken up sketching and was sketching and talking about religious themes including devils and preoccupation with devils. By the time we got to February [1992] there was also occasional evidence of some classical psychotic phenomena in that there was some thought disorder and although we got no direct evidence of hallucinations the nursing observation and certainly mine on occasion in interview was that he was probably responding to hallucinations.

When it was put to her by Mr Thorold that she did not have direct evidence of first rank symptoms of schizophrenia, but nonetheless there were present features persuasive of that diagnosis, she agreed. In her view, Jason Mitchell's personality characteristics did not amount to a diagnosis of personality disorder.

In his oral evidence to the Inquiry Dr Goddard continued to favour the view that Jason Mitchell had drug-induced symptoms rather than schizophrenia. Dr Goddard acknowledged that in the light of information that became available later the case for a diagnosis of paranoid schizophrenia appeared to be stronger, but he was not persuaded by the retrospective opinions of the forensic psychiatrists who had seen Jason Mitchell after the killings. He acknowledged the difficulty and uncertainty of the diagnostic issue:

I think the jury must stay out on this man's exact mental state and the various aetiological, causative, provocative factors in the presentation of his mental state. I think only time will tell. It is a very unusual case.

Dr Goddard persisted in the view, however, that Jason Mitchell had an antisocial personality disorder.

Post-arrest assessments

On 20 December 1994 Dr Goddard was informed that Jason Mitchell was under arrest on suspicion of murder. Although he was not the duty consultant Dr Goddard went to the police station that night ostensibly for the police purpose of determining Jason Mitchell's fitness for detention and interview. He nevertheless carried out a detailed assessment in what must have been harrowing personal circumstances. He had two sessions that evening with Jason Mitchell, who appeared calm, coherent and not in any way distressed. He showed no objective evidence of psychotic illness and his manner in responding to questions was thoughtful and considered. Jason Mitchell reported to Dr Goddard that he had not felt influenced by any abnormal experiences or beliefs at the time of the killings, and claimed that he had not experienced any auditory hallucinations during the sixteen months since his medication had been stopped. He also denied using illicit drugs for the last twelve months. He showed no features of intoxication. In a letter written the following day to Dr Knight, the police surgeon who had been present at the earlier session which lasted only ten minutes, Dr Goddard wrote:

> I concluded that Jason Mitchell was fit to be detained and fit to be questioned by police. I was not of the opinion that he suffered from a mental illness, or mental disorder for which I could recommend detention under the Mental Health Act 1983. It seems likely that Jason Mitchell suffers from a severe personality disorder of the anti-social kind which is characterised as psychopathic under the Mental Health Act, but I did not feel that detention and treatment in hospital was likely to alleviate or prevent a deterioration of the condition.

The forensic psychiatrists who saw Jason Mitchell following the killings formed diagnostic impressions that differed markedly from those of Dr Goddard. The first forensic psychiatrist to see Jason Mitchell was Dr Hadrian Ball, from the Norvic Clinic Regional Secure Unit, Norwich. He saw Jason Mitchell in police custody on 21 December 1994, one day after Dr Goddard, from whom he had obtained some background history over the telephone.

Dr Ball was immediately struck by the oddness and strangeness of Jason Mitchell's demeanour. His posture was manneristic, and his mood appeared to have an 'ecstatic' quality, which was wholly inappropriate to his circumstances. In the interview Jason Mitchell was suspicious, very guarded and appeared preoccupied with the precise words used by Dr Ball in asking questions. Dr Ball's initial impression was that Jason Mitchell was mentally ill, and would need transfer to psychiatric hospital after being remanded in custody. Dr Ball contacted Norwich Prison to let the staff know that Jason Mitchell would be coming under their care and that he should be placed in the prison health care centre.

When Dr Ball next saw Jason Mitchell in Norwich Prison on 29 December, his condition was similar. His posture and mood were abnormal, he was negativistic and denied any symptoms. Contact was made with Rampton Hospital to advise that Jason Mitchell would be referred to them for admission.

A few days later there was a marked change in Jason Mitchell's mental state and behaviour. Dr Ball's consultant forensic psychiatrist colleague at the Norvic Clinic, Dr Mark Ward, who, like Dr Ball, visited Norwich Prison regularly, saw Jason Mitchell on 4 January 1995. According to the prison staff, Jason Mitchell's condition had deteriorated considerably over the previous forty-eight hours. When observed in his cell by a hospital officer he was seen to be conversing to himself in a manner that suggested that he was hallucinating. His mental state was very bizarre. He sat on the edge of his bed smiling and giggling, repeatedly saying 'four, four, four' and other alliterative speech, using words commencing with 'f'. He rocked backwards and forwards, and made loud episodic whooping noises. Both Dr Ball and Dr Ward thought Jason Mitchell's presentation was most likely to indicate acute schizophrenia.

On 11 January 1995 Dr Goddard visited Norwich Prison. He and Dr Ward interviewed Jason Mitchell together. By this time Jason Mitchell was calmer. On occasions he continued to make strange whooping noises and both doctors noted occasional facial grimacing. He described the killings in an emotionless way that was totally incongruent with the content of what he was saying. While in conversation with Dr Goddard, Jason Mitchell's mannerisms and odd vocalisations lessened, a change which suggested to Dr Goddard that these features were a transient, personality-based reaction to his circumstances, rather than evidence of psychotic symptoms which he could not control.

The polarisation of opinion was also reflected amongst the Norwich Prison Hospital staff. Staff Nurse Jean Mason told the Inquiry:

> At Norwich prison we had many a heated discussion about Jason Mitchell and the staff were divided and I am talking trained staff and hospital officers alike. One party was convinced that Jason was totally mad and without question to their mind. The other party said that he was to an element mad, but also there was an element of badness in amongst that because of the mood swings from being totally bizarre to totally lucid.
>
> Q. Have you ever come across anybody else presenting with this range of variability?
> A. No, I have not seen anything like this before.
> Q. Did you or did any other staff think that some or all or part of his presentation might be simulation?

A. Some staff were of the opinion that it was feigned. As I say, there were two distinct camps and some people from one camp would swing to the other and vice-versa.

Dr Ian Wilson, consultant forensic psychiatrist at Rampton Hospital, visited Norwich Prison and assessed Jason Mitchell on 13 January 1995. By this time Jason Mitchell's manner and behaviour had caused a high level of concern and fear amongst prison staff. Dr Wilson's interview with Jason Mitchell was brief and carried out in the presence of four prison officers in the interview room. He was very tense, sitting rigid and staring fixedly at Dr Wilson. He showed none of the abnormal forms of speech observed previously, but was particularly reluctant to talk when asked about psychotic symptoms. Although he denied such symptoms when asked, he occasionally looked preoccupied and his concentration broke off during conversation in a way that suggested to Dr Wilson that he may have been hallucinating. Jason Mitchell's account of the killings was associated with strange ideas about the symbolic importance of Christmas. Dr Wilson's impression was that he had underlying delusional beliefs. Dr Wilson considered that Jason Mitchell's presentation was consistent with a schizophrenic illness and that he needed urgent transfer to Rampton Hospital. He was subsequently transferred on 18 January 1995 to Rampton by the Home Secretary under sections 48 and 49 of the Mental Health Act 1983.

Dr Wilson reported on Jason Mitchell's condition at the time of his assessment in Norwich Prison as follows:

> Mr Mitchell was remanded in custody and received at Norwich Prison on 22nd December 1994, when he was described as being cold, aloof, wary and suspicious, but not to present any active management problems. He was placed on the hospital wing of the prison to allow close nursing observation, and on 2nd January 1995 it was noted that there was a sudden deterioration in his mental state. According to information from the psychiatric charge nurse Mr Mitchell spent the time sitting on the edge of his bed, smiling for no reason and covering his mouth with his hand. He showed what was described as a facile and inappropriate affect and he responded to questions by endlessly repeating the number 'four'. This continued for two days at which time the repetitive four gave way to alliterative speech based on the letter 'F ', repeating such phrases as 'furry faced fucker' and 'feeling fine for fish', in the same meaningless fashion as he had repeated the number four. At about this time, on 4 January 1995, he was seen by Dr Mark Ward, consultant forensic psychiatrist

from the Norvic Clinic, who described Mr Mitchell as showing 'one of the most bizarre mental states I have seen'. Dr Ward concluded that Mr Mitchell was suffering from acute schizophrenia.

There was continued deterioration in Mr Mitchell's mental state and his alliterative speech was followed by 'whooping' and 'beeping' noises which he kept up throughout the time that he was awake, both when on his own and when staff tried to engage him in conversation. He also repetitively spat into his hands and continued to show what was described as incongruous and inappropriate giggling. The health care staff were convinced that he was responding to auditory hallucinations during this time. There were no episodes of aggression but Mr Mitchell was perceived by staff as having an air of menace about him which was sufficiently worrying for them to be very cautious in their dealings with him. At the time of my assessment visit on 13 January 1995, staff were careful to ensure that the landing was cleared in order to enable him to be kept under maximum observation when bringing him to the interview room.

Dr Wilson became Jason Mitchell's responsible medical officer after the transfer to Rampton in January 1995. Five months later, in June 1995, Dr Wilson completed a psychiatric report for Jason Mitchell's trial at Ipswich Crown Court. Dr Wilson summarised Jason Mitchell's progress at Rampton during those months as follows:

Mr Mitchell was initially very tense and agitated and intensely suspicious of staff. He was confrontational in his manner and verbally aggressive and responded to the approaches of staff with hostility although there was no physical aggression. He was periodically observed making strange noises, the whooping noises referred to in prison, laughing to himself and carrying out bizarre hand gestures. He was unco-operative with medical examination but the above pattern of behaviour was sustained over an eight week period during which time he became increasingly menacing, and anti-psychotic medication was introduced on 10 March 1995. Mr Mitchell was very resentful of this and briefly became more agitated and emotionally disinhibited, making inappropriate sexual suggestions to female nursing staff, showing marked irritability and excitability and becoming overactive, abusive and confrontational. This disturbed pattern of behaviour persisted for about three weeks and during this time he admitted to nursing staff that he had been experiencing auditory hallucinations but he did not describe the nature of these voices and subsequently denied having said this.

Mr Mitchell's response to the anti-psychotic medication, depot Haloperidol at a dose of 200 mg im fortnightly, was in keeping with the expected therapeutic action of the medication and since its introduction a clear positive response has been noted with progressive improvement in Mr Mitchell's mental state and behaviour.

As his mental state has become more settled so Mr Mitchell has been more prepared to discuss the offences with which he is charged. However, he has given different explanations on different occasions and it is not possible to be confident about which of these explanations most accurately reflects his motivation at the time.

Dr Wilson's diagnostic conclusion was as follows:

Mr Mitchell is mentally disordered within the meaning of the Mental Health Act 1983, the mental illness from which he is suffering being schizophrenia.

He has a clearly documented history of schizophrenic illness first diagnosed in 1990 which responded gradually to treatment with anti-psychotic medication followed by a relapse on withdrawal of medication. This relapse was characterised by marked behavioural changes, irritability and refusal or inability to engage in more than a brief conversation but few florid psychotic symptoms as, in the view of the consultant responsible for his treatment at the time, he was able to conceal psychotic phenomena to which on occasion he appeared to respond. This pattern of presentation described by Dr Yeldham at West Park Hospital is very similar to the way in which Mr Mitchell has presented during the period of assessment and treatment at Rampton Hospital.

Whilst an inpatient at St Clement's Hospital Mr Mitchell's medication was withdrawn for a second time and the available reports describe a pattern of deterioration similar to that observed on withdrawal of medication at West Park Hospital. The changes described, in particular in his increasingly disturbed relationships with others, emotional disturbance, socially inappropriate behaviour, extreme and bizarre changes in his presentation, preoccupied state and confrontational withdrawal of co-operation, are consistent with recurrence of symptoms of schizophrenia. It is therefore likely that he was acutely mentally ill at the time of the alleged murders.

Mr Mitchell's mental state has improved since the re-introduction of anti-psychotic medication at Rampton Hospital and he is now able to sustain rational conversations and co-operate more constructively with treatment. However, this is not a stable situation and he still shows unpredictable irritability and hostility and is inconsistent in the information he gives to staff. His treatment is at a very early stage.

In giving oral evidence to the Inquiry, Dr Wilson described how he and his colleagues had faced similar difficulties in the diagnostic assessment of Jason Mitchell to those experienced by previous clinical teams. Dr Wilson and his nursing colleagues at Rampton had been uncertain how to interpret his history and presentation on admission. There was an early occasion when Jason Mitchell was observed to be 'laughing inanely at unknown stimuli and making strange noises', and there was some suspicion amongst the staff that he may have been simulating psychotic symptoms. On balance, however, Dr Wilson thought that while the variation in intensity of Jason Mitchell's odd behaviour might be influenced by personality factors, the fundamental cause of them was psychosis. By early March 1995, the Rampton team was convinced that he had genuine psychotic symptoms and was experiencing hallucinations. He was tense and uncommunicative and no rapport could be established with him. It was concluded that anti-psychotic medication should be withheld no longer. Gradually, Jason Mitchell's condition changed after the medication was started. He became less hostile, less menacing and more approachable and flexible.

Dr Wilson agreed that the problem of establishing a diagnosis was peculiarly difficult in Jason Mitchell's case. He had an unusual ability to hide and mask symptoms, and he lacked the blunting of affect and personality that is often characteristic of chronic schizophrenic illness.

The two other consultant forensic psychiatrists who prepared psychiatric reports for Jason Mitchell's trial at Ipswich Crown Court also concluded that Jason Mitchell had schizophrenia. Dr Hadrian Ball, in his report dated 6 June 1995 concluded:

> Jason Mitchell is a 24-year-old man who is clearly suffering from a serious mental illness, namely schizophrenia. This illness has almost certainly been present since his late teenage years. It has been manifested by a number of symptoms and abnormal features including at times hallucinations, delusions, formal thought disorder (a disorder of abstract thinking characteristic of serious mental illness) and other softer signs such as abnormal moods, incongruous emotional reactions and abnormal postures.
> … Jason Mitchell's history cannot be accounted for by drug abuse or personality disorder or both.

Likewise Dr Paul Bowden, consultant forensic psychiatrist at the Maudsley Hospital reported on 21 June 1995 that in his interview with Jason Mitchell at Rampton Hospital three weeks earlier:

> Mr Mitchell's posture was abnormal and he stared in a disconcerting way. His affect was grossly abnormal and incongruous and he repeatedly emphasised that he was not, and never had been men-

tally ill, and that he was completely unconcerned about both the killings and his predicament. His sole wish was to return to prison.

He spoke sometimes in a grandiose manner referring to his coming to an understanding of the world, but when questioned about his ideas his replies were evasive, or meaningless and fatuous. He spoke of the killings and his father's dismemberment in an emotionless way ....

At times it was very difficult to understand the meaning of Mr Mitchell's statements, particularly when he spoke about being bisexual. His thinking was concrete and he used words (such as 'whim') in an idiosyncratic manner. He became threatening when these obscurities were challenged. His denial of active symptoms of mental illness was absolute, unconvincing and accompanied by a marked change in his manner – from fatuous indifference to menace.

In conclusion, Mr Mitchell has a ten year history of schizophrenia. He is insightless and non-compliant with medication. He has the capacity to lie and deceive and he is both intelligent and well versed in the symptoms of mental illness and in its treatment. He currently shows abnormalities of thinking and behaviour which are characteristic of schizophrenia ....

All three forensic psychiatrists – Dr Ball, Dr Bowden and Dr Wilson – concluded that in relation to the murder charges, Jason Mitchell's mental illness constituted an abnormality of mind which substantially impaired his mental responsibility for his alleged acts. The pleas of guilty to manslaughter on the grounds of diminished responsibility were accepted by the Court.

Conclusions

Having reviewed the various views reached by others, our impressions were as follows. First, we were impressed by the careful and considered way in which the problem of establishing a diagnosis was pursued by the psychiatrists and clinical teams. Much time and effort was spent in observing and thinking about Jason Mitchell, and in reviewing the various diagnostic possibilities. It was right, in principle, to consider whether earlier diagnoses remained valid in the light of accumulating evidence, and there was a proper concern not to continue the use of anti-psychotic medication indefinitely unless this was properly justified. Jason Mitchell's case was, genuinely and unusually, difficult.

We found the arguments in favour of a diagnosis of schizophrenia, however, more compelling than those in favour of a primary diagnosis of drug-induced psychosis or personality disorder. That is not to say that Jason Mitchell's personality characteristics and drug-taking were unimportant: they were an integral part of the total clinical picture. But they did not constitute a persuasive alternative to a primary diagnosis of schizophrenia. The evidence of illicit drug-taking that could be related in a specific way to acute psychotic symptoms was thin. We agree with Dr Christie Brown's overall appraisal that there was recurrent evidence of returning psychotic symptomatology and behaviour strongly suggestive of schizophrenia when Jason Mitchell stopped taking anti-psychotic medication. Conversely, there was good evidence of him responding to anti-psychotic medication by becoming gradually less hostile, less withdrawn and more amenable and flexible.

There is no doubt, however, that there are features which could lead to doubt about the diagnosis. The intensity of the abnormal features was variable, and Jason Mitchell did not show evidence of the emotional blunting and gradual deterioration of personality and social functioning that can characterise a chronic schizo-phrenic illness.

Two important additional sources of information emerged after Jason Mitchell's admission to St Clement's Hospital which, in retrospect, add further weight to the case for schizophrenia. First, there were the clinical observations in Rampton Hospital suggest-ing schizophrenic symptoms when Jason Mitchell was off medica-tion for two months, and gradual and marked improvement thereafter when anti-psychotic medication was restarted. Sec-ondly, there was the discovery of the extensive medical records compiled at HMYOI Feltham by Dr Latif, visiting consultant psychiatrist, in 1988 and 1989. Although not wholly conclusive, those records, as discussed in Chapter VI, appear to give detailed descriptions of psychotic features that, on first reading, are imme-diately suggestive of schizophrenia. These records, however, were mislaid. The clinical teams at West Park and St Clement's Hospi-tals, and the forensic psychiatrists who subsequently saw Jason Mitchell before his trial, were deprived of any knowledge of their contents.

The diagnostic difficulties in Jason Mitchell's case have been described at length in this chapter. The challenges they posed for the clinical staff involved in his care need to be understood. They were intrinsic to Jason Mitchell's case, and the view of Dr Goddard and his colleagues was not unreasonable. Nor did it reflect any lack of careful thought and investigation, although a second opinion might profitably have been sought. Although the differences of diagnostic opinion are a central feature of Jason Mitchell's clinical history, it is by no means certain that his treatment and management would have been different if the Easton House clinical team had accepted that he suffered from schizophrenia. It cannot be concluded that an error of diagnosis led to the killings because Jason Mitchell was in an unmedicated state. It could be hypothesised in retrospect that, had the existence of the Feltham medical records of 1988/89 been known, they may have been seen as indicating a first episode of schizophrenia at that time. Jason Mitchell's subsequent offence and admission to West Park Hospital in 1990 would then have been seen as arising from a second episode of that illness. This more extensive history might have led to a stronger presumption in favour of a diagnosis of schizophrenia and in favour of maintaining long-term medication to prevent relapse.

There is further reason why we cannot know whether a consistent diagnosis of schizophrenia would have made any difference to the outcome. The exact relationship between Jason Mitchell's mental illness and his killings remains a mystery. The degree to which he may or may not have been influenced by psychotic symptoms, and the nature of that influence has not yet been elucidated, and probably cannot be at this stage. A fuller picture may – or may not – emerge in time.

IV. Other Assessments

Without Contraries is no progression.
William Blake, 'The Marriage of Heaven and Hell'

Many of the assessments by the professional staff in disciplines other than psychiatry and nursing are of considerable interest. They contained observations and insights into Jason Mitchell's thoughts and feelings which were rarely recorded in the medical and nursing notes and which could present a different perspective on his case. They tended to be recorded in detail, but were marginalised. The status and use made of these contributions merit consideration. These assessments were infrequently referred to by the psychiatrists who reviewed the documentation, and they could also be seen as potentially challenging the uniform view of the core clinical team. Staff, who may be perceived by patients as less powerful than the core team of doctors and nurses, can be the recipients of important information. For this reason alone **we recommend** that attention should be paid to capturing the significant contributions of such staff more systematically, for example in the compilation of reports for case conferences, other reviews, such as Mental Health Review Tribunals, and hospital transfers.

Contributions of individual staff at West Park and St Clement's Hospitals are summarised below. The person whose work was most extensively discussed in the course of our Inquiry was Mrs Jackie Leaver, who was a Technical Instructor in the Occupational Therapy Department at West Park Hospital. Her contribution will be considered at the end of this chapter.

Speech and language therapy: Niki Muir, West Park Hospital

Niki Muir saw Jason Mitchell in group therapy sessions at West Park Hospital for a period of nearly two years. In her statement to the Inquiry, Mrs Muir described how Jason Mitchell initially showed poor concentration and some immature and disruptive behaviour. Latterly, however:

... Jason Mitchell became much more able to turn take (*sic*) and he was very interested in what the group was learning about the processes of communication. He appeared a young man who loved words and loved company. Superficially his communication appeared good, but my opinion is that this was misleading. His situational understanding and his grasp of interaction at a deeper level of processing were simplistic and often erroneous. He could often fail to determine the intentions of others or foresee the consequences of his communicative actions on others. He found it quite difficult to take another person's perspective. Written language was a particular problem, with omissions and errors of both form and content. This was partly because of educational and attentional shortfall, partly because of the difficulty in organising his thoughts concisely and partly because of his difficulty in selecting appropriate vocabulary and grammar in order to express his ideas.

I felt that Jason Mitchell responded to the group because it was based on cognitive behavioural principles and it therefore offered the members a structured environment in order to practise making change. It is likely that because Jason Mitchell is immature, often concrete and very often confused by his ideas and unable to organise them, he found the structure supportive. He needed very clear guidelines and when he got those he made improvement and displayed insight and sensitivity to other group members. At that time he had a weekly therapy programme and all disciplines involved kept in close liaison via note sharing and attendance at case conferences. The communication group was co-run by Occupational Therapy Technical Instructors, with myself as lead Therapist.

I did not do any formal individual sessions with Jason Mitchell. My feeling was that too much attention could produce a reverse effect and that any direct 'talking' psychotherapy would overload him. However, on some occasions within the group Jason Mitchell did disclose feelings of rejection and anger towards his family and fear of making a return to Suffolk. On those occasions coping strategies were discussed and other group members offered their experiences.

Jason Mitchell wrote to me, among others, at West Park after he left. The letters indicated that he was missing the structured week. My responses centred on further practical coping strategies for change and the need to make new relationships within the team at that time. I felt concern when he wrote regarding coming off medication and moving on. This concern was that he would begin to abuse hallucinogenic drugs again and become grossly psychotic or that, without high levels of support, he would prove unable to structure his own life adequately. Never at any time when I was involved with Jason Mitchell's care did I feel threatened.

Mrs Muir's report indicates that she had identified a number of Jason Mitchell's difficulties, his variable social behaviour, his need for structure, and his emotional conflicts in relation to his family and background. She suggested potential difficulties in working with him in a psychotherapeutic way, and drew attention to the contrast between his verbal fluency and his more fundamental difficulties of communication, understanding and empathy for others. Her view of his prognosis was appropriately guarded.

Social work: Joan Rapaport, West Park Hospital

Mrs Rapaport started work at West Park Hospital in September 1990, shortly after Jason Mitchell's admission. She described her work with him as reactive rather than proactive, and it focused mainly on the issue of Jason Mitchell's possible discharge into the community.

She formed the view that Jason Mitchell was a young man with a deprived family background, adrift from his family and with no connections in the Surrey area. Her understanding of the offence of 1990 was severely diluted. She saw it as 'a cry for help', and stated that Jason Mitchell had not intended to harm the caretaker. Even when made aware of the full details of the offence, she remained of the view that it could be considered 'a cry for help'. She did not think that Jason Mitchell posed a risk towards anyone, and pointed out that at the time of his conditional discharge by the tribunal, she had been content to drive him back, unescorted, after they had jointly visited Jason Mitchell's father at his home in Bramford.

She obtained her information from weekly case conferences and did not read the nursing or medical notes. She was aware of the work which Jackie Leaver was undertaking, and it was clear that it had been sanctioned. She was also aware of some of Niki Muir's work. She said that in her own work she was under heavy pressure at the time.

Her attempts to pursue understanding of Jason Mitchell's family relationships and his feelings towards his family were severely hampered by his 'closed' attitude towards sharing such information. She was able to make progress only when the statutory requirement arose of preparing a report for the Mental Health Review Tribunal. She was also hampered by the distance of the hospital from Jason Mitchell's home, and the fact that Jason Mitchell's father was not on the telephone and did not respond to letters.

Her report of May 1991 to the Tribunal on Jason Mitchell's family circumstances relied on Jason Mitchell's own account, which was reasonably accurate, and a report on home circumstances from a social work assistant allocated by Suffolk Social Services Department, who undertook the home visit she had requested. At that time Jason Mitchell was not seeking to return to Ipswich. Mrs Rapaport noted that Jason Mitchell was complying with his medication, accepted that he had been ill and would continue to require medication for some considerable period of time. He intended to apologise to his victim. She represented the view that Jason Mitchell was being co-operative and obliging. She considered that positive steps could be taken to facilitate the preparation of after-care arrangements.

Mrs Rapaport had also suggested that Jackie Leaver should be invited to attend the Mental Health Review Tribunal hearing.

Following the first tribunal hearing, Mrs Rapaport made efforts to obtain a community placement for Jason Mitchell in the Cambridge area. In September 1992, following Jason Mitchell's absconding to visit his father and his expression of concerns about his father's health, Dr Yeldham asked Mrs Rapaport to explore Jason Mitchell's home circumstances. At that time Mrs Rapaport felt unable to do so, because Jason Mitchell had made it clear he did not want her to make contact, and she could not proceed without his permission. In October 1992, the accompanied home visit did proceed. On 31 October she completed a detailed report of the home visit to Jason Mitchell's father, noting that he would welcome his son's return home on a permanent basis, that the family would try to be supportive, but they clearly displayed a degree of ambivalence. Mrs Rapaport subsequently formed the view that Jason Mitchell should not live with his father. She believed Jason Mitchell was also ambivalent about this and hurt by his father's failure to make contact.

The report to the next Mental Health Review Tribunal hearing in 1993 was prepared in Mrs Rapaport's absence, although in consultation with her; and she supported the recommendation that Jason Mitchell should return to Suffolk since: 'This would facilitate working with his family and the problems that lay behind that.' It had been difficult to do such work from Surrey.

Mrs Rapaport regarded the report to the Mental Health Review Tribunal as a case summary for the purpose of Jason Mitchell's transfer of care to Suffolk. Mrs Rapaport also visited the new social worker (Jane Barnett) to 'hand over' the case. She personally introduced Miss Barnett to Jason Mitchell, but did not transfer the case records, as this was not departmental policy. **We recommend** that Social Services Departments who transfer case responsibility for restricted patients should also transfer the case record.

Mrs Rapaport's work clearly focused on family issues which, to her frustration, she was unable to investigate satisfactorily because of Jason Mitchell's reluctance, the family's unresponsiveness, and the distance of the family from Surrey. She arranged a visit to the family by Suffolk Social Services Department and subsequently established direct contact with Jason Mitchell's father. She assisted Jason Mitchell in a home visit. Her approach was strongly influenced by an advocacy model. Her assessment of the gravity of the 1990 offence was clearly deficient, and reinforces our recommendation in Chapter VIII that greater emphasis should be placed by all professionals on reaching a clear understanding of the facts, as well as the patient's view of them.

Social work: Jane Barnett, St Clement's Hospital

Jason Mitchell's case was allocated to Jane Barnett in May 1993 on his transfer to Ipswich. Mrs Rapaport had made a referral by telephone and a handover visit was arranged for 24 May. At that meeting Mrs Rapaport gave Miss Barnett background information and at a joint meeting with Jason Mitchell the same material was shared. References were made to the undesirability of Jason Mitchell's discharge home to his father, and Jason Mitchell's ambivalent feelings towards him. Miss Barnett had access to the medical notes and to material transferred to Easton House from West Park.

Miss Barnett visited Jason Mitchell's father in June 1993. Jason Mitchell told her that he was missing the group and therapeutic work in which he had been active at West Park Hospital, and he said he would like to continue such work. At a case conference on 4 August 1993, it was agreed that Jason Mitchell's medication would be reduced and that Jane Barnett should commence a community care assessment to identify Jason Mitchell's housing needs.

Jason Mitchell was keen to move to a therapeutic setting, but was incapable of seeing that he would require considerable support on discharge, having been in institutional settings for several years since late adolescence. Miss Barnett was keen to find a therapeutic residential placement, and sought funding for an out of county placement since no such service was available in Suffolk.

In her summary, dated February 1994, Miss Barnett described Jason Mitchell as follows:

> ... presents as very confident and able but much anxiety and lack of confidence hidden beneath that. Periodically Jason Mitchell creates havoc – challenging, 'manipulative', unco-operative .... Nursing staff generally feel Jason Mitchell happier with clear and firm structures and boundaries. He is often well motivated but also challenging and rebellious. Jason Mitchell's reactions to his situation are typically adolescent – he has, because of his prolonged stays in total institutions still to work through this.

Shortly after this report was written the therapeutic community hostel, Greenwoods, declined to accept Jason Mitchell. Miss Barnett then sought a number of other placements and ultimately supported Jason Mitchell's proposed move to a shared house, run by MIND at Larkhill Way, Felixstowe. When questioned about its suitability, Miss Barnett indicated that it offered a degree of privacy within a supportive environment, she had confidence in the project management, and was influenced by Jason Mitchell's declining interest in therapeutic settings and his warm support for a move to Larkhill Way. When asked how much emphasis she gave to patient choice, she observed that it was necessary to have the co-operation of the client, but that judgments about where best to place a patient in after care could be finely balanced.

At the wish of the project manager, Miss Barnett did not accompany Jason Mitchell on his interview at Larkhill Way. Miss Barnett was clear that she gave a verbal briefing about Jason Mitchell's 1990 offence, his status and his needs, and that she offered a copy of his case history which was declined by the project leader. (There was dispute about the degree of information exchanged, but Miss Barnett was sure that she gave a sufficient verbal briefing, and there is no reason to doubt her.) In retrospect, she believed that in this matter, as in others, she should have been more assertive and should have made more detailed records.

When Jason Mitchell was residing at Larkhill Way, she maintained contact with him and with staff at the unit. She became aware of the deteriorating situation between Jason Mitchell and the other residents, but did not detect any features of mental illness; nor did she interpret Jason Mitchell's behaviour as indicating early signs of a relapse.

Good contact was maintained between her and Jason Mitchell's RMO, Dr Goddard, and review conferences were held throughout the period of Jason Mitchell's stay in the community. The deterioration in relationships at Larkhill Way was difficult to explore with Jason Mitchell, because the project staff were unwilling to share their concerns with Jason Mitchell, and he did not realise the impact of his behaviour on the other residents. After Jason Mitchell's readmission to Easton House, Miss Barnett continued to seek alternative independent accommodation for him outside hospital, with substantial (daily) support.

Miss Barnett saw her role as 'looking forward and seeking to find accommodation for Jason Mitchell in order to proceed with his conditional discharge'. She mistakenly formed the conclusion from her discussions with Joan Rapaport and her reading of Jackie Leaver's report that such psychological work as could be done in relation to Jason Mitchell's family history had been completed at West Park. She was conscious of Jason Mitchell's need to continue such exploration; hence her application to the Greenwoods Hostel. In consultation with her supervisor, however, she was clear that it was not her personal role to undertake such individual psychological work, and she was rightly aware that such involvement would need to be carefully structured and sustained. Within her professional role with Jason Mitchell, this was not possible. Furthermore, such support could not be obtained from the Community Mental Health Team. Miss Barnett's community care assessment was insightful. In it she described Jason Mitchell's childhood as 'dominated by a series of losses and an almost complete lack of structure or boundaries'. She described the inconsistent contact with his family, and his confident and competent manner which could mask his lack of self-esteem and the unreality of some of his expectations and hopes. She concluded:

> For five out the last seven years of his life Jason Mitchell has been living in total institutions with highly structured regimes and very clear boundaries and controls .... The transition from hospital to the community and to adult responsibility will be fraught with dangers and temptations for Jason Mitchell. He requires emotional and psychological support. If these needs are not met and Jason Mitchell returns to his past way of life, impulsive, aimless and anti-social,

then he could also become a danger to the community. Jason Mitchell recognises this and it frightens him.

These comments were written in February 1994. They draw on Jackie Leaver's observations, confirmed by Miss Barnett's experience. Miss Barnett was clear in giving oral evidence to the Inquiry that the dangers to which she referred were that Jason Mitchell might resume drug-taking and embark upon a career of burglary to support his habit. She did not expect the homicides and and had not felt intimidated by Jason Mitchell herself; indeed she liked him.

Miss Barnett fulfilled her obligations as the named social worker and social supervisor. She diligently sought accommodation for Jason Mitchell, established contact with his family, and maintained regular contact with him. She consistently identified his need for therapeutic support, but was unable to identify any alternative source of support for him. In the Inquiry hearings she displayed a becoming degree of self-criticism, but in our view she supported Jason Mitchell, sensitively and appropriately, within the level of her skill and supervision.

Clinical psychology

The notes of West Park Hospital contain a referral to the Psychology Department which reads thus:

> He at present intends to do few subjects for GCSE. We are not convinced whether he is capable. He had learning difficulties in the past and went to a special school. His verbal and performance skills will be variable according to our observation. Will appreciate an intelligence test of this man.
> D. Malcolm

All that is contained in the subsequent notes is a Wechsler Adult Intelligence Scale – Revised (WAIS-R) record form dated 28.10.92. On this form Jason Mitchell is recorded as having a Verbal IQ of 101 and a Performance IQ of 90, giving a Full Scale IQ of 97. The testers are identified on the form as 'AT & WA'. Jason Mitchell is noted to be left-handed.

There is no report based on this testing in the records. Such an interpretative report from a psychologist would be required to explain the wide variability of subtest performance which ranges from scores on Digit Span (attention span) and Picture Completion which place him in the bottom 16% of the population, to scores on Comprehension (Social Understanding) and Similarities (Abstract Concepts) that place him in the top 9% and top 16% of the population respectively. It is thus insufficient and misleading to summarise such variability by simply describing him as being in the category of 'average intelligence'.

Earlier psychological assessments

A report from W.F. Herbert, County Educational Psychologist, Suffolk County Council, to the Inquiry, dated 13 September 1995, indicates that Jason Mitchell was referred, at the age of 7, to an Educational Psychologist by his primary school headmaster and, in a report dated 15 September 1977, Jason Mitchell was said to be 'a child of average ability with limited powers of concentration'. It was noted that teachers were as concerned about his distractibility, willingness to wander out of class, and family background, as they were by his poor academic attainments. At secondary school, when Jason Mitchell was 13, he was transferred to Park Side Unit for pupils with emotional and behavioural difficulties, and was described there as a 'withdrawn, phobic and a very unhappy boy'.

Full psychological assessments were never undertaken while Jason Mitchell was a patient within his local psychiatric services. This applies both to full psychometric assessments – which were clearly indicated, given his educational difficulties and a pattern of highly variable abilities – and also a psychological assessment of his emotional difficulties and 'inner life'. This is further discussed in Chapter XIII. While psychology resources were clearly a problem, both at West Park Hospital and St Clement's, both RMOs attested to the fact that clinical psychology involvement could have been obtained, should they have deemed it important in this case.

Art therapy: West Park Hospital

Ms Christine Holloway, Technical Instructor III within the Occupational Therapy Department at West Park Hospital, produced a report, dated 11 February 1993, summarising Jason Mitchell's activities in an Art Therapy Group, and an 'Unstructured Group'. The report noted that he had 'dropped out' of these activities during recent months. When he had attended the Art Therapy Group:

Jason Mitchell's ideas and thoughts within the group were original and usually appropriate. There were times, however, when Jason Mitchell appeared to enjoy producing work that would shock, and appeared to get some delight if he succeeded.

Jason Mitchell has always been very supportive to less able members of the group, usually giving them encouragement and support.

In the 'Unstructured Group':

He relates well with two of the other members of the group and at times can become rather destructive.

Ms Holloway's report concluded:

Jason Mitchell's report reads rather negatively but we feel there are many reasons for his recent behaviour. Within the Art Therapy group Jason Mitchell was addressing many of his personal problems regarding his family circle and we feel this became too threatening for him to handle.

Art therapy: Penelope Healey, St Clement's Hospital

Penelope Healey, Senior Art Therapist and RMN, produced written and oral evidence to the Inquiry, and showed Jason Mitchell's art work to us in a closed session. Her initial written assessment of him, dated 20 August 1993, was as follows:

Jason Mitchell had no hesitation in using the art materials and spoke warmly of his previous art therapy experiences. Throughout the assessment I experienced him as a warm, friendly and engaging young man.

He chose to work with charcoal on white paper and completed two separate sets of drawings quickly and confidently. The drawings featured human figures and related solely to his immediate family members. Almost all the figures were drawn unclothed and all without exception were 'incomplete' in the sense that they had no hands or feet – the mother having no arms either!

From these drawings Jason Mitchell identified each family member to me, including himself, whom he had positioned inside his mother's womb, as yet 'unborn'. The mother was depicted as overwhelmingly tall and towering albeit 'close' to her children, whilst the father was depicted as laying prone and on a separate sheet of paper – isolated and very much 'out of the picture' in relation to the family.

Jason Mitchell had been referred to the Art Therapy Service on 12 July 1993 by Dr Odutoye, the stated reason being: '... part of rehabilitation/challenging behaviour programme.' Extracts from Ms Healey's written statement to the Inquiry, summarising Jason Mitchell's involvement in the Art Therapy Group sessions, are set out below. He attended all available sessions between 6 September and 20 December 1993 – a total of 14.

Relationships with Group Members

Jason Mitchell was, generally speaking, more 'able' than most of the other group members in that he was quite skilled and confidently experimental in his use of the art materials as well as being more verbally articulate and sometimes fairly insightful.

He was, at all times, very caring and supportive of other group members and when it came to sharing and discussing images at the end of each session he was always thoughtful and respectful towards other people's work – as he was with his own.

When he failed to return to the group after the Christmas break at the end of December 1993, his absence was noted and often remarked upon with some regret and concern by individuals in the group.

Relationship with Therapist

Initially Jason Mitchell was a little 'guarded' in his responses and it took a while before he was able to trust that I wasn't going to 'interpret' his art work for him – but would leave him free to interpret his own.

This would manifest itself in him occasionally contradicting a comment I had made about someone's image. I felt that it was perhaps important for Jason Mitchell to feel he had some control over what was happening – it was all right for him to make comments but not for me! After the first few weeks, he relaxed at this point and was able to 'hear' what I was saying and use his own judgment about accepting or rejecting what he heard.

In terms of 'group boundaries' there was never a problem. Jason Mitchell accepted all the 'ground rules' set out at the beginning of his time in the group and with the exception of a rather annoying habit of putting his 'Doc Martin'-clad feet up on the table during the feedback session, never stepped over them in any sense. (He did modify this behaviour when I complained that I couldn't see the images through them!)

Relationship with his Art Process

As I mentioned earlier, Jason Mitchell was skilled and confident in his use of art materials and took full advantage of the wide range of materials available to him. He also used the time available to good advantage and would be totally absorbed in his own process from beginning to end.

During the feedback/sharing sessions at the end of the group it was evident that Jason Mitchell was happier discussing and exploring the work of theirs rather than his own. Having said this, he obviously took some pleasure in hearing what others had to say about his work, which more often than not, engendered a great deal of interested discussion.

Jason Mitchell's images covered a wide range of differing styles, methods and approaches. There was no particular theme running through his work although he did make references to his parents and family from time to time. These references tended to be in relation to a sense of 'being distanced' or being 'out of reach' from them.

At other times, Jason Mitchell's images would range from heavily stylised angular drawings – somewhat reminiscent to the tattoos on his face to soft but powerful landscape images – often created with soft pastels and chalks.

He rarely commented upon his work and never appeared keen to explore it in any depth – or even to attempt to explain it to anyone. His reluctance to do so was honoured and respected throughout.

Leaving the Group

Jason Mitchell's leaving the group was precipitous and unexpected. He never returned after the Christmas break in December 1993 and he did not contact myself or any of the group members to explain his absence.

When he did not turn up to the group on 10th January 1994 I checked with Nursing staff on Easton House (Jason Mitchell had been readmitted to Easton House from Linkways Ward on 29th December 1993) who informed me that Jason Mitchell had begun a new OT programme. I was aware that there had been no discussion with myself about this and that there had been no opportunity for the group to say goodbye to him, or he to them.

I spoke to both Dr Goddard and Gordon Heffer about the situation, who assured me that Jason Mitchell could carry on with the art therapy group.

I then spoke with Jason Mitchell and explained that he could still attend the art therapy group if he wished. In spite of this, Jason Mitchell did not return to the Monday art therapy group.

The pictures were striking. When Ms Healey showed them to us she described Jason Mitchell as having a good ability to produce images. She commented on the wide range of styles exhibited in the pictures, from the crudely-drawn to the sophisticated, and the wide range of techniques – from pastels to pointillism pens. She said this was unusual, except amongst adolescents.

She emphasised that she did not see it as her job to give interpretations of the art work. The pictures, she said, should not be separated from the particular context of the art therapy setting, and she sought to work with patients to discuss and reflect on their work during the sessions in which the work was produced.

Occupational therapy: Erica Smiter, St Clement's Hospital

The Inquiry received a written statement from Erica Smiter, who, as Head Occupational Therapist, had contact with Jason Mitchell from his arrival at St Clement's in May 1993 until she left her employment there in February 1994.

In May 1993, an initial treatment programme was agreed, offering:

> ... structure in the form of work to create boundaries and make Jason Mitchell feel safe, to attempt to increase his motivation and concentration, and to improve his level of personal fitness. His level of personal care and domestic skills were looked at with a view to establishing a standard before discharge.

His programme began with seven half-day sessions in woodwork and one session each in cooking, art and free time.

In June 1993 it was noted:

> The content of both work and conversation was sexual, and though he socialised with both staff and patients, his frequent use of expletives was perceived by some as offensive. The staff commented that Jason Mitchell might benefit from a more psychodynamic group to allow greater opportunity for discussion, and a suggestion for an art therapy referral was made on 6 July 1993.

In August 1993, his occupational therapy programme was altered to give greater emphasis to domestic skills, and in September an occupational therapy report was considered at a case conference in which Jason Mitchell's discharge was discussed. According to Ms Smiter's statement, at that time:

> The most important points to note are that Jason Mitchell worked in concrete terms only. He was very easily distracted when in an

unstructured environment. In the structured male environment of the workshop, Jason Mitchell could be caring and tolerant but in less structured environments with females present, he became rather a bully and showed off. He really enjoyed pushing authority but usually stopped before he got into real trouble. It was suggested at the conference that it would not be a good idea to discharge Jason Mitchell directly from Easton House and he needed to get used to more freedom gradually and slowly learn to put his own boundaries in. We also wished to pick up on any psychotic behaviour early on if it was noticed. Therefore it was decided to transfer Jason Mitchell to Linkways so he could continue his rehabilitation programme in a less structured environment.

Ms Smiter also noted that, while it had been assumed that his transfer to Ipswich had been effected so that he could be near his family, it became evident that he had little reliable or continuing contact with them, and he gave inconsistent accounts of how often he saw them.

In January 1994 Occupational Therapy staff were asked to look for specific features that might indicate mental illness. Ms Smiter described the observations made as follows:

> He was changeable and lost control.
> He reported hearing voices. (This was to a new member of staff.)
> He was displaying chaotic mannerisms – we were not sure whether he was aware of these mannerisms.
> He had exaggerated mannerisms – semi-purposeful and sometimes inappropriate.
> He smiled and laughed inappropriately.

In February 1994, Ms Smiter described him as improved and showing no strange signs or symptoms, but he could be generally difficult to manage in the workshops, he absconded, and his attendance was poor. Ms Smiter's statement concluded with the assessment that Jason Mitchell was a very immature character, who appeared to feel safe within tight boundaries; he manipulated the truth and chose younger and less experienced staff with whom to talk about difficult issues.

The occupational therapy assessments indicated the extent to which Jason Mitchell was ill equipped to cope with discharge. In her oral evidence to the Inquiry, Ms. Smiter agreed that in her view Jason Mitchell needed a very slow rehabilitation programme and a great deal of support and structure. She was emphatic that she did not believe he could have survived on his own in a council flat, but such reservations were outweighed by the imperative towards discharge:

> I think the other thing that will have to be put in is that we were seen in quite a bad light that actually we were taking so long to discharge Jason Mitchell ... I can remember there were some words said when he came to us from West Park, that they were not best pleased that we were going to pull him back into a treatment regime .... Did we have the right to keep putting him back when he had actually got a conditional discharge?

Occupational therapy: Jackie Leaver, West Park Hospital

Jackie Leaver worked as an Occupational Therapy Technical Instructor during the period of Jason Mitchell's stay in West Park Hospital. She left the hospital in December 1991. She had started to work with psychiatric patients quite late in her working life and had several years' experience before she met Jason Mitchell in 1990. She had no professional qualifications in this area of work.

In February 1991, approximately a year after Jason Mitchell's offence in Epsom, Mrs Leaver produced a seven-page report based on her sessions with Jason Mitchell. It gave an account of his early experiences, family relationships and fantasy life, including homicidal fantasies and ideas. The report is reproduced in full (apart from some omitted details relating to third parties) as an addendum to this chapter. With the benefit of hindsight, the contents of the report are significant. The report was said by Mrs Leaver to have been prepared as a result of their joint work and it is signed by her and Jason Mitchell. The format of the report and some of its content are unorthodox and reflect Jackie Leaver's lack of training in this area. She also told the Inquiry that she was 'dyslexic'.

During the period of Jason Mitchell's stay at West Park Hospital, he had a number of responsible medical officers; there was no written referral or brief for Mrs Leaver to become involved. In her oral evidence she told the Inquiry that she believed that in June 1990 she and a colleague, who were working 'on the rehab', were contacted by her manager and asked to

> ... go and have a look at some young chap that was on Drummond Ward. She felt he would be suitable to work with us. Apparently Jason Mitchell had gone to the OT department and seen my manager and asked her if there was anything he could do .... We had a blanket

referral which meant really we could have anyone referred to us and then we would go and do an assessment and then we would talk to the nursing staff, and then we would talk to the psychiatrist and then we would bring people through the rehab area .... I believe that the plan was that I was asked to do some individual work with him rather than the rehab plan ... we actually had a lot of autonomy within the hospital and we worked using our own ideas.

Asked whether she was supervised, she replied, 'We had a manager', but she agreed that supervision was not structured so as to enable her to discuss the progress of individual sessions.

Jason Mitchell's individual meetings with Mrs Leaver lasted about an hour and occurred weekly. They commenced in about September 1990. After Jason Mitchell's unsuccessful transfer to the open ward Farmside in April 1991, there appears to have been conflict between the nursing staff and Jackie Leaver and Joan Rapaport, social worker, over Jason Mitchell's transfer back to the locked ward (Drummond). Mrs Leaver and Mrs Rapaport sympathised with his view that no reasons were given for this transfer. Mrs Leaver believed that her individual sessions with Jason Mitchell subsequently ceased to be productive:

> At the time I thought he felt that I had been part of what had let him down because I think that I was the main person who actually encouraged him to go forward in believing that rehabilitation would be a possibility for him.

Mrs Leaver felt unable to deal with the material that Jason Mitchell produced. He described fantasies of homicide, but she did not explore these extensively:

> It was my lack of experience that limited it, and looking back I would never attempt to counsel anybody without counselling supervision, and there was just not any supervision. I think that is why I did not explore it any further. I think I felt well out of my depth.

She attempted to communicate what she had been told in the form of her written report, so that it could be discussed by the clinical team:

> I talked to my manager about it. The secretary typed it up. I talked to the colleague that I worked with at the OT department. I cannot remember if Jason Mitchell's social worker was around at the time but if she was I certainly talked to her about it ... and I posted it off

to the ward, one to the nursing staff and I think I sent one to the psychiatrist whoever that was at the time. It was an ever moving thing on the ward. It was difficult to get anything really logged.

When asked why she was successful in getting Jason Mitchell to talk about himself, she said: 'I did not get him to talk.' She described how in her role as OT instructor she took Jason Mitchell and other patients swimming and into Epsom for coffee, and he was treated just like any other patient.

It was a very relaxed atmosphere and that is when Jason Mitchell started talking to me over cups of tea and standing outside the swimming baths having a cigarette and it concerned me that I was being told things without any framework to pass the stuff back to the team. You get put in difficult situations when that happens. I did ask if there was any sort of formal counselling available to Jason Mitchell and basically was told that there was not.
   … I kept going up to the staff meetings and kept getting told how uncommunicative this chap was and that was not what I was experiencing, or my colleagues.

She did not know how to end the work with him:

I did not know anything about it … it was a kind of blundering in the dark.

Mrs Leaver's sessions with Jason Mitchell effectively ceased when she was transferred to a different area. Concerns appear to have arisen amongst other staff about the OT sessions. An entry in the nursing notes, dated 11 September 1991, for example, suggests some conflict between the approaches of the ward and Mrs Leaver and her colleagues:

Jason Mitchell continues to manipulate staff and fellow patients. Tends to abuse his ground parole even when escorted and stays over time at OT.

During this period Jason Mitchell's records indicate deteriorating behaviour and relationships. This coincides with Jackie Leaver's reporting that, by now, Jason Mitchell's constructive engagement in the meetings with her had long since ended. Mrs Leaver left the hospital's employment in December 1991, but continued to maintain contact with Jason Mitchell.

I kept in contact with Jason Mitchell and quite a few other patients around West Park. I would drop them a line and go out and have a cup of coffee with a couple of them .... [With Jason Mitchell] it continued up to not last November but the November before [1993] and then it fell apart and I did not hear anything from Jason Mitchell until the November before he committed the offence and I got a phone call out of the blue.

When he telephoned her at work in November 1994, he had been positive:

The message I got was that life was great, basically. He wanted me to know how well he was doing and that everything was all right.

He also telephoned her following the visit at Rampton Hospital which he received from two of us [AG and PG] in October 1995.

Responses to Jackie Leaver's work

(i) Dr Lintner, Dr Crellin and the Mental Health Review Tribunal, September 1991

Dr Lintner's independent report, prepared for the Tribunal, made reference to Jackie Leaver's report in respect of family background and drug abuse. Dr Lintner's report is discussed elsewhere, but it should be noted that Dr Lintner did not refer to the issue of homicidal fantasies. She recommended absolute discharge.

Dr Crellin's report (senior registrar to Professor Merry) referred to: 'a very full report by Mrs J. Leaver, the Occupational Therapist, focusing particularly on Jason Mitchell's family and educational and occupational background.' Dr Crellin's report also did not refer to homicidal fantasies.

Jackie Leaver's report was, as is the normal practice, not included in the Tribunal papers. It would have been available to the medical member of the Tribunal, who had access to the full case notes at the time of his or her visit to assess the patient before the tribunal hearing. Mrs Leaver attended the tribunal. She told the Inquiry she had been overwhelmed by the experience and could not remember what, if anything, she said.

The Tribunal records do not indicate that her report was considered. The members of the Tribunal, giving evidence to the Inquiry, could not recall reading it. Dr Rathod, the medical member of the Tribunal, confirmed that he would have taken the kinds of fantasies referred to in the report 'quite seriously', and that he would have considered it appropriate to ask the patient about them himself.

(ii) Dr Yeldham

Dr Yeldham became acquainted with Jason Mitchell in August 1991, after Mrs Leaver's sessions with Jason Mitchell had ended. Dr Yeldham described those sessions as follows:

> She was understanding him and befriending him rather than pro-viding coherent treatment.

In her oral evidence to the Inquiry, Dr Yeldham agreed that Mrs Leaver's ambiguous role may have prevented her observations from becoming part of the way in which Jason Mitchell was under-stood by the clinical team. There were also uncertainties about the significance of the information reported by Jackie Leaver:

> One of the issues about this report is that it is uncertain where some of the boundaries are between fantasy and reality ... I mean she had a lot of information here but its consistency and exactly where it belonged I am less certain about. I mean certainly some of the information is present elsewhere and has been said at other times. Other parts of it appear to be unique to those conversations with Jackie and it was certain that Jason Mitchell at times would – well – he would say things, paint things, do things in an attempt to shock other people, to get a reaction from them. He would say things in order to obtain sympathy, he would say things because he felt that that was what somebody wanted to hear or that they would then talk to him. And I mean, I wasn't there, I don't know exactly what was going on in that relationship to know exactly what context some of these notes were in or what value to place on any of that information.

Dr Yeldham acknowledged that neither she nor, to her knowledge, anyone else continued a similar role with Jason Mitchell after Jackie Leaver's departure. Dr Yeldham's reports refer neither to Jackie Leaver's work nor to further explorations about the homi-cidal ideation.

(iii) Dr Goddard

Dr Goddard and his colleagues had considered Ms Leaver's report in preparation for the Inquiry, and had critical observations to

make. In particular, they thought Mrs Leaver had made the error
of 'being all things' to Jason Mitchell – counsellor, advocate, friend:

> An important aspect of the work of a qualified therapist is the ability
> to 'stand back' and interpret what is happening within the therapeu-
> tic relationship. It seems that Jackie Leaver's inability to do this led
> her to blindly accept all the roles that Jason Mitchell offered her.
> Perhaps it fed her need to feel significant in a way that the role of a
> Technical Instructor did not allow.

Dr Goddard commented:

> In relation to the lengthy report submitted by Mrs Jackie Leaver and
> (unbelievably) signed by Jason Mitchell, I would say that at all times
> the multi-disciplinary team and/or the consultant decide upon which
> information is taken as relevant in the context of the patient's total
> experience and which is not.

These perceived 'faults' concern the professional role of Mrs
Leaver and the status and presentation of her work. They reflect
Mrs Leaver's own statement that she was unsupervised and unable
to work with the information she was getting. It is the content of
the material, however, that was important; more so than its form
or the context of its disclosure. Also, we note that Jason Mitchell
had in fact co-signed a number of other reports.

(iv) Dr Wilson

Dr Wilson, Jason Mitchell's consultant at Rampton Hospital since
January 1995, was familiar with the report of Jackie Leaver. In
giving oral evidence to the Inquiry, he said:

> I think that the existence and admission to fantasies of a violent
> nature are highly significant in the overall context of the possible
> dangerousness it presents.

He said that this material would have influenced his assessment
and that he would have wanted to follow it up himself. It would also
have prompted him to obtain an assessment from a psychologist:

> At this stage, if he [Jason Mitchell] was not already being seen by a
> psychologist, I would have been most concerned for a detailed psy-
> chological assessment ... because psychologists have special exper-
> tise in this area and they also have the advantage of not being part

of the control over the patient ... one of the difficulties not just with Jason Mitchell but with a lot of patients, is that the RMO is seen as the one who holds the key to the door and does not always get the fullest response when investigating things that might potentially delay progress as this inevitably would.

As described in Chapter XIII, Dr Bowden also considered that the report of Mrs Leaver contained important material, meriting further exploration in relation to Jason Mitchell's developmental history and emotional life.

Commentary

The contents of Mrs Leaver's report were important, but it tended to be ignored or discounted by the doctors central to the care and treatment of Jason Mitchell. Dr Yeldham's evidence suggested that her concern about the ambiguity of Jackie Leaver's role prevented the information from being incorporated into the clinical team's appraisal of Jason Mitchell. Dr Goddard saw 'faults' in the report.

In our view, the material in the report ought to have prompted at least an assessment, if not a further therapeutic involvement, with a qualified and experienced clinician, possibly a psychologist. That assessment was not pursued at West Park and was discounted as an option at Easton House. Jackie Leaver, by her own admission, was out of her depth and unable to use the disclosures either for a comprehensive assessment or in a therapeutic way. It is possible that Jason Mitchell would not have engaged with, and benefited from, further psychological exploration. Efforts to work with him in this way might, however, have prompted further disclosures, and have provided an opportunity to monitor his inner world. It can not be inferred, however, that such work would necessarily have led to a revised judgment about Jason Mitchell's potential dangerousness.

Other doctors who gave evidence to the Inquiry had not referred in their documentation to Jackie Leaver's lengthy report. This suggests an inclination on the part of the clinician to marginalise or invalidate the contribution of 'peripheral' and unqualified staff. In contrast, the two social workers in this case, Joan Rapaport and Jane Barnett, more readily acknowledged Jackie Leaver's work, although they could not have been expected to pursue psychological exploration themselves.

It is to be expected that patients may find it easier to relate to less threatening personnel in an environment where they may not even be offered private conversations with their doctors. Such staff may gain relevant clinical insights, but may be perceived by colleagues responsible for custody and control as over involved or manipulated by patients. Jason Mitchell's case illustrates how contributions from an unqualified member of staff were disregarded, and consequently how important data were put out of sight and mind. Nothing that is relevant to the assessment and treatment of a patient should be ignored, whatever its origins. This emphasis on the importance of time spent talking to patients has recently been echoed in the 'Report of the Confidential Inquiry into Homicides and Suicides by Mentally Ill People' published by the Royal College of Psychiatrists (1996).

Jackie Leaver's Report: February 1991

Jason Mitchell Section 37/41
Admitted 5.4.90

Living in Felixstowe for the past two months. Father and brother living at 11 Acton Road, Bramford, Ipswich.

Arrived in Epsom by mistake, his plan was to go to London. Jason hid in a local church, where he was disturbed by the night-watchman. Jason told the night-watchman to lay on the floor and threatened him with a piece of wood. The man escaped and ran away. He sustained injuries when he fell over in his haste to get away from Jason. When the Police arrived Jason told them that he intended to kill the Vicar. He was found to have two knives in his possession, both knives proved to be unused. Jason's claim at that time was that he was controlled by a woman's voice telling him what to do. He also claims that there was other voices all around him, instructing him and ridiculing him. Jason now withdraws this statement and claims that the voices were derogatory and not instructing.

Past History
Remand 1988-1989. Feltham remand 23.3.90.

Youngest of 5. Father unemployed. Long history of petty thefts, drugs and homosexual activities. Hallucinating for the past 6 years. Low varieties, lived rough and in bed and breakfast since leaving school.

Report from Feltham staff was no aggression.

No contact with Father since Christmas 1989. No contact with brothers and sisters.

[details omitted]

Work History
Few days of killing chickens by stungun in a factory, could not stand the smell of blood so Jason left.

School
Left age 15 with no exams. Learning difficulties from age 8 (low concentration – dyslexic). Threatened with expulsion in senior school. Age 12 Jason went to special school.

He has no discipline, is impulsive and aimless.

Past History
When Jason was age one his Mother left the family home, leaving Mr Mitchell to bring up five children, three boys and two girls. Jason was the youngest.

Family life appeared fairly normal at first. There were annual visits from Grandparents and Aunt who lived in. Mr Mitchell was unemployed and enjoyed a drink but this does not appear a problem at this time. Jason recalls this as being a close and loving atmosphere.

Jason's Mother lived in the same small town, and it was inevitable that they would meet. Jason feels that he was rejected by her when she told him not to call her Mother as this would upset her new in-laws. He also feels that she deliberately ignored him when they met in the streets.

When Jason was age 7 both his brothers [details omitted]. Jason had no recall of his Father ever visiting the brothers. So all contact with them was cut off. Jason found this distressing. He related most to his brothers. They played rough-and-tumble-games and made a great fuss over him. Jason missed his brothers. Jason's sisters showed very little interest in amusing a small boy. They had other things to do. Jason soon found that he could get his own way by threatening to tell his Father that the girls had hit him.

[details omitted]

When Jason was aged 8 [details omitted] Jason and his Father were picked up by Police and taken to the local Police station for questioning. Jason was put in a room by himself for two hours. He was given no explanation, and his panic was for his Father's safety. He felt that the Police had already deprived him of his brothers.

[details omitted]

After this Jason found himself living in an alien world. All affection was gone. His Father had turned into a bitter and isolated man. Jason was lonely and confused. His Father's drinking increased and the home became neglected. Most of the household chores had fallen on Jason.

When drunk Jason's Father would rant and rave verbal abuse about how Jason's Mother had brought about all the family's problems. He would call her names leaving nothing to Jason's imagination. This would go on until late into the night. Jason recalls wishing his Father would just stop saying such terrible things about his Mother. When Mr. Mitchell's rage was burnt out he would put his arm around Jason and call him his mate. Jason only felt distressed and glad it was over.

Jason's schooling suffered badly. He could not concentrate and had learning difficulties. He was put in to a slow stream group of pupils. He was quiet and withdrawn. Mr. Mitchell had shut out the world and no one was allowed in to the house. Jason would not have invited anyone in even if it had been possible. He was ashamed of the state of the home. Mr. Mitchell's history was common knowledge in a small town like this, so Jason had to live with this stigma. All this set him apart from other children and no normal friendships evolved for him.

Things changed for Jason when he started to attend senior school. There he was accepted by a more boisterous group of youths. This led him in to daring and experimental way of life. Jason had no discipline or guidelines to use. No one appeared to care what he got involved with so there were no boundaries. Although he was one of a group, no individual friendship blossomed. He felt it was not safe to let anyone get too close. By the time Jason was 12 the school could not cope with him any longer. Jason was given the choice of going to a special school for learning difficulties or expulsion. He went to the special school.

Age 12 things had deteriorated. Jason found himself in serious trouble. He was out of control. Glue sniffing, and petty theft. The Police had already been involved. There still appears to be no intervention from Mr Mitchell.

Jason over the years had maintained some contact with his sisters, and visited them from time to time. On one of those occasions he met his one and only friend. This friendship led him into a homosexual relationship with an older man. Jason claims full intercourse never took place.

This man enjoyed young boys and gave them gifts, took them to places and showed an interest. All the things Jason craved from his Father.

It started as a game to swindle things off the man, but Jason found that he enjoyed the attention and affection that the relationship offered. Jason's feelings on this now, are that he took advantage of this man and 'ripped him off' not that he was taken advantage of in anyway. Jason had the odd interlude with girls but found this disappointing and unfulfilling. He thinks this was lack of experience on both parts.

During the years of puberty Jason's Father appears to have played no strong authority figure. [details omitted].

Jason feels that the special school helped him. But by then most of his spare time was taken up with a criminal element. At age 15 he left school with no exams. His home life was empty. There was no emotional or social structure to support him. Jason claims that his mental illness had started.

Jason moved from glue sniffing to cannabis. Jason explains his change in behaviour as moving from a chrysalis to a butterfly. The drugs and his mental state made him feel elated, with no sense of danger or insight into his life style. He left home to live rough on the streets of London. He thought this life would be glamorous, but soon realised that this was not true.

He returned to his home town disillusioned, living in bed and breakfast or squats, his movements appeared aimless. Jason claims his behaviour became more bizarre, he dressed, walked and talked the same as the black Jamaicans that he was living and mixing with. This fad became so consuming that Jason believed that his skin was turning black. It started with the skin on his hands. Jason's voices and fantasies became part of his everyday life. Jason did not realise that he had an illness and thought that everyone experienced these things.

Jason became heavily in debt to one of the local groups of drug dealers. He had no way of paying off this money. His petty thieving did not amount to large sums. When the drug dealers captured Jason they hurt him physically and handcuffed him. They hung him over the side of a multi-storey car park and threatened to drop him. When they released him he could not escape by running away. His family were also under threat, the men wanted Jason to thieve for them as a way of payment.

Jason then ventured on a smash-and-grab routine. He was soon caught by the Police. This offence cost him the next two years of his life. He spent from 1979-1989 in remand prison.

There his mental illness developed along with his emotional confusion and frustration. Jason coped with this by becoming withdrawn and entering into his own world of fantasy. During this time in prison Jason was still obtaining drugs and he used cocaine for the first time. For the next two years Jason used his fantasies to devise elaborate ways of killing his enemies, and how to get away with it. His hatred festered for those he felt had hurt and deprived him of his freedom. This master plan appears to have sustained him during his confinement.

On his release from prison Jason had a plan formed. If he or his family were assaulted by his tormentors, he would put this plan into operation.

In his fantasies Jason had inflicted as much pain as he could. When asked how he would have killed them, he claims with a knife. Jason feels that he would then be put away forever, because of his madness. His reasoning was that this outcome would make him the victor, and he would get away with the crime.

Jason stayed with a resettlement programme at one of the Richmond Fellowships. This lasted for six months. With hindsight Jason feels he was not treated for his illness, but should have worked at it and stayed. But he was not in full control and his impulse was to move on.

From there he went in to another Bed and Breakfast, with his fantasies, voices and loud thoughts in full flight. What little touch he had with reality, appears to have left Jason. He carried a machete around with him and fantasized how he would use it if attacked. During one of these episodes Jason chopped off most of the furniture legs in his room. He also had a thought that it would be a fun thing to do if he killed a vicar for Christmas, in his home town of Bramford.

Instead Jason went to his family home. This was November 1989. There had been no contact with his Father during his confinement.

Jason always imagined that on arrival his Father would embrace him, and all would be well. But in reality nothing had changed. By now one of Jason's brothers had returned home to live, he was established in Jason's bedroom, but the atmosphere in the home was still poor. Mr Mitchell and his son never spoke to each other. Although three people now lived in the house there was very little interaction and it was still uninviting.

By the end of January Jason had moved on, disappointed and disillusioned yet again. His next stop was Felixstowe. He slept rough on the beach for a few days. Some landlady felt sorry for him and gave him a room. Jason's plan now was to live in Amsterdam. He stole enough to get the money for a one-way ticket. Again all Jason found was disappointment. There was no excitement or glamour and he was living rough. Jason managed to swindle his way back to Felixstowe. The night before he arrived in Epsom all Jason's traumas came to a head and became too much for him to cope with. He claims that he realised that he needed help but had no idea how to get that help and no one to turn to.

He took a train thinking it would go to London and ended up in Epsom by mistake. Jason claims that when he stood over the caretaker in the Church he knew for certain that he could not kill anyone. He claims he was shaking with fear.

Jason had fully collaborated with compiling this review of his past history. He appears to have gained insight and reassurance from its disclosure.

Jason appears to have spent a vital part of his life with his basic needs denied and his immediate social structure lost. When reality became unbearable Jason formed his own fantasy world. There all things were possible and acceptable.

Over these years Jason never achieved a normal emotional growth. Although he appears strong and self-reliant, his personal needs are great. Jason sees this as being greedy. He disguises his insecurities by boasting about his fictional achievements. This motivates him to set his sights unrealistically high, and stops him making the first attempt, as he cannot cope with any more failures. Jason needs support and encouragement in a safe environment. If he is to gain self-esteem and feel safe to fail and make mistakes.

Jason was deprived of possessions and personal relationships. He coped with this by denying his need for material things and detaching himself from personal contact.

During Jason's stay at West Park he has put down roots, he is taking great pride in his new clothes and books. His bed space has taken on a homely look. He enjoys walking around the hospital and greeting people by name. He interacts well with both patients and staff. For the first time in his life Jason is building relationships that appear secure.

Working for his needs is a new experience for Jason. However there probably will be relapses when temptation proves too much. Jason is basically a truthful person and will take responsibility for his own actions, although his sense of justice appears slanted at times.

From Jason's description of his past mental illness, some of the psychotic episodes appear to have been quite florid.

He describes his voices as derogatory, but also feels that he misses them. He claims that they had fun times together as well as the bad times.

It appears for the past six years Jason's voices were the only permanent thing in his life. Jason's loud thoughts appear to have been the force that motivated him the most. Jason discussed his obsessional behaviour, he said that everything had to be perfect and he would spend a long time trying to achieve this, so that his voices would have nothing to take the rise out of. Jason is convinced that at one time his hands were turning black.

Jason appears to have moved in and out of reality and fantasy, until they both lost their boundaries.

The only saving things for him was his own insight and this made him afraid.

Jason holds no one to blame but himself. He feels that he should have understood things better. His self-image is poor and he cannot come to the conclusion that he may have been a victim or that his environment could have resulted in his impulsive, aimless and antisocial life style.

Jason has little self-esteem and he is emotionally vulnerable. He is desperate to keep improving and will comply with the treatment programme.

If Jason is in a safe and structured environment with support and understanding he could achieve a great deal. Jason has worked alongside the rehabilitation patients since June 1990.

He has a multitude of untapped potential and skills, but needs the space to learn about personal growth and to recognise the positive aspects in himself.

If these needs are not met and Jason returns to his past way of life he could become a danger in the community. Jason recognises this part of himself and it frightens him.

Jason has a shifting personality, the changes are very subtle. These changes have become less as he stabilizes and feels safer.

Jason is always ready to support others and gets a great boost from this. He needs to feel worthwhile.

Present

During the past eight months Jason has worked very well with the rehabilitation group. This group is of mixed age and ability. Jason has proved to be caring and considerate at all times. He respects the opinions of others, he listens with interest and contributes during every session. Jason copes well with change and enjoys responsibility. He will try new ideas and in doing so motivates others with his enthusiasm. During individual sessions Jason has shown a good ability to view things on a wider range and will consider new ways of problem solving.

Jason is quick to grasp instruction and theory. When he does not understand something, he will ask for clarification. This results in him giving and receiving clear messages. Although a natural leader Jason has never abused this position. He does not monopolise, threaten or force his opinion on other members of the group.

Jason shows respect for both patients and staff. He is not a gossip and his attitude towards staff is always positive. Jason appears to have no problems with authority, although he can get frustrated when talked down to.

When the rehabilitation patients discuss their weekend outings and sometimes invite Jason to join them, he has shown enormous restraint by reminding the others of his restrictions.

Jason was very upset after his unofficial visit home. He had to accept the fact that his Father cannot provide any support for him, and now realises that he must take full responsibility for his own future. Jason feels that he is well enough to deal with this and would like the opportunity to move on to one of the open wards. This would give him more responsibility and increase his independence.

Jason is now planning for the future and has expressed a wish to gain some work skills by attending a Training College for engineering or welding. He would also like to further his education by attending an English course. Jason should be encouraged and supported in these pursuits, when his restrictions are lifted.

Recommendation
A rehabilitation and resettlement programme to give Jason a safe environment to grow and achieve in.

Jason Mitchell   *Jackie Leaver*

V. Jason Mitchell's Accounts of the Killings: An Assessment

I am but mad north-north-west:
when the wind is southerly
I know a hawk from a handsaw
Hamlet, Act II, sc. ii, ll. 405-7

Jason Mitchell's state of mind at the time of the killings, and the way in which symptoms of mental disorder may have affected his behaviour at the time, were particularly difficult to assess. His accounts of his motivation and thinking at the time varied and were sometimes inconsistent.

After arrest

His first documented account was given to Dr Goddard who had two interviews with him in Ipswich Police Station at 8.30 pm and 10.30 pm on the night of 20th December 1994 after Jason Mitchell had been taken into police custody. On the following day Dr Goddard wrote a detailed account of his interviews in a letter to Dr Knight, police surgeon.

Dr Goddard described Jason Mitchell's manner in these first interviews as calm, polite, coherent and apparently free of any objective evidence of psychotic illness. He did not appear to be responding to hallucinations and he did not express any delusional ideas.

Jason Mitchell told Dr Goddard that he had experienced an urge to kill from the age of 6, when he first put a pillow over his father's head. He said that during his recent re-admission to Easton House he had thought that Mr and Mrs Wilson would be a suitable couple to kill, and he admitted that he had done so. He also admitted that he had killed his father and said that he had not killed him first because it would have led to his early detection given his known history.

When the interview resumed Jason Mitchell volunteered that he had wanted to eat the people he had killed. He said he did not regret his actions as they had served the purpose of confirming his ability to kill. He intended to go on to find someone younger to kill, but had delayed and stayed in the house. He said he cut 'Mr Mitchell' up to gain experience and help dispose of the body.

Jason Mitchell told Dr Goddard that he did not feel he was driven or controlled by outside forces to commit his acts, nor had he experienced hallucinatory voices. He conveyed the strong impression that he had acted in a controlled manner with forethought and a clear mind. He denied any ingestion of drugs or alcohol before the killings.

Jason Mitchell was interviewed at Ipswich Police Station by Dr Hadrian Ball, Consultant Forensic Psychiatrist at the Norvic Clinic, Norwich. He talked to Dr Ball of liking to stalk his potential victims and kill them in a house and live in that house afterwards. He said he had first become aware of Mr and Mrs Wilson about ten years ago and noticed at that time that their home was detached and located on a corner at which it would be possible to make a noise and not be heard. He had visited their house a few days previously waiting for them to return home, but they had not arrived. On the day of the killing, he had entered the house through an open back door. Mr Wilson was already at home and Jason Mitchell hid in a bedroom. Jason Mitchell told Dr Ball that he had killed the Wilsons on a Monday (12 December 1994) but had made a mistake in doing this as he should have killed them on a Sunday to allow seven days so that he could kill 'a family' on Christmas Day, which in 1994 fell on a Sunday. He said he therefore decided to kill his father on Sunday 18 December to allow the plan to continue. He said the family he would choose to kill on Christmas Day would have been a young family with young children. Dr Ball had the impression that Jason Mitchell's offences had been influenced by symptoms of psychotic illness. He recorded: '... although he denied it, I strongly suspected that his stated intent of killing the people as described to me was driven by underlying delusional phenomena.'

In Norwich Prison, January 1995

The next recorded interviews were in Norwich Prison. On 11 January 1995 Jason Mitchell was seen again by Dr Goddard, accompanied by Dr Ward, also Consultant Forensic Psychiatrist at the Norvic Clinic. Jason Mitchell said that he had felt he could no longer resist the urge to kill people. He had chosen the Wilsons' house because it was detached and he would avoid detection. He reported that he had experienced no particularly strong emotional reactions during the killings apart from some sense of relief after killing Mr and Mrs Wilson. He described dismembering his father's body and described the details in a very matter-of-fact, emotionless way. He had delayed the dismemberment until he knew that rigor mortis had set in. He repeated again that he had thoughts of eating flesh. He was planning to kill again on Christmas Day but could give no rational explanation about why he had chosen Christmas Day. When asked why he had not mentioned the urge to kill during his long stay in hospital, he replied 'nobody asked me'. Throughout the interview he sat upright with arms folded, and looked comfortable and relaxed. At the end he thanked all those present for visiting him.

Dr Ian Wilson, Consultant Forensic Psychiatrist at Rampton Hospital, first saw Jason Mitchell on 13 January 1995 and wrote a Court Report dated 20 June 1995, by which time he had been Jason Mitchell's RMO in Rampton Hospital for five months.

When first interviewed by Dr Wilson on 13 January Jason Mitchell appears to have given a more elaborate account of the killings, claiming that four months beforehand he had come to a decision to eat human flesh. He began by eating raw animal meat, then developed a plan to kill one person a day for the twelve days of Christmas, together with a young family. The killing of the Wilsons was a trial run, then he killed his father as a further preparation for the killings due to start on the first days of Christmas. He claimed he tasted some of his father's blood and ate a little of his father's liver. (This last claim was proved to be untrue by the findings of the post-mortem examination.)

By the time Dr Wilson reported on 20 June, Jason Mitchell had given a variety of different accounts. Dr Wilson summarised these as follows:

> When seen in Norwich Prison he described the killing of the elderly couple and his father as preparation for his need to kill for each of the twelve days of Christmas in order to be able to eat human flesh. He now denies this, and also denies having tasted his father's liver, and recognises that he was mentally ill at the time that he gave this explanation. A second explanation was that he had killed the elderly couple in the course of an interrupted burglary but in this case he was unable to account for the killing of his father. His third explanation was that he had always hated his father and had intended killing him and that killing the elderly couple was a trial run for this.

Yet another explanation was that he had known since the time he was six years old that he had to kill and that Mr and Mrs Wilson were randomly chosen victims, although he had once burgled their house, and in this explanation he described becoming strongly sexually aroused by the killing of the elderly woman.

Most recently he has reiterated that his main intention was to kill his father whom he perceived as always having treated him badly. The killing of the Wilsons in this case was to ensure that he received a prison sentence rather than a hospital disposal, his logic being his belief that people who killed their parents were sent to hospital whereas those who additionally killed strangers received prison sentences.

Dr Paul Bowden interviewed Jason Mitchell on 1 June 1995 at Rampton Hospital. He told Dr Bowden that he had left St Clement's Hospital on 9 December 1994 in order to kill someone. He had entered the Wilsons' house with the intention of killing them and later strangled his father because he hated him. He told Dr Bowden that three days after killing his father he dismembered the body. He had wanted to eat some of the flesh but was put off when he found the blood distasteful. He said that the three killings were a rehearsal for the killing of younger people, whom he intended to eat. He also said that he had an idea to kill different people on the twelve days of Christmas. Jason Mitchell also reported to Dr Bowden that he had experienced sexual arousal during the killings and masturbated later to thoughts of the strangulations. (However, there was no post mortem pathological evidence that Jason Mitchell had sexually assaulted any of his victims.)

Like Dr Ball, Dr Bowden suspected that there was an underlying psychotic basis to the killings. In his report of 21 June 1995, he summarised the evidence for a diagnosis of schizophrenia (quoted in Chapter III), and wrote:

> ... He is manifestly extremely dangerous and I suspect that many of his alleged motives for the killing are attempts to appear coldly psychopathic, thereby avoiding any hint of psychotic motivation which, in any event, may be impossible for him to describe rationally (because of its inherent irrationality).

At Rampton, post-conviction: October 1995

Two of us met and interviewed Jason Mitchell in Rampton Hospital on 1 and 11 October 1995. One of the two Inquiry Panel members had an earlier brief meeting with him before the Inquiry was opened publicly. There were three reasons for the decision to see Jason Mitchell. First, it was necessary to seek his consent for disclosure of his records, consent which in due course he gave. Secondly, we believed the contact was necessary in order that we should understand as fully as possible the difficulties of diagnosis and assessment faced by other clinicians. Thirdly, we thought we should obtain Jason Mitchell's own account of the care and treatment he had received and his relationships with clinical staff. He made no complaints about his care and treatment but did make some comments. We were greatly assisted by Jason Mitchell's Solicitor, Mr David Mylan, whose negotiations enabled the consents to be obtained and the interviews to take place. We are also grateful to Dr Wilson and his colleagues at Rampton for allowing and facilitating our visits to the Hospital.

At the time of our interviews Jason Mitchell had been taking anti-psychotic medication for about six months. He spoke willingly, was composed, courteous and pleasant in manner. He was articulate, his affect was normal in its range, he showed no obvious abnormality of mood, was attentive and did not appear to have any current psychotic experiences. His speech and thinking were generally coherent but he was fleetingly thought disordered on occasions. He said he believed he was in the right place and that the medication was beneficial. (His demeanour had been quite different when he was first seen briefly by one of us three months earlier. On that occasion he had been hostile, irritable and suspicious. He was now much more relaxed and amenable.)

In summary, his account of his background history was as follows. He said he had little contact with his mother after she left the family (before his first birthday). By the time he was 8 years old his older siblings had left home and he was brought up alone by his father. As a young child he had thoughts of wanting to kill himself. After Jason Mitchell's sisters left home his father became withdrawn and embittered. Jason Mitchell described a poor relationship with his father and claimed his father was critical and sometimes assaultive to him. He took over domestic tasks such as shopping because his father would not go out. He was unhappy, resentful, isolated and frustrated, but fearful of his father's violence. If he returned from the Co-op and the dividend sheet was two pence out his father called him a 'stupid bastard'. This was happening from about the age of 8 onwards. In Jason Mitchell's view, 'I didn't have a home-life.'

When he was aged about 6 there was a first incident of threatened violence to his father. His brother had stolen a double-sided knife with a deer foot handle and their father had removed it. Jason Mitchell found it and one morning held the knife over his father who was asleep. On another occasion he had put a pillow over his father's face. Later, aged 15, he once threatened his father with a kitchen knife.

After the age of 8 Jason Mitchell's school work deteriorated and he became unhappy and withdrawn. When teachers approached him to ask about home (because they were aware of his unhappiness), he would not confide, because he feared destructive consequences. He felt he must not let them know what was going on because his father had told him that they would break the family up: if they got into a family they would tear it to pieces. He feared what his father would do if he confided: 'If I talked he would have beaten me ... punched me – knocked me out.' He particularly recalled his father's characteristic threats to break his neck.

His favourite toy had been a teddy bear that had been passed down through the family. He said, 'I ripped its head off at the end.' When aged 13, in a state of frustration and rage with his father, he had thrown the bear around, stabbed a pen or pencil in the bear's neck and pulled its head off.

At secondary school he was picked on and bullied by pupils of his own age. He had a poor self-image and little self-confidence. He felt 'slow and backward'. He saw no future for himself.

He had no sustained, close relationships outside the family. He exploited and stole from friends. He was unconcerned about their reactions. At age 13 Jason Mitchell was befriended by an older man who made sexual advances to him, and from whom Jason Mitchell stole. He said he had also had several girlfriends.

He first took cannabis when aged 11, and from 15 onwards sought constantly to abuse glue, solvents, alcohol and cannabis. He recalled once sniffing as much butane as he could (three bottles) for self-destructive reasons: 'I wanted to damage my intelligence – wanted to get rid of it – to be stupid' (as his father had told him he was). Jason Mitchell stole and engaged in burglaries and fraud in order to fund his drug habit. He was consuming drugs frequently until his first period of imprisonment at the age of 17. In prison he was vulnerable, weak, victimised by other inmates and scared. He could not explain why he had been victimised.

The effects of cannabis had been to make him feel 'paranoid'. He thought people in cars were looking at him, and police were watching him. He also sometimes experienced hallucinations for short periods of a few hours, believing he was hearing the voice of someone who was impersonating somebody else. When the immediate effects of drug intoxication had passed and he had slept, the symptoms disappeared. In due course, however he commenced hearing voices when not taking any drugs.

After leaving prison at the age of 19 he moved to the Richmond Fellowship Hostel (Castle Project) in Cambridge. He found the individual counselling sessions too difficult and sometimes refused them: 'I blamed it on the people I was talking to, but it was me. There was painful stuff that I didn't want to remember.' He did not recollect threatening a member of staff with a blunt knife, but did describe threatening another resident with a knife (who had previously threatened him). During this period he took LSD on three or four occasions. On the first trip he began to believe he was a martial arts expert. On subsequent trips he believed he was a killer. The drug made him feel 'intensely wild – as if all moral codes were broken'. He bought knives, became preoccupied with them, and looked for victims he thought were 'killable', such as vicars, 'because they are the image of goodness ... timid ... easy targets'.

During the months before his offence in February 1990 he lived an itinerant life. He spent Christmas 1989 with his father and brother. Like most previous Christmases this one was 'abysmal – no presents, no happiness'. He said that from the age of 8 he never been given presents by his father.

Jason Mitchell said that at the time of the offence in Epsom he was not experiencing voices or paranoid thoughts, but he had experienced them beforehand. He wanted to be 'in hospital for the rest of my life ... somewhere where I would be needed – where I would be secure'.

At West Park Hospital he experienced restlessness and other side effects from the anti-psychotic medication. He was pleased to be there but was mistrustful of ward staff. He had no more homicidal thoughts. He saw Dr Yeldham in case conferences. With Jackie Leaver he had discussed his family life and other problems, but had not talked about such matters to others. He recalled the individual sessions with her in which they had prepared their long joint report. Following the Mental Health Review Tribunal Hearing he had spent six weeks of a twelve-week assessment period at Farmside, but was told he was not suitable and he was then moved back to Drummond Ward. He felt resentful that important material he had disclosed to Jackie Leaver had not been picked up by his clinical team: 'They were things I wanted to talk about and I was hindered.' He lost trust and became defensive. When he first went into hospital he had not known who he should talk to: Jackie Leaver happened to be available. He could not talk openly in case conferences, and continued to find this difficult.

While at West Park he had his arms tattooed. The tattoos on his face were done later, during November 1993, in Ipswich. On that occasion his intention was to get his whole head covered but he only had £40, which was insufficient. He chose the most that he could afford. The skull and serpent on his left cheek had cost £26; the crescent moon on his left temple had cost £14. 'The skull was the nastiest I could get for the money.' The skull and serpent was, 'a macho thing really, its a nice tattoo but it meant to me death and killing at the time'. He had wanted a dragon (which he described as 'swirly whirly') but could not afford it. The tattooed cross on the middle of his forehead had been done earlier.

At West Park Hospital, he had purchased two books by Thomas Harris: *Red Dragon* and *Silence of the Lambs*. He had found *Red Dragon* the most interesting of the two, but said he did not read it all through and he could not really remember the book. He also had books on psychiatry and psychology. (His other books, which were later recovered by the Police after the killings were: *An Introduction to Physical Methods of Treatment in Psychiatry* by Peter Dally and Joseph Conolly; *Bradshaw on: The Family* by John Bradshaw; *The Book of Runes* by Ralph Blum; *The Anthropic Cosmological Principle* by John Barrow and Frank Tippler; *Emmerdale Farm Book 2: Prodigal's Progress* by Lee Mackenzie; and Jackie Leaver's copy of *The Child, The Family and The Outside World* by Donald Winnicott.)

Before moving to St Clement's Hospital, Ipswich, Jason Mitchell had hopes that his family would get back in touch with him, but 'no one wanted to know'. When his medication was stopped, he felt happy to start with but then symptoms of feeling paranoid and hearing voices developed within a few months. The voices usually occurred when he was resting on his own in his room. He experienced them independently of illicit drug taking. He thought the voices were speaking about him, and they were outside his head, 'like someone silly next door talking'. He heard full words and sentences but they were quiet and muffled. He felt 'bad' about the voices but did not want to talk directly to medical staff because he did not want to be on medication. He tried to develop relaxation techniques and breathing exercises to try and control them. He spoke to one of the nursing staff about the voices but was eventually told that the team did not want him to restart on medication.

He found the regime at Easton House tighter than at West Park. 'It was a challenging behaviour unit and so the staff had to be quite challenging.' He thought some of the staff found him likeable and others saw him as a threat to their authority. He commented, 'I do push people away ... I'm quite warm to the touch but cold to the feel.' He smoked cannabis when at Easton House and had a source of supply in another part of the hospital. His consumption was particularly heavy during the Christmas period 1993/94. He said it did not cause voices or paranoia. He expected to 'feel good' on cannabis but instead felt depressed, not caring any more, and he isolated himself from staff.

He had wanted to move to the 'Greenwoods' hostel from Easton House, and was disappointed when the application was turned down. He covered up his disappointment with a stance of not caring and being dismissive: 'I did it then – I still do. I'm very good at it.'

When Jason Mitchell first left St Clement's Hospital and went to the MIND house in Larkhill Way, Felixstowe, he had ambitions to study philosophy or music, go to college and 'pick up my life again'. He had his own room which he initially painted red, then 'meditation grey'. He claimed he consumed no illicit drugs. At the hostel the residents were older. He had quarrels and tiffs, became frustrated, and frightened one of the other residents by threatening him with a miniature hammer. Quite quickly he found himself 'going through a bad time ... hearing voices quite strongly'. He believed that if he went outside people were looking at him, and that people on TV were talking about his life.

Living in the house at Larkhill Way had become an extreme pressure. Initially the re-admission to St Clement's Hospital was a relief but he was also upset by the failure of the Larkhill Way placement: 'I was giving up my future.' He telephoned Jackie Leaver to tell her about his re-admission but did not express his disappointment: 'I wanted to show I was making a success of my life even though I was not a success.' He told her he was leaving hospital even though he was not. He wanted to convey the impression that he was making a go of his life.

After the re-admission to Easton House he began to feel closed in and wanted to escape again. He felt 'paranoid' and heard voices. 'Things were being said on the television that I related to myself.' He talked to no one about his experiences because he was afraid of being put back on anti-psychotic medication – (he thought the medication caused attacks of anxiety and panic) – but he was also aware that he was not well without medication.

He said he had formulated the idea of killing for several months before leaving Easton House on 9 December 1994. In this part of the interview he found it difficult to give a clear, consistent or coherent account of what he had thought and experienced. It had begun 'as a feeling'. He thought that perhaps killing was something he needed to do in order to feel his emotions. He had no particular victims in mind. He did not initially have thoughts of killing his father: he had feelings of hatred, bitterness and frustration in relation to him but had not focused on him as a victim when living in Larkhill Way. At that time he had been cycling from Larkhill Way to visit his father's home. He commented: 'maybe he [father] was involved but I didn't realise it'. In Larkhill Way he had strong impulses to kill. He thought of suicide in order to relieve 'the pressure'. He went to Brighton for a day but did not have the courage to kill himself there. He also thought of using gas from the gas fire in Larkhill Way. He wanted to kill to relieve 'the pressures' on his life. These were, trying to cope in Larkhill Way and make relationships with other people; the voices and paranoid thoughts; and the struggle to avoid returning to illegal drugs. When he had homicidal thoughts he 'enjoyed them', and felt 'relieved by fantasies about murder'. They were a kind of solution and relief from pressures. He came to see killing as an achievement.

He knew the Wilsons' house because he had burgled it before. He had thoughts of burgling and then killing the occupants by strangulation. Other methods could be less effective. He knew a knife would cause pain, and it could be difficult to be sure of getting the right place. Strangling was more certain: 'It's a hands on experience.' (This remark was made in a bland manner with no sense of the human significance of what he was saying.) He also said that when he had decided to kill someone, he had to kill his father. 'I was so afraid of not succeeding – slapped wrist – you've failed again …. Once I'd succeeded with the Wilsons I realised my love was so little, I knew I could do it.'

The homicidal thoughts were intense but also inconsistent at Easton House: 'I lived a double life – I'd feel very bad and I'd think about killing and then I'd feel quite happy and oblivious to the fact that I might kill somebody.' He was aware of the consequences for himself of long-term detention in hospital or prison; this was not a deterrent but a source of encouragement: 'It appealed to me.'

He did not tell anyone about his homicidal thoughts for a variety of reasons: it was 'pointless'; he would be put back on medication; he did not want help; he did not believe he needed help at the time. His account suggested internal conflict and ambivalence. He thought he would have admitted to the homicidal thoughts if he had been asked, but also knew he would kill – it was just a question of when and how. He both wanted to kill and at the same time did not want to take life. No one asked. If he had been asked directly about his thoughts, 'I would probably have given in gracefully.'

After 9 December 1994

Jason Mitchell gave the following account to us of events from 9 December 1994 onwards. During the day he started to help Yvonne Hines with Christmas decorations, but felt paranoid – believing that in choosing the decorations he was being made to take part in a psychology test. 'I was very worried that people would find out what I was thinking.'

At the end of the day he asked if he could go out for a walk. He knew where he was going. (At this point in the interview he spoke in a more rapid, animated manner and at times was thought disordered.) 'There was something about my feet. I had to walk silently, or quietly as I could. It's on a film or something ... *Silence of the Lambs* ... A horror film. I went straight to my father's ....' He said he intended to kill the Wilsons that night, but was so sweaty and tired he decided to leave it until Saturday (the next day). He went to the Wilsons on Saturday night about 7.30 pm, and tried to break in from a back window. The Wilsons were not at home. He waited in their greenhouse to keep warm. 'It was a dark night, the moon was full, it was quite psychotic, quite psychopathic, serial killeristic, dead calm.' Between midnight and half past Mr and Mrs Wilson returned home. Jason Mitchell had the idea of pushing them into the house, but there were people passing by who might be alerted, and he therefore went away.

At about lunchtime on Monday 12 December, Jason Mitchell left his father's house, telling him he was going to St Clement's Hospital. He went instead to the Wilsons' house. Mr Wilson was in the garage, and Jason Mitchell decided to wait in the house until the night. He took off his shoes and lay on a bedroom floor with a duvet over him. He had a large knife with a compass at the end. Mr Wilson later found him, told him to leave and escorted him to the door. He told Mr Wilson he was not going to leave, hit Mr Wilson on the head with the blunt end of the knife, causing a scalp wound, and made Mr and Mrs Wilson go into the bathroom. He made Mrs Wilson tie her husband's hands, and he then tied her hands with tree binder he had taken from their shed on the previous Saturday night. He asked if they were taking any prescribed tablets because he wanted to keep them alive as long as possible. He strangled Mrs Wilson with his hands and a scarf from a drawer in her bedroom. He had told her that her husband was already dead, because 'I wanted to give her some comfort'. After killing Mrs Wilson he went to the kitchen to get something to eat. He then killed Mr Wilson, strangling him with a pair of tights and a scarf.

He demonstrated the position of his hands, explaining why anatomically this was the most effective position. He said he had retained this information from a police programme he had seen on television years ago.

At the time of the killings he felt 'very excited and very angry'. The anger was not there before or afterwards. It 'came out of the blue', and he was 'quite shocked to feel it'. He experienced 'a survival instinct feeling'. Afterwards he felt 'empty'. He had thoughts of dismembering the bodies but heard someone coming to the front door. He panicked, took £25 and left.

He commented: 'It seemed as if I was on a social ladder of killing amongst killers.'

He said he had taken no drugs or alcohol before the killings, and experienced no voices or other abnormal phenomena at the time. He was 'focused on the killing completely'. Afterwards he bought two cans of lager. He planned to kill again in about a week's time and subsequently looked for suitable detached houses for other killings. He wanted to carry on 'as much as possible'. He said:

I needed to make an impact killing – it had a big impact on me and the rest of society – because he was my own father. In *Silence of the Lambs* he says he killed his parents when he was six [*sic*] years old. It had no bearing at all on my killing my father. If a job's worth doing it's worth doing well. I'd had an impact kill. I regret I didn't finish what I'd planned and killed more people.

Jason Mitchell said he had taken a hammer from the Wilsons' house. He had thought of killing his father by hitting him on the head with it, or alternatively by pushing him down stairs, but had decided against both methods. During Jason Mitchell's stay at 11 Acton Road his father had been talking about the murders of Mr and Mrs Wilson, and had said that the police suspected Jason Mitchell. Jason Mitchell denied involvement but thought his father suspected him and was apprehensive.

He killed his father in his bedroom, strangling him from behind with his father's tie. He had asked his father if he wanted help in making his bed, and when his father was leaning over the bed, Jason Mitchell was behind him, looped the tie across the front of his father's neck, and fell on top of him trapping his arms under his body. At the time of the killing there was a quiz programme on the radio and Jason Mitchell was asking his father to answer the questions as he strangled him. He knew about the nature and timing of rigor mortis and bent his father's elbows so that later they would provide handles enabling him to lift the body. After the killing he felt 'satisfied ... found it quite amusing'.

He decided to dismember the body but had to let the rigor mortis set in first. He spent two days watching TV and sleeping. He said he had slept very little during the preceding week. During the two days after killing his father, 'I could feel grief welling in me but blocked it off ... because I wanted to go on a reign of terror.' As with the previous killings, he said he had taken no drugs or alcohol beforehand. He experienced no voices and no ideas of reference concerning the television. He said, however, that subjectively, before the killings he had felt 'very unwell ... as if I was about to hallucinate and lose control'.

Two days after the killing he used a hacksaw and kitchen knife from the house to dismember the body, partly to facilitate disposal. He knew it would be horrific, but seemed 'not to want to stop'. He planned to go to another house to kill someone else in a new area, but remained in his home. When the police came to 11 Acton Road and arrested him it was both traumatic and a relief.

He said that in his subsequent interviews with the police he elaborated his account of the killings by claiming cannibalism in order to shock and to maintain the impact of what he had done. He saw his offences as an achievement: 'I'd fundamentally established I was a killer.'

When asked directly whether he had been sexually aroused

during or after the killings he said he had not. However he said he
had experienced sexual fantasies of killing, sexual assault, rape
and necrophilia on occasions in Larkhill Way, the imagined victims
being adult men and women.

Jason Mitchell's subsequent reactions to the killings during the
months in Rampton Hospital had been more mixed. (We were
interviewing him almost a year after the homicides.) He thought
that if he had been on medication at the time, 'it would not have
happened'. On medication he was more aware of emotions, his
mood was better, he was more relaxed and experienced no voices
and paranoia. His emotions were 'more dead' when he was off
medication. He said he now no longer saw the killings as an
achievement but as the end of his life. Since killing his father he
had experienced upsetting, intrusive memories and 'flash images'
of him when both dead and alive. There were also occasional
intervals of distress when he thought about his father, and it was
therefore easier to maintain the view of his father as an evil man:

> It's worse when I think about it on my own.

> When I have a mental picture of dad happy then I sink into a big
> black hole. When I have a mental picture of him being angry then I
> have no remorse ... he was an evil man ... he deserved it.

> I loved him as a father, but I hated him as a parent .... Or I suppose
> I loved him as a human being but I hated him as a father.

Commentary on Jason Mitchell's accounts

The above material summarises, in precis form, the accounts given
by Jason Mitchell in many hours of interviews. Assessing the
significance of his accounts is a complex task, and only possible,
rather than definitive, interpretations can be put forward. The
account he gave to us differed in a number of respects from the
accounts he gave to others, and there is no *a priori* reason for giving
more weight to the account we obtained than that told to others at
different times.

It was noticeable in our interview that he showed avoidance of
painful subjects, for example by taking a sudden break or changing
the subject with a humorous aside. He was composed and showed
no emotion in recounting unhappy events of his early life and
overall, his presentation and psychiatric history revealed relatively

little evidence of the overt neurotic distress and symptomatology that might have been expected from his account of his background history. He conveyed an impression of being detached from emotional responses to his adverse early experiences. His skilled and pleasant social manner may also have hidden from view the severe personality disturbance that might be expected from his early history. Furthermore, non-disclosure of emotional pain and disappointment seemed to be a pervasive feature of his life history. In this regard, it seemed psychologically possible that the breakdown of his placement at Larkhill Way – which had been his first opportunity of independent success in the community after four years in hospital – was a major disappointment and repetition of failure, a context perhaps in which the idea of killing as a 'social ladder' of achievement was meaningful. During the latter part of our interview his account of the offences was given in an animated, fluent manner. In describing the details he conveyed no sense or awareness of the terror and suffering of his victims. Their experiences were wholly absent from the interview room.

Jason Mitchell's view of his father and their relationship was markedly at variance from accounts given by his sister and others. She recalled their father giving up work to devote himself to looking after the four children when Jason Mitchell was under a year old. As the baby of the family Jason Mitchell was particularly indulged by his father. There were always presents at Christmas. As a child he was cheerful, cheeky and he and his father were close. Later he became more wilful and difficult for his father to control. As a teenager he stole from his father to obtain money for drugs. She particularly did not believe that as a young child Jason Mitchell had threatened or thought of killing his father. She had last seen them together one Sunday when Jason Mitchell had cycled to her home shortly after he had moved in to Larkhill Way. He and his father had talked cheerfully together. She described their father as a quiet man. She and her brothers and sisters had always seen him regularly and had much affection for him. Their bereavement was considerable. Initially they did not believe that Jason Mitchell could have killed their father.

These discrepant accounts remain, and no doubt will be further explored. Jason Mitchell did not convey to us the impression of giving deliberately misleading or fabricated accounts: he seemed to be trying to answer questions honestly. The discrepant accounts indicate at least that Jason Mitchell's descriptions of his father should be understood as referring to his own subjective experience of the relationship, rather than the character of Mr Mitchell and the father-son relationship that others observed. No doubt a narrative that selects the bad memories of an ambivalent relationship with his victim is easier for Jason Mitchell to bear.

Dr Bowden's perspective

As described in Chapter III, the problems of psychiatric diagnosis were considerable in Jason Mitchell's case. The relationship between his psychopathology and the killings is also unlikely to be unidimensional, and an account of the relationship may need to consider the combined influences of psychosis, Jason Mitchell's personality and emotional life, and family dynamics. Although the forensic psychiatrists who assessed Jason Mitchell all thought that his psychotic illness of schizophrenia was of primary importance (and the basis for a diminished responsibility plea), this was also the aspect that was most difficult to relate in a precise way to his acts of killing. It was thought likely that the killings had a delusional basis, but the content of those delusions was, and remains, obscure.

Dr Paul Bowden, who gave oral evidence on the final day of our hearings, had the unparalleled experience of having carried out psychiatric assessments on over a thousand individuals charged with murder, over a period of twenty years. We were greatly helped by the perspective he could bring to the particular difficulties in Jason Mitchell's case.

Dr Bowden placed particular weight on the earliest psychiatric reports, principally that of Dr Pugh at West Park Hospital (10 August 1980), because at that early stage Jason Mitchell seemed best able to describe his experiences clearly. Dr Bowden said:

> I think that as his illness continued, his ability to explain it disintegrated. I suspect that, speaking generally, his abnormal mental experiences became increasingly chaotic and ... he was unable to communicate them.

Dr Bowden thought this was evident in the recent interviews conducted by us, interviews in which Jason Mitchell's accounts were 'completely chaotic and mostly un-understandable'. Jason Mitchell was, also, clearly unreliable in reporting psychotic symptoms. Dr Bowden reported:

When I interviewed him it was difficult to rely on anything he said because he contradicted himself. He made it very clear that there were areas of his mental life he would not discuss by becoming threatening, so he was limiting what he would discuss in the interview situation. He was unreliable and he said things ... which not only contradicted things he said to me but contradicted what he said to other people.

For example, ... I, ten years on in 1995, would not place any reliance on what he said about auditory hallucinations. There may be other reasons for that than the deterioration of the mind with schizophrenia, and his mental life becoming more un-understandable to him. He might be learning that if you say certain things, people do not believe you. He might be learning that if you say certain things, I am going to be treated in a way that I do not want to be treated, so he may over a period of years ... avoid saying things other than for an end, so he would only admit to voices perhaps if he thought there was a point to it, that he saw some gain in it. Whether ... he experienced them or not is a totally different matter.

In Dr Bowden's view the progressive deterioration in Jason Mitchell's ability to describe his symptoms would have made the assessment of risk more difficult, and it may also have explained why so little was known about Jason Mitchell's emotional life. In accounting for the homicides Dr Bowden considered that his emotional state may have been of particular importance.

The point I wanted to make was it is the emotional content in which people's abnormal mental experiences occurred. It seems to be the most important in determining violence. It is not the experience itself. Lots of people are walking around with instructing auditory hallucinations intending to kill people, probably thousands at this very moment who are not in maximum security hospitals who will never do anything about it, but it is the emotional context and the context of the personality of that individual ... that is important, not the experience itself, and that area is missing.

Dr Bowden was then asked by Mr Thorold whether the clinical teams lacked a clear understanding of Jason Mitchell's emotional life. He replied:

In the papers that I have read, I have almost no understanding of his emotional life.

The fact that Jason Mitchell was thought to have a severe mental illness, should not preclude him ... from that type of enquiry. That is, into his emotional life, his relationship with his family, his relationship with his father ....

Although sure about the diagnosis of schizophrenia, Dr Bowden did not regard this as a sufficient explanation for the killings. Other important aspects were Jason Mitchell's affective state, his personality and early development, and the anger he felt to his family and the world in general:

> All these things make as important a contribution to understanding him as thinking of him as a schizophrenic.

Although drug abuse was also an important feature of Jason Mitchell's background history, and Dr Goddard and his colleagues at Easton House had suggested that Jason Mitchell might have carried out the killings in a drug-induced psychotic state, Dr Bowden saw no indications of this. In his experience killings under the influence of drugs tended to be much more 'chaotic' in manner than those carried out by Jason Mitchell. We agree with Dr Bowden's view. Jason Mitchell himself also denied any drug taking and described a state of clear consciousness at the time of the killings.

The difficulty of relating the killings to specific features of Jason Mitchell's schizophrenic illness was not unusual in Dr Bowden's experience:

> it is not at all uncommon for us not to be able to link the actual abnormal mental state with the acts. In fact it is more usual than unusual.

It was also not uncommon for mentally ill prisoners to exhibit periods of apparent calm and self control, as well as acutely disturbed states, as happened shortly after Jason Mitchell's remand in custody.

Dr Bowden argued that the question of diagnosis should not be given undue prominence:

> I wonder whether one issue ... is whether the diagnosis is all that important and relevant. Whatever occasioned what happened in 1990, it was an abnormal state of mind and it was with the intention of killing a stranger who could have been killed ....
>
> Moving between schizophrenia and paranoid personality and drug-induced psychosis, it may influence management, but not com-

pletely ... I think there is an undue emphasis on questioning the diagnosis if there is still someone to manage who had behaved homicidally in an abnormal mental state four years previously.

He also cautioned against assuming that some indication of the impending killings should have been evident to clinical staff before Jason Mitchell left St Clement's Hospital on 9 December 1994. It was entirely plausible that he could have had grotesque thoughts in mind but an apparently normal exterior:[1]

> Of course we know that there are people ... who live in the community who commit absolutely horrendous acts over long periods of time and we all ask ourselves the question, 'How could they possibly? I used to work with them and they seemed quite normal'. Why should we think that the mentally ill would behave differently to people who we consider not to be mentally ill? Why should we expect mentally ill people to say, 'I am thinking of killing' because non-mentally ill people do not say that?

Dr Bowden was sceptical of Jason Mitchell's admission that he had been sexually aroused during the killings:

> As the interview was proceeding, I got the strong impression that he was playing a part, or was trying to impress me in a certain way, and towards the end of the interview he was becoming more and more grotesque ... in his attempts to impress me that this had been part of a sort of cannibalistic ritual and I did not believe that was necessarily the case nor did I believe I could rely on his attempts to impress me that that was what he did in the killings.
> I asked him towards the end of the interview about sexual matters and he picked it up very quickly and said that there was, which again reinforced my belief that I could not rely on what he was saying because I knew this was the first time he had said that. That is in none of the papers I have read. ... I believe it was unreliable and was said in the context of an attempt to impress me with a certain persona.

[1] Jason Mitchell's case is perhaps similar in this respect to another local case report sent to the Inquiry by Dr Andrew Mason. Dr Mason's historical paper describes the case of a Suffolk man with probable schizophrenia, Samuel Ward, who killed the Reverend John Ashburne near Bury St Edmunds on 1 August 1661. A contemporary account of the killing noted that Mr Ward had previously been 'Distracted' but '... was now become very sober, and carried himself very civilly and orderly, and was suffered to go without any keeper ...' Mr Ward made a sudden attack on Mr Ashburne, killing him with a fork and Mr Ashburne's own knife. (A. Mason (to whom we are grateful for having sent us his paper) 1994, 'The Reverend John Ashburne (c. 1611-61) and the origins of the Private Madhouse System', *History of Psychiatry*, v, 321-45).

Jason Mitchell conveyed a different impression in his interviews with two of us (AG and PG). He denied to us any sexual arousal during the killings and gave a glib assurance that he now had a settled sexual orientation and a normal fantasy life. We suspected there may have been sexual feelings associated with the killings more than he was acknowledging, principally because he had given a detailed account of this to his solicitor in an earlier interview which we have seen (Mr Craig Marchant's copious notes of an interview were made available to us as a result of Jason Mitchell waiving his legal privilege to their contents).

A final aspect that requires mention is the possible influence of the two books Jason Mitchell possessed, *Red Dragon* and *Silence of the Lambs*. At Larkhill Way Jason Mitchell had watched the video of the latter and had lent the two books to a fellow resident. Speculations about the significance of the material need to be approached with great caution. Dr Bowden told the Inquiry that he had seen individuals who had been heavily influenced by such material and believed they were characters in such books, but these cases were unusual. In Jason Mitchell's case Dr Bowden was sceptical:

> I had the very strong impression that this was what he wanted to believe himself, but this does not necessarily of course mean that that was the reason he behaved as he did. ... It is interesting but I would not put any reliance on that.
> ... He may be playing a part to make what was inherently irrational seem reasonable or understandable.

It should be remembered that people with serious mental illnesses,

> do have the capacity to be disingenuous and to play different roles and we should not think that that capacity is in any way impaired.

In our interviews Jason Mitchell tended to deny and minimise any influence of the books on his thinking. What was of interest was that an examination of the books revealed more parallels of content than Jason Mitchell had acknowledged. We hesitate, however, to draw any conclusions from this observation.

Thomas Harris's two novels, *Red Dragon* and *Silence of the Lambs*, were first published in the UK in 1982 and 1989 respectively. The editions referred to below are the paperback versions published by Arrow Books (*Red Dragon*, 1993) and Mandarin

Paperbacks (*Silence of the Lambs*, 1991) The latter was made into a well known film; the former into a lesser known film, *The Manhunter*.

Both novels contain the character of the imprisoned serial killer Hannibal Lecter. In *Red Dragon* the serial killer on the loose is Dolarhyde, a deformed and socially humiliated man who had been abandoned by his mother at birth. Subsequent attempts at their reconciliation fail, his mother remaining distant and disinterested. His father is cut in two by a taxi. He is reared by his grandmother who is at times emotionally abusive and physically threatening. Dolarhyde addresses his need for identity and self esteem by becoming a serial killer: '... a projective delusional scheme which compensated for unbearable feelings of inadequacy' (p. 144). He stalks families with the intention of killing them. This is deemed by him his 'becoming'. His becoming is his transformation into the 'Red Dragon'. Dolarhyde engages in necrophilia, and uses rubber gloves when killing (as Jason Mitchell claimed to do when dismembering his father). Dolarhyde ties and gags one of his victims, describes a strangulation technique and takes food from the refrigerator of one of his victims. The importance of moonlight at the place of killing is referred to (p. 64).

Dolarhyde obtains a spectacular new tattoo of a dragon (p. 158) 'the brilliant tattoo of the tail that ran down his lower back and wrapped around his leg'. Tattoos are referred to throughout both novels quite frequently. Dolarhyde wears a kimono in his bedroom. (A resident at Larkhill Way described Jason Mitchell wearing a similar garment.)

Also in *The Red Dragon* is the imprisoned high status serial killer Hannibal Lecter. He is famous, highly 'respected' and feared. He is very important to the FBI in catching Dolarhyde. He is a trained psychiatrist, evading psychiatric definition and understanding by his colleagues, although he is described as a 'sociopath' (p. 52). (At Rampton Jason Mitchell asked to attend educational classes in sociology, 'because I'm a sociopath'.)

In *Silence of the Lambs* Hannibal Lecter had carried out horrific killings involving cannibalism. He claims once to have eaten a victim's liver (p. 23). The serial killer on the loose in this novel (Jame Gumb) was abandoned by his mother when aged two and murdered his grandparents when he was aged 12. Jame Gumb is concerned with his own transformation of identity through killing women and is obsessed with the 'becoming' of moths and butterflies

– the Imago. (Jackie Leaver's 1991 report contains the phrase 'Jason Mitchell explains his change in behaviour as moving from a chrysalis to a butterfly'.)

Lecter escapes at the end of *Silence of the Lambs*, evading capture by means of a disguise, including changing his nose by means of silicone injections. (Pauline Cornford's witness statement to the Police dated 30.1.95 reports Jason Mitchell saying he had no ambitions other than to kill and eat people. He went on to say he would have to change his identity by means of using wigs, having plastic surgery and using false noses.)

The above comparisons suggest that Jason Mitchell may have been familiar with the content of the two novels, and that at various stages he offered accounts of his intentions and actions which had parallels with, and may have been drawn from their content. It is conceivable that he identified with their main characters and that he entertained the idea of becoming a serial killer. When he was interviewed by the two of us, ten months after the killings, he was still speaking of the 'social ladder of killings' and making an 'impact kill', but he was denying consciously being influenced by the novels. He also denied having said that he had eaten his father's liver (although he undoubtedly had said this). Both of us noted how reference to *Silence of the Lambs* and serial killing spontaneously came into the content of Jason Mitchell's interviews. There are also, however, many points of difference between Jason Mitchell's behaviour and the stories of the novels.

Conclusions

The attempts to understand Jason Mitchell's killings have been multiple and time consuming. Uncertainties and gaps in knowledge characterise each of the factors that together may have played a part – schizophrenic illness, his personality development, emotional life, abnormal sexuality, and family psychodynamics. The above review illustrates, perhaps above all else, the limitations of clinical methods in this area and the complexities of judgement that are involved in weighing and evaluating different accounts. Furthermore, the accounts that are compiled cannot be regarded as definitive causal explanations; they are narratives of how events were psychologically possible and understandable. Plausible alternative narratives can always be constructed. Ultimately, none can be wholly relied upon.

In the hearings Dr Bowden was reminded of what he had written in his court report for Jason Mitchell's trial:

> I suspect that many of his alleged motives for the killings are attempts to appear coldly psychopathic, thereby avoiding any hint of psychotic motivation which, in any event, may be impossible for him to describe rationally (because of its inherent irrationality).

Mr Thorold's subsequent questions and Dr Bowden's answers were as follows.

> Q. Does this mean that in this case we get little or no assistance as to motivation from what the patient himself says?
> A. I believe that to be the case.
> Q. Would you say that outsiders trying to make sense of it are likely to find it unfathomable?
> A. Yes.
> Q. Probably indefinitely?
> A. Yes.
> Q. So that time, if anything, is not going to help and he will become more confused about it?
> A. The reverse happens. I think that as time goes on, people provide explanations which become more and more elaborate and concrete because they feel more comfortable having an explanation.

Social expectations of clinicians' abilities to understand and predict patients' offences have to be tempered by recognition of how limited those abilities are. If achieving an understanding of what happened after the event is so problematic, how much more so is foreseeing the event before it occurs. Hindsight appears to provide no better means of explaining past events than does foresight enable us to predict future events.

Part C

Mental Health of Jason Mitchell in Youth Custody, 1988-89

VI. Medical Records at Feltham Young Offender Institution

VI. Medical Records at Feltham Young Offender Institution

With the same cement, ever sure to bind,
we bring to one dead level ev'ry mind.
Alexander Pope

Jason Mitchell was sentenced to a term of two years' Youth Custody on 19 February 1988 in respect of property offences committed in 1987. He served his sentence mainly at Feltham Young Offenders Institution, sandwiched between two short periods, at the beginning and end of his custodial period, at Hollesley Bay Young Offenders Institution. From the latter institution he was discharged to the Richmond Fellowship Hostel in Cambridge, without any specific psychiatric oversight being put in place. Jason Mitchell's Inmate Medical Record (IMR) for that period, held by the prison authorities, did not surface after the day of his discharge on 12 May 1989 until 12 October 1995 during the Inquiry hearings at Bury St Edmunds. (We deal in Chapter XXV with the circumstances whereby these records were mislaid, and the general provisions for the transmission of documentation within and outwith the prison service.) When recovered from the archives of the prison service they revealed the first signs of an emerging psychiatric problem.

Chronology	
6/8/87	Remanded in custody HMP Norwich.
19/2/88	Sentenced to two years imprisonment for offences of robbery and theft. Returned to HMP Norwich.
24/2/88	Transferred to HMP Chelmsford
2/3/88	Transferred to Hollesley Bay Colony Young Offenders Institution.
31/5/88	Transferred to HMYOI Feltham
14/3/89	Transferred from Feltham to HMYOI Hollesley Bay
12/5/89	Released from Custody and took up residence at Richmond Fellowship Hostel, Cambridge

The first indication of any mental disorder, evidenced by a note on file within Jason Mitchell's IMR, came in early 1988 from a prison officer at Norwich Prison where he was held on remand for the 1987 offences. Prison Officer N.G. McPhee, in a memorandum of 9 January 1988 to his group manager, stated that, after having been on leave for a fortnight and on returning to duty, there had been a noticeable change in Jason Mitchell's behaviour. He wrote:

> Unknown to him I observed him for a period of 15-20 minutes during the lunch hour on Saturday 9.1.88. During this time I saw an excessive behaviour pattern, i.e.:
>
> (1) he talked to himself and answered himself back;
> (2) danced around the cell – no radio was playing;
> (3) kept on jumping on and off his bed;
> (4) laid on the bed and pulled his knees up to his chest and rocked backwards and forwards while whimpering.
>
> None of these actions were done in the above sequence but were continual. On checking Mitchell's F1150 I found he had been on a charge recently for shaving his head. *In my opinion the matter should be brought to the attention of the medical officer* (italics supplied).

At Hollesley Bay YOI, Jason Mitchell was referred by the Governor to the visiting consultant psychiatrist, Dr Berry, asking for advice 're feasibility of medical transfer, as it is unlikely he will survive here for much longer; staff say he is "not all there".'

Dr Berry reported back to the Governor on 24 March 1988:

> Re your memo of 22.3.88; I saw this lad on 21.3.88. I note the history of self-injury but do not regard him as a suicide risk.
> Bizarre behaviour was described at HMP Norwich in January, but the SMO regarded him as normal after investigation.
> I have read his petition which agrees with his verbal account to me. I agree that he is unlikely to survive on normal location, but I cannot agree with staff that he is 'not all there'.
> As he is not ill, and I have not made a diagnosis or offered treatment, I cannot arrange a medical transfer without deceiving my colleagues. You may quote me as saying that a change of location would be in the interests of his health if he was enabled not to be afraid. If he goes on R46 [segregation] surely Region will transfer him rather than have him on it here for 12 months.

That same day Jason Mitchell temporarily barricaded himself in his cell. He wrote a note actively seeking segregation. During the next two months Jason Mitchell was almost continually segregated; he was, predictably, transferred to Feltham YOI on 31 May 1988 where he remained until 16 March 1989 on transfer back to Hollesley Bay YOI.

Chaplain's assessment

Extracts from a report prepared on 8 May 1988 by the Prison Chaplain, Rev. E.A. Giles, illustrate that Jason Mitchell presented differently to different staff and produced disparate evaluations:

> Staff opinion is dismissive of Jason Mitchell to the point of being derisive. While I can certainly understand why this should be I have to report that I found Jason Mitchell to be a great deal more than the extremely poor specimen portrayed in staff comment. During the course of my interview with him he presented as a good conversationalist displaying considerable perspicacity and imagination. His conversation was fluent, always polite, and he displayed considerable sense of humour. I think that he has deliberately chosen to act the part of a 'drop out' and that his lifestyle is of his own making.
>
> He described his father as sad and lonely (thereby displaying a good deal more insight than the majority of his peers). He himself appears to be equally lonely having been in custody from October 1987 and having received no visits .... Looking to the future Jason Mitchell expresses the gravest doubts as to his ability to stay out of trouble. He even spoke of being 'scared' of leaving custody.

Having made this assessment, the chaplain did not recommend parole.

Probation assessment

This assessment, of 19 January 1988 by Mrs E. Ashton, a probation officer, highlights Jason Mitchell's evident difficulties at 17 years of age. Her report contains a particular pointer towards subsequent aspects of personality disturbance relating to a lack of empathy for others. In relation to his burglaries and robbery, she noted:

> He says he did not intend to hurt the victims of his crimes but in discussion with him he appears to lack any awareness of the fear he must have caused or the invasion of others' privacy.

Mrs Ashton's view was:

Jason Mitchell seems to lack boundaries to his behaviour normally learned during childhood. He appears to be unable to conform to rules and regulations and drifts around in what can only be described as a state of day dreaming. It is likely that he is an isolated, lonely and unhappy young man, who uses his day dreaming activities as an escape from reality. However, despite efforts to befriend him, it has not been possible to gain the respect and confidence of this young man.

Jason Mitchell's letters

Probation records during the period of Youth Custody contain a dozen or so letters written by Jason Mitchell to his probation officer. They express a range of hopes and fears for his release, and while they suggest sustained efforts during this period to communicate his thoughts and feelings, they are at times difficult to follow and show variability of mood and guarded prognosis for social survival on release.

(15.7.88)
I'm overjoyed at my place in the Fellowship and I will say yes, 'yes', I'm delighted and excited but I know my excitement has spread to parts of me that I don't want it to spread to and I feel more and more in the mood I used to be when I would do crime ....

(23.7.88)
It is my birthday and it's Saturday and I could think of better places than prison to spend it. I didn't want to write to my dad or family as his just blanks my letters. I thought I would cheer myself up and write to you ....

(18.8.88)
I've been thinking of what I would be doing if I was out and it's difficult to think straight about it. It seems prison is a place that has taken over my very existence ....

(18.1.89. Writing in thanks for a gift of a radio)
It really made Christmas a memory rather than an excuse to say my time is coming close and not even think of it like Christmas, but with some help and a radio I could feel the importance of it. I know my life is going to take off with a vroom, can't see any other way it can go except better so I'm going to try and, who knows, this time next year, I could be the boss of Harrods and a multi-millionaire .... I think feelings, love and happiness, are too important to disfigure with luxuries, living and drugs .... I would prefer to get my kicks from life

it has so much to offer in the natural buzz, just for instance being nice and helping someone out ....

(16.3.89. Introducing himself to his new probation officer)
I don't want to commit crime and I'm looking for help in religion. Even the thought of being free from temptation is a great lifting of the pressure.

These letters are concurrent with Dr Latif's many entries in Jason Mitchell's IMR reporting the progress of psychological symptoms such as hearing voices.

At Feltham YOI he was placed for most of his time in Bittern Unit. Mr Arthur de Frisching, Area Manager (Chilterns) in the prison service, who at the relevant time was the Governor of Feltham YOI, described to us the special nature of Bittern Unit. It was designed to cope with the young men who presented difficulties of management without having to be placed in the hospital wing or undergoing treatment by medication. It could be described as a half-way house between a normal location for an inmate and hospital. Mr de Frisching also told us that, because of its staffing levels and the composition of the young offenders, he thought it unlikely that illicit drugs were freely available. Since Jason Mitchell had no visits from family or friends, and appeared to be low in the pecking order among the inmate population – at HMYOI Hollesley Bay other inmates had taken his tobacco off him – he would not have been likely to have had ready or continuous access to drugs. Furthermore if the prison staff had suspected that he might be using drugs, this would almost certainly have been recorded in his disciplinary record, but there are no such references.

On 24 July 1988 Jason Mitchell was seen by a locum medical officer at Feltham who wrote:

He is a disturbed youth who wishes to discuss psychiatric problems that have been with him over the last two years. I feel that he is genuine in his approaches and concerns. Please would Dr Latif [visiting consultant psychiatrist] see and advise.

Dr Latif saw Jason Mitchell on 27 July 1988; thereafter he saw him on no fewer than 30 separate occasions over the next $7\frac{1}{2}$ months. On the first occasion Dr Latif wrote:

Seen as requested. He is co-operative and appears keen to talk about himself and try to resolve certain emotional conflict that he has at the moment. He feels totally rejected by his family. No one from his family has visited him since he has been here [then two months]. Says at times his inner feeling is different from how he responds to others outwardly .... He thinks his nose and lips are changing shape. He has marks on one side of his face and not on the other. He remains concerned about this. He denies feeling depressed and he sleeps well and his appetite is normal. This is an interesting young man. He needs to be observed further for assessment.

We quote some extracts from Dr Latif's notes to indicate the extraordinarily commendable recording of the interviews that, whatever Dr Latif's conclusions, have an immediate impact upon the clinician reading them. Dr Goddard, when asked by Dr Grounds for his reaction to the detail of the description of reported symptoms said:

> like you, when I first saw them I thought, 'my God, look at this. Has this man got very obvious schizophrenia and it has been going on all this time and nobody has bothered to do anything about it'.

19.8.88
Says he thinks everyone knows his life and everything about him. He believes the whole world knows everything about him. TV talks to him and people communicate with him through TV. He thinks could be special power of his brain which makes him communicate with the rest of the world.

There is no evidence of thought disorder. Says he hears voices talking to him about him and very rarely they talk to each other about him. Says 'its so unbelievable that its incredibly believable'. Observe.

25.8.88
Says he still hears voices talking about him e.g. if he reads a book, voice questions the other voice including him asking why he enjoys reading the book. While reading he hears voices repeating what he has just read and finalising spelling ... of the difficult words that he reads. Thinks they go all the time about other things, e.g. if he washes the sink in his room they ask him not to do that and so on. He clearly recognises the voices as coming from outside his head and they are not his own voice. He is not afraid of the voice. He is not sure whether they are real voices but he thinks they might be.

He thinks that these voices are the voices of people. He wonders why they waste their time talking to him, or talking behind his back. He is positive about his belief that people whose voices talk about him never eat any food. He tends to neglect his personal hygiene deliberately and when he finds himself unclean he begins to feel very small inside of that feeling. Beginning to sink in his soul. He continues to neglect himself until he suddenly feels that he need to improve his personal hygiene.

To him all these things are real. He does not think that there is anything wrong with him. Observe.

2.9.88
Today he was encouraged to pursue rational conversation. He could carry out normal and rational conversation and talked most of the time to the point. With some direct guidance he could be dissuaded from talking past the point. He did not volunteer any of his hallucinatory experiences during the course of the session.

9.9.88
Says he feels fine. Today I guided him to pursue rational and normal conversation and I encouraged him to answer all the questions to the point. He was able to carry out normal conversation for a short while, only to start talking past the point immediately after. Says he hears voices talking to each other and occasionally to him 'with negative attitude towards him and positive attitude towards themselves'. He was unable to expand any further. Observe while living within normal location.

14.9.88
Recently he has been allowed to work in CES. Since then he has been keeping himself occupied and now talks less about his hallucinations. He appears cheerful today and his emotion quite appropriate. His insight too seems to be of fair amount. Observe.

21.9.88
Says he is able to change the shape of his eyes, nose and lips at will, making them look better if looking at the mirror. He feels that they look bigger. He claims he has done this on several occasions.

Although he continues to express ideas of delusional intensity his affect and personality is fairly well preserved. He appears keen to share his feelings and views with me which makes him feel relaxed. Since he has started to see me he has made steady improvement behaviourally.

28.9.88
Says he does not hear voices talking to him as long as he remains occupied doing something, but when he hears voices talking at him those voices come from a distance according to pitch of those voices and seem as normal voices. However, he is not scared by them. As advised, he has been trying to dismiss them as being unreal but could not get rid of them.

12.10.88

Says he hears voices talking to him instructing him to do things and interrupt his thinking which is annoying for him. But he is not scared of those voices.

Within the unit he keeps himself to himself and this is how he finds it easier to cope. Outwardly, he is OK and free of any psychotic symptoms.

19.10.88

He appears to be coping well within Bittern Unit. He found it quite stressful working in CES and gave up that job because of that reason. Now he appears relaxed and cheerful. My impression is that he does not suffer from any schizophrenic illness at present.

28.10.88

During the whole session he did not mention about his auditory hallucination even once. At present he is unable to differentiate between fantasy and reality. I help him to learn how to do that. In a supportive environment he is unlikely to have a breakdown.

4.11.88

Says he does not feel like eating but once he starts to eat it is difficult for him to stop. Says he is trapped in between two feelings i.e. either not to do things at all or if start doing it, he feels compelled to continue doing the same e.g. reading.

9.11.88

Says he does not feel depressed today but feels strange. He feels big for himself. He feels closed in as within a small square. Says talking to me and sharing this feeling with me relieves him of heavy emotional burden.

16.11.88

He still hears voices talking to him, telling him not to do certain things. But he is no longer afraid of them although they make him angry.

30.11.88

He does not seem to be affected by the hallucinatory voices. He has learnt how to avoid hearing the voices by keeping himself occupied.

7.12.88

Says he now has certain amount of authority over the voice that he hears. Says I have been able to create doubts in his mind that voices that he hears could be unreal.

14.12.88

He spent last week writing poems which reflect his day-to-day feeling. His poetic expression seems to be of paranoid and insecure nature. However he appears relaxed.

21.12.88
... today he did not talk about hearing voices. I did not enquire about this either. His thought process appears normal and his emotions fairly stable.

30.12.88
... he appears bright and cheerful. Bittern unit environment seems to have helped him a great deal.

6.1.89
... The voices have changed now. They are more sensible not so childish. When they say things to him he can laugh at them as they are not so powerful now.

10.2.89
... Voices do not bother him as long as he keeps himself occupied. He does not talk so much about hearing voices any longer as he used to do before. There is no indication of any psychosis and he does not need treatment with any drugs. He does benefit by individual counselling.

The last time Jason Mitchell saw Dr Latif was on 8 March 1989. Dr Latif ended his counselling role on an optimistic note: 'He appears calm and relaxed. He has gained reasonable degree of emotional maturity and should be able to manage his own affairs.'

Jason Mitchell was transferred to Hollesley Bay YOI on 14 March. On 22 March 1989 he threatened to hang himself: 'Noose made from sheet removed from cell.'

Jason Mitchell's medical record for 23 March 1989 states:

23.3.89
Seen 21.3.89 after scratching wrist, bullying and lost time. Advised. Transferred Feltham .... He has been threatened. Made a noose as cry for help. Has been attacked in showers at Feltham, there is a risk of assault. He can't stand up for himself. There is a risk of self injury or suicide gesture rather than suicide. He is not depressed and does not need treatment. I would advise rule 46 and send back to Feltham. Why did he come here?

For the remainder of his time in youth custody – two months – the medical record is silent. As a result of being absent for a short time on arriving back at Hollesley Bay, Jason Mitchell spent the rest of his sentence in the closed unit, Warren Hill. He did not go to Feltham. His IMR of Youth Custody days having travelled with him to Hollesley Bay, thereafter remained there, stored in the muniments room, and its contents were unknown to those who subsequently became involved in his psychiatric care and treatment.

At the time of compiling his notes, Dr Latif recorded that he did not consider Jason Mitchell was suffering from a psychotic illness such as schizophrenia. He maintained this opinion before us on two grounds. First, he said that Jason Mitchell did not display any thought disorder; and secondly, that the hallucinations which Jason Mitchell frequently mentioned were not genuine but were 'pseudo-hallucinations'. While it is understandable that a clinician may be reluctant to make a firm diagnosis of schizophrenia in a young person presenting with a first episode of psychotic symptoms, we think that Dr Latif's contemporaneous records strongly suggest that Jason Mitchell may have had symptoms of schizophrenia. Dr Latif's detailed and copious notes are replete with references to hallucinations, and he did not record at the time that they were not authentic, nor did he describe them in his notes as pseudo-hallucinations. Secondly, the opinion he expressed in his written statement to the Inquiry that Jason Mitchell did not exhibit thought disorder was not consistent with his own documentary evidence. The entries in his medical notes for 2 September 1988, 'He could be dissuaded from talking to past the point' and for 9 September, 1988: 'Today I guided him to pursue rational and normal conversation and encouraged him to answer all the questions to the point. He was able to carry out normal conversation for a short while, only to start talking past the point immediately after' – both suggest that on occasions Jason Mitchell may have been thought disordered.

Dr Latif's detailed descriptions of Jason Mitchell's abnormal experiences are also suggestive of schizophrenia. Jason Mitchell described auditory hallucinations of voices outside his head talking to him and to each other; they talked about him, commented on his actions, and repeated his thoughts (for example, when reading). He described them instructing him to do things and interrupting his thinking which he found annoying. He expressed abnormal beliefs in a firm manner suggestive of delusions, for example, a belief that the whole world knew everything about him, and that the people whose voices he heard never eat any food. He believed the television talked to him and that people communicated with him through the television. He also had abnormal beliefs that were dysmorphophobic in content, for example, that his nose was changing shape.

However, there are also other features in the records that might cast some doubt on a diagnosis of schizophrenia. There was an improvement in Jason Mitchell's mental state without the aid of anti-psychotic medication, and he appeared to be assisted by the advice and counselling sessions given by Dr Latif. Jason Mitchell was not admitted to the hospital wing of the YOI, nor considered for transfer to an outside psychiatric hospital. This is attributable, in part at least, to the kind of regime that operated in the Bittern Unit, as described to us by Mr de Frisching.

Although it seemed to us that the records were suggestive of a first presentation of schizophrenic illness, Dr Latif, in his written and oral evidence to the Inquiry, maintained his opinion that Jason Mitchell did not have schizophrenia, and went on to argue for an alternative diagnosis. In his written statement to us of 31 October 1995 he concluded:

> While under my supervision at HM Feltham YOI & RC Jason Mitchell had presented symptoms strongly suggestive of drug-induced psychosis of delayed nature (ICD 10: F19.75). He was not a danger to himself or to others.

We have to say that, having read and re-read Dr Latif's high quality notes, and having taken oral evidence from senior management at Feltham during the relevant period – the Governor, Mr de Frisching and the Health Care Manager, Mr D.A. Strong (now Governor, Huntercombe YOI) – we cannot conclude that there was anything present in the documentation to support a diagnosis of drug-induced psychosis.

The ethos at Feltham, Jason Mitchell's low status among his fellow inmates within the institution, and the absence of any reference in both the IMR and the general file to illicit drug-taking in the counselling sessions with Dr Latif argue powerfully for the improbability of any drug-induced psychosis. The sustained symptomatology over a long period during 1988-89 also seemed incompatible with such a diagnosis.

Dr Latif's excellent notes nevertheless provide a valuable contemporary record of psychotic symptomatology which would inform any future carer or treater as source material towards later diagnosis. The records were not without ambiguities, but at the very least any diagnostician would have been bound to view the psychotic episode on 8 February 1990 as something other than the first symptoms of schizophrenia. That terrifying episode needed to be assessed against the backcloth of the earlier recorded symptoms.

Copies of the Feltham records were sent by the Inquiry to clinicians previously involved in Jason Mitchell's case in order to seek their observations. Dr Richard Penrose, the consultant psychiatrist who assessed Jason Mitchell at Feltham in March 1990 with a view to his reception into West Park Hospital, would have found the mislaid IMR confirmatory of his diagnosis. Dr Penrose told us that Jason Mitchell 'was seriously mentally ill and required treatment in a secure setting. The opportunity of examining the previous records [the Feltham IMR] although doubtless interesting and perhaps providing a more complete picture would not materially have altered my opinion ....' Likewise Dr Denise Yeldham, who became Jason Mitchell's RMO after he became the subject of the Hospital Order in September 1990, did not think that the information, while providing additional support in her diagnosis of schizophrenia, 'would have greatly influenced my view or actions'.

Her predecessor as Jason Mitchell's RMO, Professor Merry, who had been an advocate for Jason Mitchell's absolute discharge, told us that the fresh evidence would have led him to support the conditional discharge which the Mental Health Review Tribunal ordered in September 1991. Professor Merry's senior registrar, Dr Crellin, who made the main report to the Tribunal on that occasion, said that the 1988/89 material would have provided no more than a confirmation of the appropriateness of a conditional discharge. Dr Brenda Lintner, the independent psychiatrist who supported the conditional discharge, noted that no definite diagnosis of mental illness had been made at Feltham, although there were suspicious symptoms. She did not think that her report to the Tribunal would have been couched in different terms.

Dr Ian Wilson thought that overall the records added weight to his own view that Jason Mitchell had a schizophrenic illness, although there were discrepancies and inconsistencies in the Feltham notes. Both he and Dr Lintner noted the sharp variations there appeared to be in Jason Mitchell's state over short time periods.

Dr Christie Brown, in a supplementary report to the Inquiry, wrote:

The prison medical records contain the same themes as I earlier encountered in the documents I studied before making my first report. Jason Mitchell had an unhappy background and felt neglected by his father. By some who saw him he was thought weak and inadequate but others found positive aspects in him. He described clear symptoms of mental illness. It is noteworthy that while he was in prison these descriptions were nevertheless not thought to represent a true mental illness. It would certainly appear that trained observers found something unconvincing about his descriptions.

Dr Christie Brown concluded his supplementary report by saying:

> ... the prison record provides some evidence to suggest Jason Mitchell had developed a mental illness by the time he was in youth custody. At the same time the difficulty in assessing him is highlighted in that it appears that there was something about him which meant that his descriptions of his psychotic symptoms were not believed.

Dr Goddard (who spoke in this respect for the whole of his team at Easton House) said that, subject to the qualification that the question of how he would have acted in the light of the undiscovered records was hypothetical, the records would have enabled him 'to have a much more thorough picture' of Jason Mitchell's background. He added:

> I think it would have certainly influenced my views about his ability in terms of where he might be placed in the community following such a long period in institutions ....

and he agreed with our Chairman's question:

> You would put a question mark against his ability to survive in the community on his own?

Whatever impact the lost records might or might not have had on the diagnosticians and those responsible for the care and treatment of Jason Mitchell while he remained in hospital, they would undoubtedly have assisted in informing discharge planning in May 1989, including the insertion into the discharge plan of psychiatric oversight. Jason Mitchell was on licensed supervision from the date of his release from custody on 12 May 1989 until 28 October 1989, the expiry date of his licence. During the earlier part of 1989 Mrs Christine Turnbull, a probation officer in the Suffolk Probation Service, was responsible for the initial negotiations with the Rich-

mond Fellowship hostel in Cambridge as to Jason Mitchell's suitability for accommodation on release.

Placement in Cambridge

On 1 June 1988, Christine Turnbull (probation officer) made an
application to the Richmond Fellowship for a placement for Jason
Mitchell. In describing his needs she said, 'Jason is a loner and
lacks many of the skills with regard to forming and sustaining
relationships and this area will need a great deal of attention.
Jason states that he has the necessary practical skills in this area
(Personal Care) but in terms of his personality he needs to learn to
respect himself.'

The supporting Social Enquiry report made reference to the
possible effect of his childhood on his poor self image, to his most
recent offence 'when he took money from a till and pulling out a
screwdriver as he left the premises telling people to back off'.
Reference was made to him tending to live in his own world and
withdrawing into his own imagination but that 'he is nevertheless
in touch with reality'. It stated that Jason Mitchell admitted to
using glue and that he was smoking 7-8 joints of cannabis a day
before his imprisonment.

His probation officer stated in a report dated July 1988: 'Mr
Mitchell has not unnaturally shown some concern that he may not
have the ability to change. Nevertheless, the commitment he displayed during his period of assessment is such that I feel it is a risk
worth taking if this young man is to have any chance of being
diverted away from a criminal career.'

In May 1989, after his discharge from Hollesley Bay, Jason
Mitchell was re-assessed for admission by the Richmond Fellow-
ship and, after a seven-day assessment, admitted to the Castle
Project in Cambridge.

His first three-monthly review was held on 17 August 1989. The
section on the referral process refers to the fact that 'Jason can
often confuse people with his language frame and that some of his
reasoning seems sideways/lateral'. A review of his family history
states that the level of deprivation 'was extremely serious (more
serious than at first suspected) and has had very long-term effects
on Jason's behaviour'. It was suggested that this had led to Jason's
creating a false ego, but the report writer stated: '... my feeling is
that the core problem for Jason is a non-integrated ego ....'

In reviewing his needs, it was noted that he had presented in a number of different ways being skilled at making relationships but having problems in sustaining them. Some of this was felt to be due to Jason's quick mood changes and his (almost random) dumping of anger.

The review of Jason Mitchell as a member of the community at Castle Project noted that he could be both caring and very destructive. He had dominated other residents and been very aggressive towards staff, including threatening a staff member with a blunt knife. He had shown resistance to working with his own needs in group sessions and had missed a number of individual counselling sessions. It was noted that Jason had used complex and confusing language and that questioning Jason on what he meant often produced tension or open confrontation.

Jason Mitchell had given his notice in at the project in July, but had been persuaded to withdraw it. A week later he told his probation officer that he had been forced to sign a contract agreeing to his departure from the project on 29 July 1989. The probation officer expressed concern to the project that he had not been consulted, was informed about the episode with the knife and the notice was again withdrawn. It was, however, noted that a mutually agreed end to the placement was likely to be the outcome of the three-monthly review. A leaving date of 31 August was agreed. Jason Mitchell's comments are noted: 'It's a shame and sad it never turned out right that I couldn't work it out. I jumped and changed from day to day. My emotions stick. It's hard to move on from difficult emotions. That's because of me.'

Jason Mitchell had expressed the wish to stay in Cambridge and was eventually found accommodation at the Church Housing Project in Cambridge to which he moved on 21 August. At first he wished to move on and an application was made to another project. However, on 21 September, Jason reported on a visit to his probation officer that he might be offered a place at one of the cluster flats attached to the project. The probation officer records that this was a positive possibility and seemed a little surprised. Jason Mitchell's order was due to end on 29 October and he failed to keep his final appointment with his probation officer which was scheduled for 16 October.

The two questions we asked of Mrs Turnbull and her successor, Mrs E. Booth (now of the Staffordshire Probation Service) were: (1) had they known of an earlier diagnosable condition of mental illness, what steps would they have taken to link up with the community psychiatric services; and (2) would Jason Mitchell have been a suitable candidate for residence at the Richmond Fellowship hostel?

Mrs Turnbull told us that, had she been aware of the nature and extent of Jason Mitchell's contact with Dr Latif, she 'would have sought his opinion on Jason Mitchell's needs following release' and would have passed the information to Cambridge Probation Service and the Richmond Fellowship. She added that had there been signs of mental illness that needed to be followed up, it was important for the Richmond Fellowship to be aware of it. It might have been the case that the Castle Prospect hostel was not suited to Jason Mitchell's needs. Furthermore, consideration would have to be given to a psychiatric follow-up upon Jason Mitchell's release from custody.

Part D

The Provenance of the
Hospital Order 1990

VII. The Criminal Event, 8 February 1990

> No florid prose, nor honeyed
> lies of rhyme,
> can blazon evil deeds, or
> consecrate a crime.
> Byron, *Childe Harold's Pilgrimage*,
> Canto the first, III (1812)

What precisely happened at St Barnabas Church, Epsom, on the morning of 8 February 1990 ought to have been of the greatest significance to the clinicians and others who subsequently became responsible for assessing the risk of future harm by Jason Mitchell, if and when he came to be considered for discharge, either absolutely or conditionally, from the Restriction Order. If only because the best predictor of dangerousness is past behaviour, those assessing risk needed vitally to know the full nature and extent of that past behaviour.

Jason Mitchell had found shelter overnight in the church on 6/7 February, being at that time of no fixed abode and wandering aimlessly around the London area. He had landed up, by chance of British Rail, in the Epsom area. The next day he had obtained permission from the vicar, Rev. Michael Preston, to continue to shelter from the rain. This he did on the night of 7/8 February 1990. Counsel for the prosecution of Jason Mitchell at the Central Criminal Court on 10 September 1990 described the incident in ample detail:

> He spent a second night there and the next morning was awakened, according to him later in interview, in hiding waiting for the vicar; but in fact at a quarter past eight the gentleman, aged 70, who part time cleans the church, went to the church for his usual reason. He spent about an hour doing so, being unaware of the fact that the defendant was there, until there came a stage when he was in the vestry, became aware of someone, turned and found the defendant standing in the doorway of the vestry, asked him what he wanted and the defendant produced a piece of wood, some three feet long, which certainly looked like a baseball bat, although I do not think it was, and told the cleaner to get on to the floor and, according to the

cleaner, tried to hit him with the implement, repeated demands for the cleaner to get down on the floor.

The cleaner tried to protect himself and then at the first opportunity ran from the church, falling down the steps causing the injuries to which I have referred and ran towards the vicarage. While he did that, the defendant, after a little distance, stopped and returned to the church but the cleaner asked the vicar to call the police which, of course, happened and the defendant remained in the church until the police arrived.

In answer to their [the police's] initial questions (on the journey to Epsom Police Station), he told them that he had been sent to the church by a voice. He agreed that he tried to hit the caretaker and that was because the voice had told him to kill the vicar, at least to kill someone and the caretaker had come in first. He asserted then that he had tried to kill the caretaker and really would have done so, and he would have kept hitting him until he was dead because the voice had said that the time was right to kill.

In interview, [at which a social worker as the appropriate adult was present] apart from repeating certain of those matters, he indicated that he had been waiting for the vicar having been told what to do by the voice. He had not done so the previous day when he had seen him, because there had been too many people about. He denied actually using the weapon to take a swing at the cleaner, but accepted that he had chased him and that the cleaner had run because he had threatened to make him lie on the floor. The reason he tried to make him do that was so he could strike him more easily and in the right place. By the right place, he said he meant the right place to kill him, that is to say, on the head.

Then he was taken to the police station. On the way in it was noticed that he had got a couple of knives in a back pocket and when asked about those, he said that he had had the knives for some two months; he had got them to kill but had never used them.

By any standards of criminality the incident revealed a terrifying and potentially homicidal event. Jason Mitchell was initially charged by the police with an attempted murder on the cleaner, and with threatening to kill the vicar, the latter charge being dropped at some point along the prosecutorial road. No indictment was preferred on that charge, probably because the only evidence came from an admission by Jason Mitchell to police officers. The response of the prosecuting authorities was, instead, to prefer two indictments. One indictment was for attempted murder of, and an assault occasioning actual bodily harm to, the cleaner. The second indictment related to the discovery on Jason Mitchell of the two knives; the charges alleged possession without lawful authority or reasonable excuse of offensive weapons in a public place. The resulting criminal offences to which Jason Mitchell pleaded guilty only reflected very partially the true criminal event. The crimes to which he ultimately pleaded guilty became the 'index offences', which were repeatedly cited in any response to a query about Jason Mitchell's past behaviour for the purpose of predicting future conduct and for deciding what form of care and treatment was appropriate.

Central Criminal Court, 10 September 1990

When, on 10 September 1990, Jason Mitchell was brought to trial, it could be confidently expected that a Hospital Order under Section 37 of the Mental Health Act 1983 would be made. This was because he had already been identified by the Senior Medical Officer at Feltham Remand Centre as suffering from a treatable mental illness, and had been remanded by the Crown Court to West Park Hospital for treatment in accordance with Section 36 of the Act. He was admitted to West Park Hospital on 4 April 1990. By Section 36(6) an accused cannot be remanded or further remanded for more than 28 days at a time or for more than 12 weeks in all. Jason Mitchell's stay in West Park Hospital beyond 4 July, therefore, continued as an informal patient, on bail to appear for trial two months later.

When the matter came before Judge Rant QC there were available the two psychiatric reports required for the making of a full Hospital Order under Section 37 of the Act. The case was instantly adjourned for the two advocates to engage in plea-bargaining. Since a Hospital Order may be made in respect of a conviction for any imprisonable offence, however minor the crime might be, there was every incentive for the prosecution to accept a plea of guilty to the least serious offence against the person in the criminal calendar. (A common assault does not even need to be an infliction of a blow, but merely the threat of physical contact.) Accordingly, after a short adjournment, a third count in the indictment charging the attempted murder and the assault occasioning actual bodily harm was added to include common assault. To that third count, Jason Mitchell pleaded guilty, as he did to the other indictment which charged possession of offensive weapons (they were forfeited). The prosecution was content that verdicts of not guilty to the offence of attempted murder and an assault occasioning actual bodily harm should be entered. The offence of assault occasioning actual bodily harm was ordered not to be proceeded with unless the court subsequently gave leave for it to be dealt with. The court was aware of previous convictions in 1986 and 1988, but unaware of the history of psychiatric problems experienced at Feltham YOI in 1988-89, a matter to which we advert in Chapter VI.

When aged 16, Jason Mitchell had been convicted of theft and shoplifting; he was ordered to undergo a total of 24 hours at an Attendance Centre. Later in 1986, he was convicted of house burglary and was placed under a Supervision Order for 12 months. In February 1988 for a number of property offences in 1987 and a robbery of £117 from a wineshop (which involved threatening a young pregnant shop asistant with a screwdriver) he was given a total of two years' Youth Custody which he served mainly in Feltham Young Offenders Institute, sandwiched between two periods at the extremities of the sentence in Hollesley Bay Young Offenders Institute from which he was discharged to a hostel in Cambridge in May 1989.

Hospital Order with restrictions

Two psychiatrists recommended a Hospital Order. Dr Pugh, who had previously sought to obtain, without success, the medical records from Feltham YOI, thought that it was unnecessary to add a Restriction Order, because Jason Mitchell was continuing to take his medication and the prognosis for recovery from mental illness was good. Dr Penrose also thought a Restriction Order was contra-indicated. Neither of the two psychiatrists considered, nor was the issue canvassed, whether a Restriction Order limited in time – say, 12 months – would have been appropriate. Judge Rant merely asked: 'If he lapses into his ill state, he is capable of being very dangerous, is he not?', to which Dr Pugh replied: 'I think I could not say that was not the case; he could be.' It was clear that the judge considered that the making of a Restriction Order or not was finely balanced. He said:

> I do not think it is right for me to take a risk unless it is absolutely *de minimis* and therefore ought to be ignored with the safety of the public. I do not think this is a case where I can say the risk is so small that it can be completely ignored.

The judge accordingly made a Hospital Order under Section 37 of the Mental Health Act 1983, together with a Restriction Order, unlimited in time, under Section 41. Jason Mitchell returned to West Park Hospital.

Restriction Orders may be imposed for a definite period or without limit of time. The Percy Commission in 1957 did not consider that the court should be bound to relate the period of a Restriction Order 'to the term of imprisonment which might otherwise have been imposed, though in many cases it may think it appropriate to do so'. Since the purpose of a Restriction Order is not, unlike a prison sentence, to reflect the seriousness of the offence, but to ensure that the patient is not discharged prematurely, the courts, since a leading case in 1967, have stated that Restriction Orders unlimited in time, should be made, unless the medical evidence proves convincingly the prediction of recovery of mental health within a definite period of time. Rarely nowadays is a Restriction Order properly limited in time. Jason Mitchell's case was considered to be no exception. The Butler Committee on Mentally Abnormal Offenders in 1975 recommended (para 14.25) that the power to make orders of limited duration should be removed from the statute book. This was rejected in the Government's consultative exercise in a White Paper, 'The Review of the Mental Health Act 1959' (Cmnd. 7320) on the grounds that in certain cases where there is a good ground for expectation that an offender will soon recover from the disorder that has prompted his offence, 'it may be possible for the court, in the light of medical evidence, to make a reasonable prediction of when an offender will cease to be dangerous' (para 5.28). The situation was left unchanged in the Mental Health Act 1983 (section 41(1)).

Jason Mitchell's case exemplifies two general problems of ensuring that there is adequate knowledge on which to base a decision about imposing a Restriction Order. First, it may be difficult to establish a complete account of an individual's past history of psychiatric illness and offending behaviour. (In Jason Mitchell's case information about his first episode of psychotic illness in prison in 1988 was not available to later psychiatrists.) A confident recommendation for a time limited Restriction Order would be contingent on a full psychiatric history. Given the inherent difficulties in achieving this, there would appear to be merit in reconsidering the proposals of the Butler Committee that the power to impose time limited Restriction Orders should be abolished, and that all such Orders are made without limit of time.

Secondly, Jason Mitchell's case illustrates the inadequate appreciation of a patient's past offending history that can arise because of the absence of a full, authoritative and detailed account of the index criminal event. The witness statements from the church cleaner and the two police officers amply substantiated the prosecuting counsel's description of Jason Mitchell's offence. But witness statements, in the process of being edited into prosecutional language, inevitably lose some of the flavour of the event. To demonstrate the point, we include a statement written for the Inquiry by the cleaner. Our only comment is that the award of £1,500 by the Criminal Injuries Compensation Board would appear to reflect rather more psychological harm than any physical pain or injury.

Letter from Mr J.R. Powell

THESE ARE THE TRUE FACTS TO THE BEST OF MY KNOWLEDGE AND BELIEF

Dear Mr Morden,

On the morning of 8 February 1990, as usual I arrived at St Barnabas Church 8.15 am after visiting the church hall in Hook Rd, Epsom, which was also part of my duties. Arriving at the church itself, I spent the next hour checking for broken windows etc. then carrying out my cleaning programme.

All this time, Jason Mitchell must have been hiding and watching my every move. However, I did notice items had been hidden behind the high altar. I thought they had been left by workmen who were carrying out repairs to the church. These were later found to belong to Jason Mitchell.

I eventually returned to the vestry and put away my materials which included the dust pan and brush. I had my back to the open vestry door leading to the main church. I was conscious of someone standing behind me. I turned and found Jason Mitchell standing there with a wooden club in one hand. I asked him what he wanted; he said, 'On the f...ing floor.' I said, 'No.' He became very angry and his face was livid. He said, 'I'm telling you, get on the f...ing floor.' I replied 'I don't get on the floor for no one.' This was not bravado on my part but sheer bluff, hoping to bide time.

Then Jason Mitchell came at me swinging the club. I managed to evade the first assault. He again swung the club knocking the dust pan and brush out of my hands which I was using to defend myself with. All this time I was retreating towards the open vestry door.

On the opposite side of the vestry room was the door which led to the outside of the church. I managed to slip the Yale catch before Mitchell's next effort and ran for my life. After flinging the door open, I completely missed a small flight of steps and landed on the concrete path which surrounds the church. I hit a wooden fence and eventually finished on the grass verge next to the concrete path. My knees were cut and bruised, my clothes ruined and my right shoulder and right hip badly bruised.

I managed to pick myself up and stumbled making my way to the vicarage some 10 yards away. In the meantime, I saw Mitchell standing at the top of the steps, club in hand. He was hesitating. I am sure he was not quite sure where he was which gave me that bit of extra time. All this while I was trying to shout for help but no sound seemed to be coming out.

On reaching the garden gate, my voice came back. I was shouting army abuse and crying for help. At this point Mitchell turned back and vanished from my view. Half way up the garden path to the vicarage I collapsed. My cries were heard by the vicar, Michael Preston, who came out of his house, I shouted 'Get the Police, I have been attacked.'

After he had phoned the Police he helped me into his home where I stayed till I was eventually taken across to the church to identify Mitchell, who was now detained by the Police. I told the Sgt in charge that Mitchell was the man and I never wanted to see him again. I was then taken by the Sgt back into the vestry. He said, 'You must prosecute this man because I am sure he will do this again'. I had no hesitation in agreeing with him and gave him the signed statement.

During my statement, the Sgt asked my age and said I was getting too old for this game. I said I had to take on Mitchell because it was self-preservation. The Police then wanted to take me to hospital for examination and treatment but relented to my request to be taken to my own GP. I was examined by Dr R. Watts, my GP, who has since retired. He found no serious injuries, treated my cuts and bruises and prescribed medication.

For approximately 7 months I was in trauma and had nightmares. I feel sure at this point I should have received counselling but none was forthcoming.

On 5 September 1990 I was awarded £1,500 for general damages by Miss Shirley Ritchie QC representing the Criminal Injuries Board, with an option to appeal. At that time I did feel the award was inadequate but as I was still in trauma and having nightmares, I could not stand further hassle.

On reflection, I think someone must be made accountable for this grave error or errors. They had Mitchell's previous criminal history before them *before* he attacked me. He was then placed in a hospital a mile away from my home, knowing I was the person who had him convicted, which made my family and myself liable for revenge. Then, to crown it all, he was set free into the community to commit 3 murders. I feel deeply for the families of the 3 people who were murdered.

For the people who are responsible for this, I wonder if they would have made the same decision if, one miserable February morning, they had been subject to an attack in a church similar to the one carried out on me by Jason Mitchell?

It's time the system started to think a little more about the victims and their families.

Trusting you will find the enclosed sufficient for your needs,
I am, sir, yours respectfully
J.R. Powell
(Signed, 7 October 1995)

The fact that the two criminal charges of which Jason Mitchell was eventually convicted (common assault and possession of offensive weapons) were minor, and the fact that subsequent descriptions of the event were usually in brief common summary form, may have enabled the reality of what happened to be minimised and misrepresented. **We recommend** that in any case where the criminal event involving a mentally disordered person is serious or dangerous it should be the responsibility of the Crown Prosecution Service to prepare a full account of the criminal event before criminal proceedings have been finalised, and the CPS should ensure that this account is transmitted after the criminal process has run its course to all those involved in the criminal proceedings, including C3 Division of the Home Office, and the clinicians subsequently responsible for the care of the patient, in respect of restricted cases. The account should become an established part of the patient's clinical record. The preparation of such an account at an early stage of the criminal process will also serve one of the aims of the Victims Charter to provide criminal courts with information regarding the impact of a crime upon the victim.

Regardless of the absence of Jason Mitchell's Inmate Medical Record for the period of his Youth Custody in 1988-89, there was nevertheless ample evidence to question the nature of his mental illness for which appropriate care and treatment needed to be provided. No one involved in the criminal justice proceedings appeared to direct attention to the appropriateness or otherwise of general psychiatric provision available at West Park Hospital, or whether the specialism of forensic psychiatry in a Special Hospital or a Regional Secure Unit was indicated. Viewed from that perspective, the trial of September 1990 misfired in terms of the appropriate response of criminal justice and the mental health system. The judicial focus was on controlling discharge – should there be a Restriction Order or not – rather than an inquiry about the nature of the treatment for Jason Mitchell.

Dr Bowden told us that he would have regarded Jason Mitchell as a candidate for a place in a Special Hospital. Had the case been referred to one of the doctors at Broadmoor Hospital, Dr Bowden was confident that the criteria for admission to Broadmoor would have been met, and Jason Mitchell would, very likely, have been admitted; and hence unlikely to have been discharged within five or six years.

Dr Bowden's concern was for the wider range of psychiatric and psychological services which the Special Hospitals alone provide, and was much less concerned with the extra security which Broadmoor or a Regional Secure Unit (for which none was available in the South Thames region) provides, as against that of a general psychiatric hospital. Jason Mitchell's needs indicated, he thought, provision from forensic psychiatry rather than general psychiatry.

While, no doubt, it is generally a duty of psychiatrists to seek advice and assistance (in the form of second opinions) from those specialising in the care and treatment of mentally disordered offenders, it is also a duty of the Crown Prosecution Service to seek out, in the interests of public safety, the opinions of independent forensic psychiatrists in such cases. This is particularly necessary where general psychiatrists are already involved in treating the patient, with all the in-built optimism engendered by a well established doctor-patient relationship. (By the time of the trial Jason Mitchell had spent six months at West Park.) **We recommend** that the Crown Prosecution Service reviews its procedures in relation to the prosecution of mentally disordered offenders destined to be routed into the mental health system through a Hospital Order.

VIII. Rendering of the Criminal Event, post-September 1990

How often misused words generate misleading thoughts.
Herbert Spencer, *Principles of Ethics*,
bk. I, part ii, ch. 8.152

The fact that Jason Mitchell's convictions at the Central Criminal Court in September 1990 were for the minor offences of common assault and for the possession of offensive weapons (the latter for the most part was dropped from later references) could have misled, and did so easily mislead the Clinical Team at Easton House into thinking that the incident was comparatively trivial. Indeed, when Mr Ken Dunnett, a highly experienced manager employed by East Suffolk Local Health Services NHS Trust as its Mental Health Act Administrator, visited West Park Hospital with Mr Gordon Heffer on 15 February 1993 to assess Jason Mitchell's suitability for transfer to St Clement's when Easton House opened in May 1993, he said that 'we were given information about the index offence which was relatively minor' – note the singular index offence – 'and was presented as low-key and foolish behaviour rather than a seriously dangerous act. On the evidence we saw no reason to disagree with the assessment.' When giving his evidence to us Mr Dunnett acknowledged that his description of the incident on 8 February 1990 was totally misleading, although he made an unavailing attempt to interpret the factual ingredients shown as altogether less frightening than adherence to reality would demand. Mr Dunnett must have communicated the devalued incident to Dr Goddard and the rest of the Clinical Team.

Dr Goddard explained that the reference to seriousness emanated from a remark in the literature on the professional approach to risk assessment. An index offence disclosing a minor conviction should not be too troubling when judging dangerousness. Nevertheless, Dr Goddard's terse comment that Jason Mitchell's index offence 'was one of Common Assault' is an exemplar of the Spencerian dictum. Throughout the handling of Jason Mitchell's case there was no serious questioning among the staff at Easton House that the index offence masked the reality of the criminal events, although there were occasions when questions about Jason Mitchell's violent propensities might have been seriously addressed.

One exception to the view that medical and other staff at St Clement's Hospital were seeing the criminal event of 8 February 1990 ('the index offence') as minimal misconduct, if not bordering on the trivial, was Dr K. Odutoye, who did a review on Jason Mitchell's admission to Easton House on 5 May 1993. His notes on record state:

PC (presenting complaint) – First presented to the psychiatric services in Epsom, Surrey in early 1990 following a threat to kill a caretaker with a baseball bat in a church. The caretaker ran away (slipping and hurting himself in the process) and called the Police who apprehended Jason Mitchell in the church. (He had been waiting for them and made no attempt to escape.) He was initially taken to the Feltham Remand Centre and eventually transferred to West Park Hospital, admitted in April 1990. He was an informal patient while on bail until his Court case in September 1990 where he was found guilty of common assault leading to his current detention under Section 37/41.

On initial interviewing by the police, he told them his attempted assault of the caretaker was as a result of hearing voices telling him to do so. He had arrived in Epsom having caught the wrong train from London (he had just arrived from Amsterdam having lived rough there for 1/52 [one week] and had intended to go to Romford (only enough fare to get there) and then on to his father in Ipswich. It was raining and he took shelter in a church. He was found by the vicar the next day who allowed him to stay there. He says it was at this point that he had an intuitive feeling that if he killed the vicar he would be able to escape from all the persecution and derogatory voices that had plagued him for the previous six years. He said although he'd told the police he'd responded to voices, this wasn't strictly true and he had later withdrawn this statement while in hospital. 'I lied because I thought everyone heard voices and I thought this would be the best way to explain to them.'

The following morning, the caretaker came into the church and he realised he would have to kill the caretaker as well as the vicar to cover his tracks. He asked the caretaker to lie down so he could strike him cleanly on the head with a baseball bat. However the caretaker declined this polite suggestion and took to his heels, slipping and falling in the process. Jason Mitchell says he chased him out of the church but made no attempt to strike him. He said that he was shaking whilst wielding the bat and realised that he 'could never ever kill anyone'. He then waited in the church for the police to arrest him.

In a report of 8 June 1994 from the occupational therapists the event was described as 'threatening a church cleaner with a base-ball bat with intentions to kill, and also had two knives in his possession'. Another undated report from the Easton House files described Jason Mitchell as having 'threatened a 70-year old church cleaner with a baseball bat but with apparent intentions to kill. The man managed to escape and call the police, and later two knives were found in Jason Mitchell's possession.'

Little if any attention seems to have been paid either to Dr Odutoye's account, given apparently by Jason Mitchell himself, or to the written reports from the occupational therapists. A not dissimilar, if rather shorter account than Dr Odutoye's was re-corded by Dr M. Mohamed, SHO to Dr Goddard in her psychiatric report of 14 December 1993. She stated:

> On his return to England he intended to go back to his home in Ipswich but took the wrong train and arrived at Epsom. He says that it was raining at the time and he took shelter in a church where he met the Vicar for the first time. The Vicar allowed him to take shelter. Mr Mitchell then experienced a voice saying, 'You should kill the Vicar, this is the time you should kill that man.' The next morning the church caretaker came and Mr Mitchell decided he should kill the caretaker with the Vicar so that he would not be apprehended. He believed that the Vicar was responsible for the psychological distress he was going through. He had a lump of wood with him with the intention of assaulting the caretaker. He asked the caretaker if he would kindly lie down on the ground so that he could knock him out with the minimum of damage. The caretaker ran away and Mr Mitchell waited for the Police to arrive. He was convinced that his voices had tricked him this time.

Elsewhere in the medical records there does not appear any account remotely resembling Dr Odutoye's or Dr Mohamed's re-cord. Indeed, Dr Goddard and Mr Dunnett could hardly have said what they did, had they been familiar with Dr Odutoye's entry.

We detect that there is a confusion among non-lawyers about the nature of an individual's criminality. Proceedings in criminal jus-tice involve labelling acts or omissions in terms of convicted of-fences enumerated in the criminal code. Often the label disguises the reality of the offence, particularly where (as here) pleas of guilty to lesser offences are accepted in the criminal process. But criminal responsibility, which is the exclusive interest of the criminal courts, is not to be confused with the criminal event which gives rise to criminal proceedings. It is imperative that it is the criminal event – the whole of the circumstances leading up to and surrounding the action dubbed a criminal offence – which must be revealed to those caring for and treating the patient in the mental health system. **We recommend** that the Royal College of Psychiatrists, the Royal College of Nursing, and other relevant professional bodies, should issue guidance to their respective members not to rest content with information about 'index offences' but inquire thoroughly into the criminal event. This is particularly necessary in cases of restricted patients.

The confusion is not dispelled in administrative circles in the field of mental health. In the statement of the Secretary of State, for consideration by the Mental Health Review Tribunal which sat on 3 September 1991, the circumstances of the offence leading to Jason Mitchell's admission to hospital were stated thus:

> It was reported that the circumstances of the offences were that at the time of the offence, Mr Mitchell was of no fixed abode and had spent two nights in St Barnabas Church, Epsom. Early in the morning of 8 February, he was seen by the clearer. Mr Mitchell attacked the man with a baseball bat he had found in the church, but did not manage to hit him.
>
> The cleaner ran away but fell, grazing his hands and knees. He managed to get up and called the police.
>
> When Mr Mitchell was questioned, he stated that he had intended to kill the vicar and the cleaner. He was then arrested and taken to Epsom Police Station, and when searched, two knives were found.

The statement, while no doubt an accurate summary, failed to convey the full flavour of the frightening incident to the cleaner, and made no mention of Jason Mitchell hearing voices urging him to kill.

In her report to the same tribunal Dr Brenda Lintner, an independent psychiatrist, underplayed the significance of the criminal event. She said:

> He had returned to London from Amsterdam and on 6 February 1990 arrived in Epsom by mistake, having taken the wrong train from London. He slept overnight in St Barnabas Church, Epsom and next day was disturbed by the elderly church cleaner. Jason Mitchell threatened the cleaner with a piece of wood which he describes as being the same size as a baseball bat. He says that he asked the

cleaner to lie down, but the man managed to escape and Jason Mitchell was arrested. It appears that Jason Mitchell made no attempt to run away realising that he needed help. He was convicted of common assault and possession of an offensive weapon. Psychiatric opinion was given that Jason Mitchell was suffering from a long standing paranoid schizophrenic illness and an order was made under Section 37/41 of the Mental Health Act.

There is no doubt from the evidence that Jason Mitchell was mentally ill at the time of the offence and that he was in a profoundly confused and disturbed state. His view now is that he would not have been able to hurt anyone and that he was more afraid than aggressive. He also felt very tormented by his auditory hallucinations. Jason Mitchell now feels very remorseful about the entire incident. He was shocked to think he could have threatened someone and has written, via the hospital vicar, a letter of apology to the cleaner whom he realises must have been badly upset. He describes himself as not being a violent person and this seems to be borne out by the history.

Dr R. Crellin, Senior Registrar to Professor Merry, Jason Mitchell's RMO at the time, simply stated the formal legal position at trial:

> Jason Mitchell is currently on a Section 37/41 imposed on 10 September 1990 following an offence committed on 29 March 1990 [*sic*]. I understand he was found not guilty on count 1 of attempted murder and not guilty on count 2 of assault occasioning actual bodily harm but was found guilty on count 3 of common assault and count 4 of having offensive weapons.

Dr Crellin did not attend the tribunal hearing, but was represented by Dr Mawala who was unacquainted with Jason Mitchell's case. Mrs Joan Rapaport, a social worker, attended. Her report of 13 May 1991 corresponded, rather more shortly, with Dr Lintner's report. It said:

> Reports state that Mr Mitchell came from London to Epsom on 6 February 1990. He had intended to board a train to Romford but by mistake had taken a train to Epsom. He slept overnight in St Barnabas Church, Epsom. The following day he threatened a seventy-year-old church cleaner with a baseball bat. The cleaner hurt himself whilst making his escape but managed to call the police. Mr Mitchell told the police that he had intended to kill the Vicar and Caretaker and later two knives were found in his possession.

Giving evidence before us, Mrs Rapaport was unable to elaborate on what she thought in September 1991 about the criminal event of 8 February 1990. She may have conveyed to the tribunal the incomplete account of the event she has recorded in her report.

Judge Anwyl QC, who as Ms Shirley Ritchie QC presided over the September 1991 tribunal, was quite adamant that, even if she and her colleagues had read the prosecution statements about the criminal event of 8 February 1990, they would not have altered the way in which she and her colleagues had approached the tribunal's task. She said:

> No, I do not think so, we had before us evidence that the man had been violent and frightening as a result of hearing voices which he was hearing at a time when he was ill and not being treated. We also had overwhelming evidence that almost from the word go, once he started to be treated, the voices had disappeared. He gained insight and was controlled by his medication. As a result he was no longer suffering from an illness of a nature that required him to be detained.

Judge Anwyl did concede, however, that any information about the true nature and extent of the criminal event would always be useful to tribunal members.

We wish to emphasise the important point that the gravity of the offence of which a person is convicted is not necessarily an accurate guide to the seriousness and danger of the criminal behaviour. And this recognition is especially important in relation to mentally disordered offenders when the primary interest may be in securing a disposal by means of a Hospital Order which can be made following a conviction for any imprisonable offence. In the circumstances of a minor, imprisonable offence the prosecution and the court may justifiably consider that nothing is to be gained in contesting a more serious charge when the practical outcome of hospital disposal would be the same, and is appropriate for the defendant. As we indicated in the previous chapter, the compilation by the Crown Prosecution Service of a full account of the criminal event will serve to avoid any potential downgrading by those who will read the reports for the purpose of clinical diagnosis and risk assessment.

This is of general importance. However it does not imply that in Jason Mitchell's case a more accurate account of the criminal event of 1990 would have enabled the killings of December 1994 to be foreseen. With hindsight, Dr Ball and Dr Bowden, both experienced forensic psychiatrists, commented on the inherent uncertainty and

difficulty in assessing Jason Mitchell's risk and potential dangerousness before the events of December 1994. Dr Ball said that if he
had seen Jason Mitchell at the time of his West Park admission:

> I think ... I would not have considered him to be as dangerous as he
> subsequently turned out to be. I think I would have come to the
> conclusion that he would be potentially dangerous in the untreated
> state when he was floridly psychotic, but when he was given medi-
> cation and detained in hospital his dangerousness would not have
> caused me a great deal of concern.
>
> The reason why I come to that view is that it is how I view the
> vast majority of my own criminal patients at the regional secure unit,
> the majority of whom are subject to restriction orders, and the
> majority of whom have committed far more serious offences than the
> index offence comitted by Jason Mitchell, and most of those are
> dangerous in the untreated state.

Dr Bowden was asked whether he thought there was any way in
which one could predict, monitor or in some way manage the
question of risk in this case that was not in fact done. He replied:

> I do not think before December 1994 that any practising psychiatrist
> could confidently have predicted with any degree of accuracy that
> Jason Mitchell within a specified time would have committed an-
> other serious act of violence. I think it is a possibility but it is
> impossible to quantify the likelihood of him behaving in a seriously
> violent way again. He was a risk. Different people would quantify
> the risk differently.

Dr Bowden observed that compared with other mentally ill people
who commit serious violent acts, Jason Mitchell did 'not actually
score very highly' in relation to the psychiatric phenomena that
may generally be asociated with such acts. In considering his
individual case what may have been more important was understanding the impact on Jason Mitchell of what was happening to
him:

> ... what was happening in Jason Mitchell's mind, and that is the
> thing, in terms of risk assessment, that we knew least about.

Part E

Restriction Order and its Discharge

IX. First Mental Health Review Tribunal, 3 September 1991

> Lawyers should be prepared to reconcile themselves to techniques
> of analysis and investigation which are different from those in the
> common law courts.
>
> Report of the Commonwealth of Australia's
> Administrative Review Committee 1971
> (the Kerr Committee Report)
> Parliamentary Paper 144/71, para 334

Jason Mitchell took the earliest opportunity to apply for a review
of his compulsory admission to West Park Hospital. On 25 March
1991, just beyond the expiry date of six months from the date of the
Hospital Order of 10 September 1990, he applied, as a restricted
patient, for his discharge. He had every encouragement to think
that he was, exceptionally, a candidate for discharge, either absolutely or conditionally. Immediately after the hearing at the Old
Bailey in September 1990, his RMO, Professor Merry, was forthright in declaring Jason Mitchell as not suffering from any mental
illness and recommending absolute discharge. Professor Merry's
senior registrar, Dr Crellin, in a report of 29 April 1991 to the
Mental Health Review Tribunal, more cautiously indicated a conditional discharge. His report stated:

> His present mental state examination shows Jason Mitchell to be a
> rather tall and intimidating man on initial appearance. He has a lot
> of poorly executed tattoos which contribute to this, particularly one
> on his forehead. Despite his appearance, it is easy to establish good
> rapport with him. He is co-operative and open and very friendly.
>   His mood shows him to be neither depressed nor elated. The
> flattening of his affect and the rather inappropriate blandness of
> affect referred to in the previous report is not as noticeable. Although
> he is rather flat in his moods, he does show appropriate emotional
> responses. His speech is normal in volume, flow and content. His
> thoughts show no abnormality of form and he has no delusions and
> no abnormal thought experiences. He no longer experiences any
> auditory hallucinations. He appears to have insight into his condi-
> tion, accepts that he has been ill and appears to recognise the need
> for continuing stay in hospital and medication.

His progress in hospital since his admission in September has been good. In many ways he is a model patient. He is helpful on the ward, friendly to staff and patients and works well with the occupational therapist and the industrial therapy unit. He has open access to all parts of the hospital grounds ....

Our present plan is for him to undergo rehabilitation through Farmside, one of the rehabilitation wards at West Park. We feel his present mental state is as good as it is likely to be and that there is no benefit in him staying on Drummond Ward indefinitely. Referral to the rehabilitation services was therefore the next logical step and he was transferred to Farmside about a month ago. Some decision will have to be made on his Home Office restrictions as rehabilitation will necessarily involve him leaving the hospital grounds etc.

Neither Professor Merry nor Dr Crellin attended the tribunal hearing. Instead Dr Malawa, who appeared to have had no responsibility for the care and treatment of Jason Mitchell, attended. Support from the social worker at West Park Hospital, Mrs Joan Rapaport, was forthcoming. The Home Office, in formalistic fashion, offered the Secretary of State's observations:

In the light of these reports and all the previous evidence in this case, the Home Secretary is satisfied that Mr Mitchell continues to require continued detention in West Park Hospital for treatment. This treatment is necessary both for his own health and safety and for the protection of others.

In response to an independent psychiatrist's report from Dr Brenda Lintner of 7 June 1991 which recommended discharge 'with the obvious proviso that there is suitable accommodation for him in the community', the Home Secretary opposed an absolute discharge, 'believing it right to maintain the special restrictions which the Central Criminal Court felt necessary to impose less than a year ago'. The Home Office was, however, willing to consider any proposals which the RMO might wish to make for a conditional discharge. There followed these words of bureaucratic caution: 'The Home Secretary would wish to be assured, in particular, that Mr Mitchell has good insight into the effect illicit drugs could have on his mental state and for him to be generally monitored and tested on a graduated programme of leave outside the hospital grounds.' The only cautionary note (rather a detailed and perceptive account) was implied by Mrs Jackie Leaver, Occupational Therapy Technical Instructor, who in February 1991 reported disturbing signs of Jason Mitchell's psychopathology. Dr Crellin, in his report to the tribunal, recorded that 'there is also a very full report by Mrs J. Leaver, the Occupational Therapist, focusing particularly on Jason's family and educational and occupational background'. Jackie Leaver's report was not enclosed, and it is common practice not to include such reports. The report lay in the hospital file and would have been available for the medical member to see and to communicate its contents and import to his two non-medical members on the Tribunal.

The scene was set for a conditional discharge. Given the nature and source of the material (before the Tribunal), and given that Dr Rathod told us that if he had read the Jackie Leaver report he had not appreciated its true significance, no reasonable tribunal could have come to any conclusion other than that it should grant a conditional discharge. Mrs Shirley Ritchie QC (now Judge Anwyl QC) who presided over the Tribunal, told us that she and her colleagues would not have decided differently, even if they had been in possession of the full details of the criminal event of 8 February 1990.

The law provides that a tribunal may be satisfied that hospital detention is no longer necessary, provided that the patient can be placed in suitable accommodation in the community and be required to submit to treatment as an outpatient by a suitable psychiatrist. The tribunal may also defer the conditional discharge, which means that the tribunal will require the detaining hospital to submit proposals for the patient's after-care for the tribunal's approval. That was precisely what the Tribunal did on 3 September 1991. The Tribunal ordered that Jason Mitchell be

> conditionally discharged, but that such discharge be deferred until such arrangements as are acceptable to the Tribunal are made:
> The Conditions of his discharge are:
> 1. Residence in a hostel approved by the RMO.
> 2. Acceptance of medication as advised by the RMO.
> 3. Submission to ongoing out-patient monitoring as advised by the RMO and social worker.

The Tribunal sat for an hour and a half to hear the evidence, and met for a further 20 minutes to compose its reasons for the decision.

> The reasons for the decision of the Tribunal are as follows: The Tribunal is satisfied that the patient continues to suffer from mental illness, but not of a nature or degree which makes it appropriate for him to be liable to be detained in a hospital for medical treatment.

The Tribunal, however, considers that it is appropriate that he remain liable to recall in the event of relapse.

The Tribunal was satisfied about these reasons because:

1. There is no sign of mental illness at present; that is the view of Professor Merry, Dr Malawa and Dr Lintner. Until reduction of medication has been tried, the Tribunal cannot be satisfied that the current mental state is not dependent upon medication.
2. There are arguments for absolute discharge in that the patient has insight into his problems, and is well motivated as far as treatment is concerned. Nevertheless the Tribunal feels that the patient would be assisted by conditions to discharge to ensure practical, therapeutic and medical support.

The Tribunal proceeded to make recommendations:

1. That there be gradual reduction in medication with a view to eventual cessation.
2. That, pending discharge to a hostel:
    a. the patient be moved forthwith to an open ward; and
    b. be granted unescorted leave outside the hospital as deemed appropriate by the RMO.

The tribunal was in effect saying that Jason Mitchell should get the benefit of a deferred conditional discharge, the three conditions relating to provisions for after-care. On the other hand, in its recommendations, the Tribunal was advocating a therapeutic experiment to see what happened if Jason Mitchell's drugs were reduced, and then all medication discontinued. If the RMO were to act on the recommendation the result would be to undermine the possibility of discharge, were Jason Mitchell to relapse on the reduction and/or discontinuance of medication, simply because the RMO would have to wait several months after discontinuance to ascertain the emergence of psychotic symptoms. Judge Anwyl, before us, accepted that the combination of a deferred conditional discharge with a recommendation for experimenting without medication during the period of deferment was suggestive of incompatible directions, at least if the directions were treated by the hospital as compelling. Such compulsion appeared even more compelling by the recommendation that 'the patient be moved *forthwith* (italics supplied) to an open ward'. It provoked an audacious demand from Jason Mitchell's solicitor (who had appeared at the tribunal) calling upon compliance, 'failing which we shall have no alternative to ask the Tribunal to reconvene'. Indeed the clinicians were fully compliant. They transferred Jason Mitchell, unsuccessfully, to an open ward; within a month the placement broke down.

A further problem is posed by the Tribunal's recommendations. The clinical preference to reduce medication would necessitate close nursing observation to detect recurrence of psychotic symptoms, and hence require in-patient care and treatment. That situation conflicted directly with a decision that Jason Mitchell was clinically ready for discharge. How would a doctor at one and the same time confront the situation of having to search for accommodation in the community in pursuance of the deferred conditional discharge and perpetuate psychiatric treatment in conditions of continued detention? When faced with that dilemma, and the fact that the Tribunal cannot legally adjourn a case to wait and see whether a patient's condition changes, Judge Anwyl acknowledged that the two threads of the reasoned decision 'could' cut across each other. Reluctantly she accepted that any psychiatric relapse on withdrawal of medication might open up a situation of potential dangerousness in Jason Mitchell. Mr Thorold finally put the question:

> Q. If you were taking the view that he needed to have a reduction of medication and that it remained possible that he might hear voices advising him to kill and equip himself with weapons, can you explain why you felt, in those circumstances, legally forced to reach a discharge decision?
> A. I cannot legally, no. Practically, yes, but not legally.

Recommendations, other than where the patient is being discharged, may often be helpful in promoting care and treatment with a view to later discharge. We think that this case exemplifies, however, the need to avoid making recommendations whenever they are likely to sit uneasily alongside a decision to discharge. We shall deal with this more fully in Chapter XX in the context of the thorny issue of deferred conditional discharges. The case throws up other aspects relating to the proper functioning of Mental Health Review Tribunals.

Lay members

Each panel for a Mental Health Act Tribunal has three types of member: (a) legal members appointed by the Lord Chancellor: they are normally senior practitioners in the legal profession, although legal academics have been appointed; (b) medical members appointed by the Lord Chancellor after consultation with the Department of Health; they are usually consultant psychiatrists, often in retirement, but other doctors with psychiatric experience may be appointed. Forensic psychiatrists are infrequently available. **We recommend** that efforts should be made to ensure that the medical members of tribunals dealing with restricted patients are forensic psychiatrists. The third type of member is dubbed 'lay'. Lay members are appointed by the Lord Chancellor, after consultation with the Department of Health, who have 'such experience in administration, such knowledge of social services or such other qualifications or experience as the Lord Chancellor considers suitable' (Schedule 2 to the Mental Health Act 1983). More often the 'lay' member is a magistrate or social worker. As Professor Hoggett (now Mrs Justice Hale) observes in the 4th edition (1996) of *Mental Health Law*, at p. 184, the appellation 'lay' is a misnomer, since the lay member is expected to have a basic understanding of the health and social services and preferably some experience or interest in mental illness or learning disabilities. In their second annual report (1994, para 3.4 (iii), p. 10) the Mental Health Review Tribunals state:

> Lay members need reasonable familiarity with health and social services to enable them to understand why the patient is appealing, what they have experienced in hospital and what community facilities and social supports might be available to a patient on discharge. Lay members should preferably have some interest in or experience of mental health and/or learning disability. This may have come through membership of a mental health voluntary organisation, being a hospital visitor or befriender, or from life/work experience which brings them in contact with a range of people – for example through being a magistrate, teacher, trade union official, managing a business or being involved in local government or charitable organisations. In practice 'lay' might be thought a misnomer in relation to the present Tribunal lay members who include mental health professionals, hospital administrators, social workers and nurses. A detailed description of the lay member's role is given at Appendix 13 [which among other attributes for this category of member, asserts that the lay member's role is 'to supply the responsible lay person's view'].

While we do not dissent from the view that the non-professional has a place in the tribunal system, we think that more emphasis should be placed on expertise from those engaged in the mental health system. It is noticeable that no mention is made of psychologists in the extract from the Mental Health Review Tribunals Annual Report. We have no doubt that in the difficult cases of restricted patients – particularly if the patient has learning disabilities – a clinical psychologist should be seriously considered to fill the place of the third member as the non-medical, non-legal, professional input to application for discharge. In the case of Jason Mitchell it was apparent from his educational background that he had been assessed as needing special education; some psychological input might have teased out some of the underlying problems of Jason Mitchell's bizarre behaviour. **We recommend** that the third category should be named 'other relevant disciplines' and that the Lord Chancellor's list should include a number of psychologists.

The only difficulty that we envisage in having a psychologist as the third member of a tribunal is that it might be thought to disturb the balance between legal, medical and other – primarily social – expertise. Substituting the last for another clinician would disturb the balance. There might be a case for having a psychologist instead of the psychiatrist in some readily identifiable cases, but that would mean replacing the medical component, which at present cannot be done. There is, of course, the question of whether the system is well enough organised either to identify the cases where a particular expertise is called for, or to arrange for such expertise to be available. None of this detracts from our recommendation that the tribunal system should be reviewed (see Chapter XX). The question of membership of tribunals will inevitably be encompassed in such a review.

Judge Henry Palmer, the regional Chairman for the South Thames Area, who helped us on a number of matters touching on the role and functions of Mental Health Review Tribunals, told us that he knew of no qualified psychologists on the panel. When asked why this was so, he said:

> My guess is that it is because it has never occurred to anybody that it would be a good idea to appoint psychologists, and indeed I don't think it would be a good idea.

When pressed to say why he thought there was no advantage in picking a psychologist, Judge Palmer gave a revealing answer. He was asked whether a psychologist might not make a distinctive contribution to the deliberative process in cases where there was a conflict of primary diagnosis, where issues of personality or personal development arose, or where fantasy life and insight were important aspects. Judge Palmer answered: 'Well I think, if I may say so, even to ask the question suggests a misunderstanding about the role of the three tribunal members, because the three tribunal members sitting at the tribunal are acting in a judicial capacity. And people acting in a judicial capacity act on the evidence presented to them. They don't substitute their own views and attitudes and knowledge for the evidence which is submitted to them .... To suggest that one of the members of the tribunal can bring his own knowledge and experience to bear and substitute his own views for those of the witnesses seems to me to suggest a fundamental misunderstanding of the role of the judicial tribunal.'

Judge Palmer was asked first whether putting the appropriate questions may not depend on a knowledge of psychological expertise; and secondly, whether the role, which Judge Palmer said was inappropriate, is more or less precisely what the medical member does. He or she does bring his or her expertise to the hearing. To which Judge Palmer responded: 'The first point, of course, I agree with, that the knowledge that a psychologist lay member would have might well enable him to ask more pertinent questions. But I have to say that judges frequently have to judge matters about which they know themselves absolutely nothing and they become experts in the course of the case based on expert evidence presented to them. And a judge can deal with, let us say, a complicated case involving matters of chemistry without having the first idea of chemistry himself, but he does it because expert witnesses come into court and give their evidence and then the judge makes his decision about it. It is not anything different about Mental Health Review Tribunals. I do not see that a chemical judge has to be appointed to a chemical case.'

We think, with genuine respect to Judge Palmer who has almost unrivalled experience and expertise in tribunal work over the last 35 years (since the 1959 Act), this is an outmoded attitude to tribunal functioning. We cite Mrs Justice Hale's view in the 4th edition (1996) of her textbook (p. 177):

> However, Tribunals are not part of the ordinary court structure. In fact, they have many advantages over traditional courts of law. Their membership can be tailored to the particular problem and their more flexible and informal procedures to the peculiarities of the subject-

matter. They are not stuck in the adversarial model of British court procedure and can adopt elements of the inquisitorial approach. This is most important in mental health cases, where it is vital that the tribunal should not be too overawed by the hospital evidence, but also that the experience should not have an adverse effect on the patient's health and treatment. The difficulty lies in deciding how far it is possible to go in balancing these considerations against the traditional requirements of natural justice.

It is to the aspect of fairness (*alias* natural justice) to which we turn in considering the role of the medical member in the eliciting of material for the consideration of the tribunal in its decision-making process.

The special role of the medical member

Before the tribunal sits to hear an application, the medical member is required to examine the patient with a view to forming an opinion of the patient's mental state. Included in this function is the power to examine all the medical records. Rule 11 of the Mental Health Review Tribunal Rules provides that the medical member 'may take such notes and copies' of the medical records as he or she requires for use in connection with the application. Whether the medical member communicates his findings to his colleagues will depend on what is uncovered from the medical records to illuminate the patient's mental condition and how much (if at all) is passed on to the other tribunal members by copied documentation or word of mouth. We have seen, for example, that in September 1991 Jackie Leaver's report of February 1991 was never relayed to the tribunal members, even if Dr Rathod himself had read it – which he could not remember.

We recommend that the medical member should expect the hospital to prepare for his use a set of summary documents from each of the professions involved in the multi-disciplinary team responsible for the patient's care and treatment.

Assuming that anything of significance about the patient's mental condition is brought to the attention of all three tribunal members (which may be a rash assumption) what is the status of any information gleaned from medical records? Two issues of fairness arise. First, the medical member is at one and the same time a witness giving evidence to his colleagues – that is, if he actually communicates any material – and is a decision-maker adjudicating on evidence for which he is in a privileged position of exclusive access to it in its context of an undisclosed medical record. Being witness and part-judge is hardly conducive to adjudication before an impartial tribunal.

The second anomaly is that the medical member's opinion on the patient's mental condition is treated as part of the tribunal's deliberations, rather than a piece of evidence, undisclosable to the applicant-patient or any other participant in the hearings. There is thus no formal opportunity to learn what there is to challenge in the medical member's opinion (or what it is based on). There is the added complication about the timing of the medical member's information. If he tells his colleagues what he has learned at the outset of the hearing, will that produce a pre-conceived result? If the information is postponed until the tribunal withdraws at the end of the evidence to deliberate, there may be no opportunity for the information to be tested. Since the decision in *R* v. *Mental Health Review Tribunal, ex p. Clatworthy* [1985] 3 ALL ER 699 indicated that a tribunal cannot properly decide a case on the basis of material known only to itself, it would appear that the parties must be aware of the material adduced by the medical member and have an opportunity to deal with it. That would point to an early disclosure of the medical member's information rather than it being held back to the deliberative stage. The matter deserves clarification in the Mental Health Review Tribunal Rules.

That leaves open the question of how to cope with the dilemma of the medical member as both witness and judge. We put the suggestion to Judge Palmer that there was something to be learned from the procedure of the Discretionary Lifer Panel (DLP) in the penal system. (It is noteworthy that Jason Mitchell, as and when he comes to be considered for release from Rampton Hospital or any penal establishment to which he may be transferred in the future, he will be dealt with under the DLP system and not by a Mental Health Review Tribunal: unless, of course, the Court of Appeal substitutes a Hospital Order for the three sentences of life imprisonment imposed by Mr Justice Blofeld.) Is there, we asked, any merit in replicating the DLP system of preparing for the panel and the parties a dossier which would include a background social and medical history, a full account of the index offence and up-to-date reports on the prisoner, his family circumstances and an assortment of experts of the risk element of any release? Judge Palmer replied:

The system we have at present is a compromise. The only member of the three panel members of the tribunal who is entitled to see the clinical notes is the medical officer. And the problem in restricted patient cases comes in this way, that if all three members of the tribunal panel saw the clinical notes, then they would all have to go to the Home Office with their comments. So we have now a compromise where the medical member sees it and is in a position to bring out any important matters and the other two members of the panel do not. You are suggesting yet another compromise which is that somebody should settle down with the clinical notes and make a resume of all those notes, and I find it hard to believe that this is going to be of any great advantage.

The problem is that medical members on tribunals are also expected to be witnesses of fact, which members of a discretionary lifer panel are not. It could be argued that it is unnecessary for medical members to be witnesses of fact, now that there is independent psychiatric evidence in many (but not all) cases. It might be that in restricted patient cases such evidence should be compulsory. On the other hand, it is not reasonable to expect a doctor sitting as a member of a tribunal not to form a professional opinion about a detained patient. If that is so, it may be better for the doctor to see the patient in a clinical setting outside the hearing before the tribunal. But at the very least, the substance of the psychiatric opinion (and preferably the full reasoning for that opinion, whether written or oral) should be disclosed at the outset, on precisely the same footing as the other evidence. This would not require a change in the Rules. But a change in the Rules would help. We would add that the quality of evidence might be improved, were the tribunals to become more receptive to their inquisitorial role. Tribunals might, more often, adjourn for more information to be gleaned. Again, that may depend on the ability of the system to cope with additional work engendered by adjournments.

Alternatively, we think there is merit in Judge Palmer's proposal, at least for the restricted cases which bulk large in their importance and hence deserve a more elaborate treatment. Their cases should, in any event, equiparate with those mentally disordered offenders who are given discretionary sentences of life imprisonment, although we note that there is no 'tariff' element in a restriction order, and should not be. **We recommend** that the Home Office give serious attention to bringing the two procedures into line. There is no warrant for continuing the discrimination between the lifer system and the restricted patient system.

X. Second Mental Health Review Tribunal, 6 April 1993 and 10 August 1994

Confusion is not an ignoble condition.
Brian Friel, *Translations*, 1981, p. 67

The decision of 3 September 1991 granting Jason Mitchell a deferred conditional discharge did not immediately have an easy passage. Deferment was lengthily, if not abnormally, protracted. (He remained in hospital until May 1994.) A search for accommodation in Cambridge was overtaken, first, by an almost immediate deterioration in Jason Mitchell's behaviour at West Park, and a decision in late 1992 to move him back to his home area in Ipswich. On 25 February 1992 the clerk to the Mental Health Review Tribunal inquired of the hospital what progress had been made in meeting the conditions set by the Tribunal for Jason Mitchell's conditional discharge. Dr Yeldham, Jason Mitchell's RMO from 27 October 1991 onwards (replacing Professor Merry) wrote on 1 April 1992 as follows:

> Whilst we have followed the Tribunal's recommendations, the situation for Jason Mitchell is now different to that of September 1991 only inasmuch as it is clear to his professional advisers – though less so to Jason Mitchell – that he has a continuing mental illness which is medication-dependent and that an overly hasty rehabilitation plan has failed, so that we must all adopt a graduated process.

This was followed up by Dr Yeldham's report of 29 December 1992 to the Home Office as follows:

> Jason Mitchell is now stable, psychiatrically, on depot medication. In my opinion, this stability would be threatened should medication be withdrawn, or excess illicit drug use occur. He has been a danger to others when psychotic in the past and has been irritable and verbally (but not physically) aggressive during relapses this year. I think it essential, therefore, that psychiatric supervision continues and, having obtained purchasers' (Health Authority) agreement, am exploring whether this could be available, should Jason Mitchell

transfer to his home area. I am in contact with Dr Ray Goddard, a Consultant for Rehabilitation and Challenging Behaviour, St Audrey's Hospital, Melton, Woodbridge, Suffolk. I think rehabilitation could best be successfully carried out in Jason Mitchell's home area, with family support, now that his psychiatric state is reasonably stable. I will be grateful if you could indicate your views as to this proposal, the conditions the Home Secretary would require and the steps by which this could be achieved, assuming all parties remain agreeable.

On 21 January 1993 the Home Secretary gave notice of a reference of Jason Mitchell's case to the Mental Health Review Tribunal. Since the 1991 Tribunal was disqualified from reconvening to reconsider its own decision that the patient be discharged, the reference was made to a fresh tribunal which had to start from square one and determine whether Jason Mitchell was at the time of that hearing to be discharged or not. The inability of the 1991 tribunal to re-examine its own decision was the result of a House of Lords' decision in *Secretary of State for the Home Department* v. *Oxford Regional Mental Health Review Tribunal* 1988 AC 120. **We recommend** that this decision should be reversed by law, so as to allow a tribunal to adjourn an application in order to give time for a further examination of the patient's mental health before any decision to discharge is made. Jason Mitchell's case came, therefore, before another tribunal in the context of an impending decision by West Park Hospital to transfer him to St Clement's Hospital. In the *Oxford* case, the House of Lords went further than was necessary in order to dispose of the appeal. The failure of the system in that case to ensure that the Home Office was aware of the tribunal proceedings should have sufficed, requiring the tribunal to think again about its decision, without limiting its power to adjourn. Rule 16 is wide enough to permit that procedure. This aspect of the law adds to the case for a thorough review of the procedure, if not the role of Mental Health Review Tribunals, which we recommend in Chapter XX.

By March 1993 the Home Office was consenting to Jason Mitchell's transfer to St Clement's Hospital, and Dr Goddard was writing to Dr Yeldham to say that he was prepared to admit Jason Mitchell, but would prefer to do so on the basis of him transferring as a restricted patient, with a view to later discharge. He wrote:

I was pleased to have the opportunity to meet briefly with Jason Mitchell at St Audry's Hospital together with his social worker on

17 March 1993. I understand that a mental health tribunal may be held as soon as May and I think it is important to make clear that I would only be prepared to accept Consultant responsibility for Jason Mitchell provided this could be as an inpatient in the first instance under Section 37/41. In the past, I have found it far better to develop a personal relationship with restricted patients on an inpatient basis in order to develop mutual trust and to set the ground rules before moving on to conditional discharge. Ideally I would like to see the tribunal delayed for six months following a proposed transfer here but if this cannot be organised and the tribunal remains set for May, I will delay a final decision on his transfer until the outcome of the tribunal's deliberations are known. Should an early tribunal result in conditional discharge, then transfer for inpatient care to Ipswich would clearly not be appropriate and I would not accept responsibility for Jason Mitchell on a Section 42. I am happy for this letter or its contents to be made known to the Home Office.

As a result of the reference of Jason Mitchell's case to the Mental Health Review Tribunal for further consideration 'because of the considerable alteration in Mr Mitchell's medical circumstances and the change of plans regarding rehabilitation back into the community', the case came on 6 April 1993 before a tribunal composed of Judge Uziell-Hamilton, Dr David Duncan and Mrs Sandra Fox (all of whom willingly came and gave evidence to us). Jason Mitchell, who was by that time poised to be transferred to Ipswich – he eventually moved on 5 May 1993 – was represented by his solicitor, Mr John Sellars. Dr Yeldham and Mrs Joan Rapaport submitted reports. No oral evidence appears to have been given, and the proceedings lasted only 15 minutes, both very unusual features of a tribunal hearing.

Since the 1991 tribunal had directed that the conditional discharge be deferred for the purpose of the hospital authorities making practical arrangements to enable compliance with the conditions, it (the 1991 tribunal) was not entitled later to reconsider its decision whether the patient should in fact be conditionally discharged. The law provides moreover that the tribunal cannot even subsequently alter the nature of the conditions anticipated on the occasion of the deferred conditional discharge, save for correcting points of minor detail.

The conditions imposed by the 1991 tribunal had not been satisfied, and no approval for the conditional discharge had been granted. The case, therefore, went back to square one. Given the prevailing circumstances of Jason Mitchell's mental condition and potential transfer to Ipswich, the question for decision on 6 April

1993 was: should Jason Mitchell be given a fresh conditional discharge, deferred or otherwise? There is the rub. Judge Uziell-Hamilton thought at the time that all that was being asked for was approval to the transfer from West Park Hospital in Epsom to St Clement's Hospital in Ipswich. No one else concerned in the proceedings thought likewise. Every other person thought that a conditional discharge was being granted or at least endorsing the 1991 decision. The contemporary documentation similarly recorded a conditional discharge.

The tribunal's decision, as recorded by the tribunal clerk under Judge Uziell-Hamilton's instructions, disclosed the confusion of the legal position and the Tribunal's function on that day. The Tribunal directed:

> The statutory situation remains unchanged since 3 September 1991 when Mr Mitchell was conditionally discharged, such discharge being deferred until suitable arrangements could be made subject to the approval of his RMO.

That the tribunal thought that it was simply endorsing the conditional discharge of 3 September 1991 is apparent from the reasons given for its decision:

> The tribunal heard from Dr Yeldham, RMO and read the reports of Dr Yeldham and Mrs Mitchell [*sic*] the social worker. The Tribunal also read the letter dated 16 March 1993 from the Home Office. It is clear that all involved in this case recommend the transfer of Mr Mitchell to St Clement's hospital, Ipswich in order to facilitate his conditional discharge. The Tribunal endorsed this course of action.

Jason Mitchell's solicitor, Mr John Sellars, wrote to us on 26 September 1995 as follows:

> I recorded that the Tribunal sanctioned arrangements for a transfer under deferred conditional discharge. My recollection was that there was no formal taking of evidence and that all parties were agreed as to the disposal hence the most unusually short hearing of only 10 minutes. I had earlier acted for Jason Mitchell on the 3rd September 1991, when a deferred conditional discharge had been ordered and my understanding of the situation on the 6th April was that a further conditional discharge was being made. Had I had occasion to think otherwise I would have pressed for a full hearing which of course would have taken far longer and involved proper examination of the witnesses.

At the end of July 1994, when Jason Mitchell was ready for his move officially (as opposed to his placement there on leave of absence) to the MIND shared accommodation at Felixstowe, the Tribunal members were asked to confirm the conditional discharge. Both Dr Duncan and Mrs Fox expressed their agreement to the conditional discharge. No conditions were attached to the Order. Judge Uziell Hamilton returned the following form to the tribunal officers:

MENTAL HEALTH REVIEW TRIBUNAL

DEFERRED CONDITIONAL DISCHARGE

PATIENT: Mr Jason Mitchell

HOSPITAL: West Park

It is confirmed that the conditions specified in the decision of
_____ have now been met to the satisfaction of
the Tribunal.

Signed: A Uziell-Hamilton
His/Her Honour A Uziell-Hamilton

Date: 10 August 1994

The 'conditional discharge' of the 1993 Tribunal was legally flawed. There was no proper legal authority permitting Jason Mitchell to enjoy the fruits of a conditional discharge from 10 August 1994 onwards.

There was, however, no reason why anybody at St Clement's should have realised the fact. Indeed, they were entitled to proceed upon the assumption that the conditional discharge was fully operative. It is probably the case that, even if the 1993 Tribunal had treated the case as an application for a conditional discharge, it would have granted it, even though there had been a relapse in Jason Mitchell's mental condition. Nothing that we have heard leads us to believe otherwise. Only the omission of any knowledge of Jason Mitchell's psychotic condition in 1988-89 when he was at Feltham Young Offenders Institution could conceivably have altered the course of events in 1991 or 1993. Nothing untoward flowed from the fact of illegality, although the strict legal position remained unaltered: Jason Mitchell was an undischarged restricted patient until his arrest on 20 December 1994.

Our counsel, Mr Oliver Thorold, stated in his opening remarks at the Inquiry:

> It must be a matter of considerable concern that the decision by the 1993 tribunal not to grant a discharge to a restricted patient can, through a sequence of misapprehensions, metamorphose into an apparently valid order to discharge the patient.

We agree. We add only that, while the Jason Mitchell case may have been unusual in its factual situation and legal application, it appears to disclose some confusion among the practitioners in the management and functioning of tribunals, if not a lack of professionalism. We are not hesitant in so concluding, because we have uncovered a defect in the 1991 Tribunal hearing in respect of recommendations of a therapeutic nature. Other disquieting aspects of the tribunal system were canvassed with all the members of the two (1991 and 1993) Tribunals which indicated some unease among themselves about the jurisdiction of Mental Health Review Tribunals. We have addressed some of these issues in the previous chapter and will discuss the acute problem of deferred conditional discharges in Chapter XX.

XI. Role of C3 Division, Home Office

I could be worse employed
Than as watcher of the void,
Whose part should be to tell
What star if any fell.
Robert Frost, 'On making certain anything has
happened', Christmas Poem, v.1 (1945)

The Mental Health Section of C3 Division of the Home Office first became aware of Jason Mitchell's case on 12 October 1990, on being notified of the Hospital Order made by the Central Criminal Court on 10 September 1990, coupled with the Restriction Order. In accordance with the computerised language in the Mental Health Caseworking Caseworker's Guide issued to civil servants in C3, their duty was to 'create a patient'. Jason Mitchell became dischargeable from the Hospital Order only by the Home Secretary or on application to a Mental Health Review Tribunal, to which he could apply annually. The two powers exist in parallel, because a patient may be fit to be discharged some time before his or her next time to apply for a tribunal comes round, in which case the Home Secretary could act. And secondly, while the tribunal can discharge the patient only if the criteria for detention no longer exist, the Home Secretary has discretion and can discharge the patient with some residual mental disorder where treatment in hospital is inappropriate.

Since the tribunal route for a conditional discharge was successfully obtained by Jason Mitchell within a year of becoming a restricted patient, the Home Secretary's powers came only marginally into play in the transfer of Jason Mitchell from West Park Hospital in September 1990 up to his conditional discharge to the shared accommodation in Felixstowe in August 1994, via St Clement's Hospital, Ipswich. It is thus the role of the Home Office in the quadripartite – patient, RMO, tribunal and Home Office – functioning of tribunal discharges in restricted patient cases that primarily attracts our attention.

Following Jason Mitchell's application to a Mental Health Review Tribunal the Home Office submitted on 4 June 1991 the

Secretary of State's observations to the Tribunal. Part A of the statement read as follows:

A. *Circumstances of the offences leading to admission to hospital.*

On 10 September 1990 at the Central Criminal Court, Mr Mitchell was convicted of common assault and having offensive weapons.

He was reported to be suffering from mental illness and the court made an order under section 37 of the Mental Health Act 1983, authorising his detention in West Park Hospital, together with an order under section 41 of the Act, restricting his discharge without limit of time.

It was reported that the circumstances of the offences were that at the time of the offence, Mr Mitchell was of no fixed abode and had spent two nights in St Barnabas Church, Epsom. Early in the morning of 8 February, he was seen by the cleaner. Mr Mitchell attacked the man with a baseball bat he had found in the church, but did not manage to hit him. The cleaner ran away, but fell, grazing his hands and knees. He managed to get up and called the police.

When Mr Mitchell was questioned, he stated that he had intended to kill the vicar and the cleaner. He was then arrested and taken to Epsom Police Station, and when searched, two knives were found.

While this account constituted a fair summary of the criminal event of 8 February 1990, it lacked the full flavour of a terrifying incident. When the members of both the 1991 and 1993 tribunals gave evidence before us they were given the full details of the criminal event. All said that they viewed it in a different light. It was no longer a minor offence. The Home Office summary did not bring out the fact of Jason Mitchell experiencing directive voices; it made no reference to the fact that the church cleaner had been instructed, two or three times, by Jason Mitchell to lie down on the floor; and it did not indicate Jason Mitchell's admission on interview that he carried the knives with the purpose of killing. The summary also did not mention the charge of attempted murder to which Jason Mitchell's plea of not guilty was accepted.

All these matters were discoverable from prosecution witness statements, any PACE interview of the accused and from the opening address of prosecuting counsel on a plea of guilty being entered. None of these statements was available, although at a late date a transcript of the proceedings before Judge Rant QC was to hand for us.

Paragraph 10.59 of the Caseworker's Guide states:

Information for which the Home Office is responsible

> This consists chiefly of information provided to the Home Secretary
> by the police or the courts. It should *always* (italics provided by the
> guide) include an account of the circumstances of the offence(s) (or
> alleged offence(s) where patients have been found 'under disability')
> which resulted in the current admission to hospital and include a
> full list of previous convictions .... Care should be taken to ensure
> that the account of the offence(s) is accurate and unbiased. Our
> account should be based only on information provided directly to us
> by the police, the courts, the DPP or the Crown Prosecution Service:
> we should not use accounts of offences written by RMOs. These may
> be inaccurate or biased. The account, which should not be unneces-
> sarily lengthy, should be a summary of the circumstances of the
> offence(s). It should *not* refer to names of witnesses or victims; the
> conclusiveness or otherwise of forensic evidence; or quotations from
> witness statements.

Mr Jonathan Potts told us that the Home Office sees its role as
assisting the tribunals, but wondered whether it was necessary
that all the prosecution material and information should 'pass
through us'. It seems to us that the Home Office as the primary
repository of the Restriction Order should simultaneously receive
all the relevant prosecution documents. As and when required to
make submissions on behalf of the Secretary of State to a mental
health review tribunal, the 'circumstances of the offences leading
to admission to hospital' should provide an adequate account of the
criminal event from a mental health perspective, and not be just a
'summary'. We also do not understand why the statement 'should
not refer to names of witnesses or victims'. Since they will already
have been in the public domain, in the Criminal Court proceedings,
there should be no absolute bar. Discretion should be used whether
to confer anonymity on witnesses and victims. We think also that
it would alert the caseworker to what was required if, instead of
giving 'an account of the circumstances of the offence', the account
was of the circumstances leading up to and surrounding the criminal event. It is the event and not the label of a criminal offence,
that needs to be the focus of the account leading up to the making
of a Restriction Order.

We have referred to the limited nature of the documentation
provided by the Home Office to the Mental Health Review Tribunal
about Jason Mitchell's 1990 offence. **We recommend** two general
measures in respect only of restricted patients, because they would
assist tribunals and clinicians in their handling of these cases.

(1) C3 Division of the Home Office should act as a repository of information about the patient's index offence(s), and should take responsibility for compiling and making available a full documentary account of the criminal event(s).

(2) As we have outlined in Chapter IX, the procedures and practice of C3 Division could usefully be compared with Home Office practice in relation to Discretionary Lifer Panels (DLPs). It is the task of Home Office officials, on behalf of the Home Secretary, to provide the Parole Board with a dossier of information and reports on the prisoner for the DLP Hearing. Schedule 1 to the Parole Board Rules 1992 sets out clearly, and in detail, the reports and information which the Home Secretary is required to submit. The structure of the dossier includes offence-related papers consisting of full details of the offence, and, where available, any post-trial police reports; pre-trial and pre-sentence reports examined by the court; any comments by the trial judge in passing sentence; and any relevant remarks by the Court of Appeal in appeal against conviction or sentence. The dossier also includes the 'life sentence plan', focusing on areas of concern which arise from the prisoner's offending behaviour, and suggests how these areas might best be tackled during sentence; a full range of current reports on the prisoner's performance and behaviour in prison prepared by a variety of specified members of staff; and a full account from the home probation officer of considerations relevant to release. The resulting dossiers are comprehensive. The requirements for compiling information are laid out in a much more thorough way than is the case for Mental Health Review Tribunals. Consideration should be given to whether a similar approach would enhance the quality of the documentary evidence that comes before tribunals. We were pleased to learn from C3 Division that a comparison of these two areas of practice is currently planned. While there are differences between the discharge procedures for mental health patients on restriction orders and the release on parole of life sentence prisoners, there is much to be said for equating the two processes. After all, it is often fortuitous whether a mentally disordered offender finds himself in a prison cell or a hospital bed.

During 1991 and 1992 the Home Office was in occasional correspondence with Jason Mitchell's RMO at West Park Hospital. On 28 September 1992 worry was expressed at the lack of progress in giving effect to the deferred conditional discharge. Thereafter Home Office consent to various unescorted leaves of absence was granted and in March 1993 transfer to St Clement's Hospital was approved. Meanwhile the Home Secretary's reference to a mental health review tribunal was made. (We have dealt with that matter in Chapter X.) A letter from the Home Office to Jason Mitchell's Social Supervisor, Miss Jane Barnett, indicated the official understanding of what the tribunal had directed and filled in the terms of the conditional discharge. The letter said:

> As you will be aware, the Mental Health Review Tribunal for the South West Thames Regional Health Authority considered the above-named patient's case on 6 April 1994 [*sic*: should read 1993] and exercised their powers under section 73(2) of the Mental Health Act 1983 to direct his conditional discharge. The Tribunal considered that the patient's discharge should be subject to the following conditions:
>
>   1. The patient shall reside at the MIND Hostel [*sic*: it was not a hostel, but shared accommodation] 19/27 Larkhill Way, Felixstowe, Suffolk, or at such other address as approved by his supervisors.
>   2. The patient shall attend a psychiatric out-patient clinic as directed by Dr R. Goddard, or his successor, and comply with any treatment he may prescribe.
>   3. The patient shall be under the supervision of Miss J. Barnett, a social worker of Suffolk Social Services, or her successor.

The Home Office never received from the tribunal office a formal notice setting out the conditions of Jason Mitchell's discharge (which it should have done) but constructed the detailed conditions from Dr Goddard's office at St Clement's Hospital without reference to the tribunal office. If this amounted to an act of maladministration it did not result in any injustice.

While the Home Office performs certain functions in reaction to Mental Health Review Tribunals, its main responsibility is directed to those mentally disordered offenders upon whom the criminal courts have imposed Restriction Orders under section 41 of the Mental Health Act 1983. An aspect of this responsibility is the grant of leave of absence. This became important following Jason Mitchell's transfer to Ipswich and his two abscondings in February and March 1994 which were duly reported to the Home Office. By this time the clinical team had become wedded to the view that such psychotic symptoms as were exhibited related

entirely to substance abuse. Dr Goddard was then reporting that
no useful purpose was served by Jason Mitchell remaining a
detained patient, and was displaying frustration at the inability to
find suitable accommodation. He regretted the 'lack of suitable
after-care facilities' which delayed the implementation of the conditional discharge.

During April 1994 Jason Mitchell was granted three separate
leaves of absence as follows:

6 April   Unescorted short term leave, without overnight
           stay, of up to 3 hours per day.
18 April   Unescorted short term leave, without overnight
           stay, of 3 hours daily outside hospital grounds.
27 April   Leave of absence with overnight stay at Larkhill,
           Felixstowe, MIND shared accommodation.

These visits away from the hospital, although made only weeks
after the two unauthorised absences, were undertaken without
incident.

Prior to confirmation from the Tribunal of the conditional discharge – which eventually came on 10 August 1994 – Dr Goddard
requested leave for Jason Mitchell for the purpose of visiting the
MIND shared accommodation in Felixstowe. Leave was granted on
28 April 1994. (Further leave for the same purpose was sought and
approved on 13 and 16 May 1994.) The Home Office letter of 28
April 1994 reads as follows:

> I am directed by the Secretary of State to refer to your letter dated
> 27 April about the above-named patient and to say that he hereby
> consents in accordance with section 41(3)(c)(i) of the Mental Health
> Act 1983 to the patient being granted:
>
>> unescorted day leave on 3 May and overnight unescorted leave
>> during 6/9 May 1994 to the MIND Hostel, Larkhill Way, Felix-
>> stowe, Suffolk.
>
> The Secretary of State's consent is given on the understanding that
> the grant of leave involves no undue risk to the patient or to others.
> The local police and this Department should be informed at once if
> the patient fails to return to hospital from leave.

The grants of leave of absence were made on the sole say so of Jason
Mitchell's RMO, Dr Goddard. Such solid reliance on the medical

officer responsible for the care and treatment of the patient seems
in effect to operate as a delegation of the Home Secretary's responsibility to ensure, as far as possible, the protection of the public.
We were told by Mr Jonathan Potts, the Head of C3 Division that
at no time during which the Home Office had responsibility for
supervising the Restriction Order on Jason Mitchell was any Minister's approval sought for the granting of leave of absence. We
think that the Home Office should be more searching in its granting
of leave instead of putting the whole burden of responsibility on the
patient's RMO. **We recommend** the updating of the Caseworker's
Guide to require information to be obtained not just from the RMO
but from others who will bear responsibility for the after-care
placement of the patient.

A good example of the divergence of view about the safety of the
public arises from this case after Jason Mitchell had obtained
confirmation in August 1994 of his conditional discharge. Dr Goddard, as Jason Mitchell's psychiatric supervisor, reported to the
Home Office on 8 September 1994. He recorded that Jason Mitchell
was free of psychotic symptoms. He was said to be adopting a very
positive attitude and was abstaining from the use of alcohol or illicit
substances.

Miss Jane Barnett, as Jason Mitchell's social supervisor, wrote
a report received at the Home Office on 26 October 1994. It lacked
the positive opinion of Dr Goddard. She referred to the two other
residents finding Jason Mitchell intimidating and manipulative.
She alluded also to the curious episode of Jason Mitchell reporting
to his local police station to 'confess' to crimes. Miss Barnett
thought that Jason Mitchell might 'act out his anxieties'. These
expressions by Miss Barnett of worry about Jason Mitchell reflected her earlier (pre-August 1994) concerns about his ability to
survive in the community without social support. It is such matters,
emanating from social workers and other non-medical professionals, that should be sought by the Home Office when considering
applications from RMOs for grants of leave for their patients.

Part F

The Management and Culture
of Easton House

XII. Aims and Policies

We had the experience, but missed the meaning.
T.S. Eliot, *Four Quartets, The Dry Salvages*

Introduction

The Easton House Challenging Behaviour Unit at St Clement's Hospital, Ipswich, opened in April 1993. Previously, services for inpatients with challenging behaviour had included sixteen beds at St Audry's Hospital, which was scheduled for closure.

Early in 1993 the East Suffolk Local Health Services NHS Trust proposed to East Suffolk Health Authority that the challenging behaviour service be enhanced so as to reduce the need to refer patients to the Norvic Clinic regional secure unit in Norwich, and to reduce reliance on secure hospital beds in the private sector. The development of the service was also intended to assist the acute wards at St Clement's Hospital.

Dr Goddard, as medical director for the Trust and consultant with responsibility for the challenging behaviour wards, took the lead in formulating and developing proposals for the new service. He envisaged that the new service at St Clement's Hospital would enlarge the role of the old long stay wards at St Audry's Hospital, catering for disturbed patients. The new unit would require an increase in nurse staffing levels, and East Suffolk Health Authority proposed that the service should be open to all Suffolk residents – the previous service had only catered for patients from East Suffolk. It was also envisaged that the unit might enable the return of any Suffolk patients currently being placed out of the county. Jason Mitchell was the only such patient at the time.

In comparison with the previous service at St Audry's Hospital, the new service at St Clement's was intended to have more stringent admission criteria, a stronger emphasis on a therapeutic environment, and reduced length of stay. The operational policy for the unit was jointly agreed, and the new unit took admissions from April 1993. Its development was a major contribution to local and regional services that owed much to Dr Goddard's drive and vision.

We visited Easton House during the course of the hearings and spoke to staff there informally. We are grateful to Mr Ken Dunnet, Mr Gordon Heffer and their colleagues for their openness and helpfulness in arranging our evening visits. The Easton House unit impressed us as well designed, pleasant and reasonably spacious internally. The unit consists of two inter-related areas manned by a single multi-disciplinary team. Easton Two is described as a ten-bedded intensive care locked unit, and Easton One as a four-teen-bedded area for disturbed patients requiring less intensive treatment and observation. Each unit is self-contained for leisure, dining, kitchen and washing and toilet facilities. Easton House has dedicated occupational therapy facilities, a multi-gym and a closed-in garden area.

The operational policy for Easton House, dated June 1994, commences with the following mission statement:

> To enable each individual to achieve their optimal level of inde-pendence with the aim of discharge to their home or other accommo-dation in the community as appropriate to their own specific needs and abilities.

The stated philosophy and aim of the unit is to create a safe, therapeutic environment to help each individual patient reach his or her best possible level of social functioning and acceptable behaviour. To that end, the unit sets out to provide individual treatment programmes based on multi-disciplinary assessment of each patient's needs, the patient being involved in this planning as far as practicable. The individual treatment programmes are to be monitored by the team at regular intervals.

The categories of patient for whom the unit is designed are defined as follows:

1. *Mentally ill offenders*
Offender patients being under the jurisdiction and responsibility of Suffolk Health Authority and referred by courts, prisons, special hospitals and the regional secure unit, as being persons who exhibit challenging behaviour or require a higher level of security as part of the conditions of the court order.
   Some will be detained under sections of the relevant parts of the Mental Health Act (1983).

2. *Chronic behavioural problems*
Patients whose continuing behavioural problems require greater input than is expected to be provided on other long stay wards.

3. *Medium term placements*
Short/medium term placements for specific time limited therapeutic programmes.

4. *Short term emergency placements*
Patients from acute wards within St Clement's Hospital who require intensive care for periods of no more than one or two days other than in very exceptional circumstances.

The two criteria for admission are that patients must be assessed to be suffering from treatable mental disorders; and that they are displaying violent or difficult to manage behaviour beyond a level that their present carers or supporters can manage in that present environment. Multi-disciplinary assessments before admission are carried out by the Easton House team as far as possible and admissions are agreed with the consultant in charge of the unit. The operational policy of the unit also refers to multi-disciplinary assessment following admission, agreed care plans, regular reviews of them, and adherence to Trust policies on discharge and after-care. The operational policy is clear and reflects aspirations of good practice.

The medical staffing of the unit includes the consultant, a senior clinical medical officer and a senior house officer, all of whom have other responsibilities outside the unit. Nursing staff include a clinical specialist in challenging behaviour and deputy nurse manager, two assistant ward managers, staff nurses and enrolled nurses. There is also input from a senior occupational therapist and an art therapist. The clinical psychology post was vacant.

During the first six months after it opened the new unit admitted 38 patients, and compared with the previous service at St Audry's the staff were coping with a higher level of disturbed and aggressive behaviour. The turnover of the unit was also quite substantial. The report of a monitoring visit by Catherine Lavers and Mary Burns from the Health Authority in March 1995 noted that departures from the unit numbered 32 in 1993/94 and 40 in 1994/95. The average length of stay reported by the clinical co-ordinator at that time was 15-20 days on Easton Two and six months on Easton One.

We were impressed by the good organization, appearance and general atmosphere of the unit, the morale and cohesiveness of the staff, and their sense of purpose. There were strong and experienced senior staff. They displayed immense support and loyalty towards Dr Goddard.

It was also our impression that in practice, the ethos and the clinical approach of the unit were in certain respects more limited than ideally they should have been. While there was a proper primary focus on careful diagnostic assessment, the use of effective medical methods of treatment and the encouragement and maintenance of socially acceptable behaviour, these tended to be at the expense of psychological approaches to understanding the experience and emotional lives of patients. This is of particular importance in the management of patients with histories of offending, and is considered in more detail in Chapter XVIII.

Care Programme approach-compliance and aftercare section 117 arrangements

During the period of Jason Mitchell's care and treatment in East Suffolk the policies relating to Care Planning were set out in 'Guidelines on assessment and care management for hospital discharge' which were issued in January 1993, the procedures established to support the Care Programme approach in 1991 and the Social Services procedures introduced to support the Care in the Community legislation.

There is evidence of a sequence of Care Plans which describe problem areas, set objectives, establish a Care Plan and include an evaluation process. A particularly clear example of such a plan is to be seen in the Linkways plan of 4 November 1993, part of which is set out below.

Problem	*Objectives*
1. Future Accommodation. Jason wants to leave hospital and live with other people.	To find suitable accommodation which will provide Jason with help and support.
2. Section 37/41 MHA has ground parole only at present.	To increase Jason's freedom gradually.
5. Family structure. Poor relationship with father wants to get to know estranged mother but she's reluctant. Sees his sisters periodically no contact with two brothers.	For Jason to establish the relationships he feels he needs with his family.

Care Plan	*Evaluation*
1. Liaise with social worker and look at all available options.	Seen Greenwoods. Application to be sent.
2. Liaise with MD Team and gradually extend Jason's boundaries.	Ongoing continue.
5. Give support while he tries to build relationships. Help him to cope with any rejections.	Has seen his mother, meeting affable. Will meet again.

The plan contained six problems, all of which were dated for evaluation and signed when evaluated.

Between 11 May 1993 and 9 March 1994 eight Care Plans were completed. No Care Plans exist thereafter, save for an Emergency Plan on his readmission. However, section 117 discharge planning meetings and review meetings were held in September and October 1993, in June and August 1994, and an undated meeting was held probably shortly after Jason Mitchell's admission to Easton House. Reference is also made to a review meeting on 16 November 1993 for which no records were identified.

Oddly, while the Care Plans are clearly dated, the section 117 meetings are very poorly date identified.

Social Services Care Assessments and Plans were completed in February and November 1994.

All the staff from St Clement's who gave evidence placed great emphasis on the Care Plan as the tool for ensuring a co-ordinated approach to patient care. All plans save one accord with the guidance and show evidence of change and adjustment over time. Consistent with the general emphasis on a behavioural regime, they are clear in both setting objectives and adequate in evaluation where the objectives are concrete and focus on behaviour. Those objectives which relate to Jason Mitchell's relationships and feelings are more cursorily dealt with. For example, in the plan of 8 July 1993 the following entry is typical of those which relate to Jason Mitchell's feelings:

Problem	*Objective*
Difficulties in expressing his feelings with regard to his circumstances (that is, being in hospital, restrictions brought about by MHA, prospects, expectations and family relationships).	To be able to express his feelings and to feel comfortable with these feelings whether positive or negative.
Care Plan	*Evaluation*
Staff to be approachable and accessible – use active listening skills and allow time to vent feelings. Offer support and encouragement when appropriate and to promote security and psychological safety.	Remains current.

Jason Mitchell's personal contribution to the care planning process on 20 October 1993 included the following:

Problems	Objectives
1. Difficulties in getting it together in terms of positives for family and feelings time spent in hospital and after hospital and after care.	Need to express my feelings negative or positive to overcome disruptive (disrupted) thoughts and emotions.
2. Parole	To work towards regaining previous privileges.

Care Plan	Evaluation
1. I will keep a daily (?) diary sheet for myself in the way of a diary around attitudes, feelings towards problems.	??
2. I will meet three times a week with my key worker Sue. This is for the next two weeks commencing 21st October. This will be for a period of one hour.	??
3. Unescorted parole to OT and back.	Successful. May have further unescorted parole in hospital grounds.

Various other adjustments are made to the parole arrangements but typically no evaluation comments other than the two question marks are made on the more personal objectives.

The final Care Plan is dated 9 March 1994:

Problems	Objectives
Maladaptive behaviour leading to unsuccessful social relationships including violence to others and risks to himself.	To provide structure and regain acceptable social skills prior to discharge ASAP.

The plan then lists things which Jason Mitchell values and goes on to plan a sequence of tasks for a daily programme which include a number of sanctions. Shortly thereafter Jason Mitchell absconded and was absent for a period of ten days.

A review of the care plans reinforces our view that while the care and treatment programme was consistently recorded, less importance appeared to be attached to issues to do with Jason Mitchell's feelings and relationships than to his behaviour.

The section 117 procedures were complied with, with the exception of the date recording. A wide number of professionals were invited to attend, including GPs and project leaders from MIND. It was noted that Jason Mitchell did not wish a relative to attend. A summary of the past history was prepared which touched on the intention to kill, described his experiences of unusual phenomena; hearing voices; ideas of reference and paranoia for six years before hospital admission, that these were controlled with medication and that he relapsed when medication was withdrawn. (After care co-ordination meeting dated 29 September 1993 and also dated 29 October 1993.)

The need to register with a GP, to receive support if required from the CMHT and to have his financial support and benefits advice from his social worker were identified. The programme proposed was:

1. To live in a supported hostel.
2. To attend day hospital (how often?).
3. CHT support initially, if appropriate.
4. Social supervisor Jane Barnett.
5. RMO Dr Goddard.

The next meeting proposed the move to Linkways which subsequently failed. The After Care meeting, held on 8 June 1994 after Jason Mitchell's transfer to Larkhill Way and attended by Lawrence Markwell from MIND, his social worker and hospital staff, identified his key worker as Jane Barnett and noted that the following programme was in place.

1. Supervised accommodation (MIND).
2. Social supervisor Jane Barnett.
3. Social activities arranged through MIND: Day hospital offered but did not want it. No need for CMHT due to care network that has been arranged.

The complex interaction between case conferences, care planning and section 117 meeting is illustrated by this brief summary, as is the potentially confusing overlap in nomenclature and responsibilities. The tool which appears to hold the system together is the case conference. **We recommend** that case conferences are recorded more fully.

The two Social Services Community Care Assessments were full and completed in accordance with the Department's guidance. The first contains a thorough and detailed family history, an intelligent assessment of Jason Mitchell's needs and a good description of his personality. The brief description of the index offence included the threats to kill, and the conclusion (quoted in full in Chapter IV) points to 'the dangers and temptations with which a transfer into the community will be fraught', recommends a therapeutic placement, and points out that if Jason Mitchell's needs are not met he could become a danger to the community.

The second was completed at the time of the breakdown of the placement at Larkhill Way. This summarises the history, describes the achievements to date and describes the reasons for the breakdown as having needs other than the practical support available at the placement and the MIND decision not to renew the tenancy. It does not point to the deteriorating relationships with fellow residents and staff. The proposed care plan describes his needs as:

1. Rehousing to single self-contained flat, preferably Felixstowe.
2. Support in setting up home, getting back to work and possibly further education.
3. Support and structuring time and developing networks/friend-ships in the community.
4. Monitoring mental health.
5. Monitoring Care Plan and conditional discharge.

No mention is made of any service deficit. In evidence Jane Barnett pointed to the absence of a setting in which Jason Mitchell's emotional needs could be explored in safety and the scarcity of counselling services, although she pointed out that the latter would have been inappropriate unless delivered in a structured setting. Staff are often reluctant to record unmet need in face of the threat of judicial review and ambiguous guidance from central government on this point. Without such information it is difficult to see how a real picture of unmet need or need for a reshaping of existing investment can emerge.

The Care Planning, Section 117 system and Care Assessment system were all complied with, were all appropriately multi-disciplinary in approach and form the basis of a sound process. **We recommend** that a system of review where breakdown occurs, e.g. the Larkhill placement, should be implemented.

In this context it must be remembered that these procedures operate within a wider recording network. We were impressed by the detailed nursing records at both West Park and St Clement's, which gave a very clear picture of Jason Mitchell's behaviour and its effects on others. We noted an absence of a picture of his feelings and thoughts about himself, his offence and his family. Only glimpses of these issues emerged (albeit powerfully) in the main from the records of the professions supplementary to medicine and in the Suffolk Social Services records.

Purchaser/Provider

The evidence of joint working in Suffolk between Social Services, Health Purchasers and Health Providers in the field of mental health is impressive. The contracts with the MIND provider and hospital discharge procedures were jointly signed by the two authorities. Furthermore, there is evidence in the material presented to us which shows that when such procedures were implemented they rapidly found their way onto the agendas of provider team briefings. There was also evidence of a multi-disciplinary approach to case conferences.

The Social Services Department had managed its post-Community Care managerial arrangements in such a way as to preserve a focus on the needs of people with mental health problems. The Health Purchasers had established clear contracts with their provider trusts and there was evidence of an appropriate degree of flexibility in the contractual arrangements as well as evidence of emerging quality assurance and contract monitoring strategies.

We have already expressed our view that the range of community and hospital-based services was impressive, but **we recommend** that the Health and Social Services purchasers could usefully review the balance of expenditure to see if a more specialised focus could be developed within the range of community-based residential services in order to provide a locally based therapeutic service. We also note that Suffolk Health's current contract specifications do not include quality standards specific to patients with histories of violent offending (although various standards are set for detained patients, seclusion, individualised care and the use of control and restrain). **We recommend** that the Purchasing Authority should consider developing quality standards that apply to patients with histories of violent offending. Such standards might include requiring Providers to ensure that a full range of assessment approaches, including access to forensic psychiatry services, are available for such patients. It will be seen from our review of the management of Easton House that there is at least a question as to the balance of therapeutic strategies at the unit. **We recommend** that an externally facilitated multi-disciplinary review should be undertaken of the balance between behavioural and psychodynamic approach at Easton House and the skills available to develop a greater degree of flexibility. Dr Goddard expressed the view that his unit's approach was eclectic. A reading of the Care Plans, and the evidence presented in this case, would suggest that this approach and this skill mix were not always in evidence. Where a staff team is so clearly and appropriately sensitive to the dangers of 'splitting', which were frequently referred to in evidence, there is a danger that the team may become inward-looking, and there was some evidence that new members of the team, who might have been presenting valid differences of perspective, were seen as being manipulated. To avoid what could be incipient problems, **we recommend** that some form of peer-group audit or external audit be incorporated into the Trust's quality assurance programme, and that the purchasers, perhaps in concert with the Department of Health, should develop contract-monitoring measures more finely-tuned to the needs of services for people with mental health problems. **We recommend** that Purchasers ensure that there is clinical audit of hospital psychiatric teams to examine multi-disciplinary working and the representation of varied and possibly contradictory perspectives in clinical records. In making this suggestion we are aware that such measures are notoriously elusive. An approach which samples care plans and reviews might be a starting point.

We found that social workers may occupy a number of roles: Named Assessor, Care Manager, Social Supervisor, Appropriate Adult and Approved Social Worker. In the relationship with a service user a social worker may experience not just a lack of harmony, but frequently conflict, because the roles fulfil competing functions. The most obvious example is the Care Manager role, which may include advocacy work, and the Social Supervisor, where the worker adopts an independent position. These concerns were particularly evident in relation to those roles where the service user is subject to statutory provisions. It is, of course, possible to combine these roles, but to do so presents considerable challenges to managers and staff alike. This problem is compounded when the worker concerned is also operating with colleagues who are working in the Care Programme approach, set out by the Department of Health. Local managers are well aware of these problems and have sought to address them by developing the 'Suffolk Approach' which seeks to clarify differences of nomencla-

ture and potential overlaps of responsibility. In this context a very
helpful paper has been prepared jointly by the Social Services and
Health agencies and this is commended to the Department of
Health.

The recent document of guidance published by the Department
of Health, 'Building Bridges', says nothing about the role of the
Social Supervisor. Indeed, it is quite explicit in stating that the
Mental Health Act and its Code of Practice are the documents
which govern people subject to statutory provision and states: 'This
guide does not seek to replace the Code in any respect.' **We recommend** that the Department of Health be invited to draw together
the existing fragmented policy guidance on the role of Local Authority and Health Service staff in the care and after-care of mentally
ill people in an integrated document of guidance.

We recommend that the Home Office Notes for the Guidance
of Social Supervisors of restricted patients be reviewed and revised
to take account of potential conflicts in the roles of social workers
arising from recent changes in the Community Care, Mental
Health and Criminal Justice legislation.

The Social Services Department conducted a thorough case
review and made a number of recommendations which we endorse.
Indeed, we were heartened by the level of self-criticism and openness to learning which was displayed by the staff and management
of the department. Among the recommendations for change which
they made are proposals that staff who are required to act as social
supervisors to restricted patients should be Approved Social
Workers, that Social Services Departments should make the
records of clients, particularly clients who are restricted patients, readily available to Departments into whose area they
are discharged. These are incorporated into our summary of
recommendations.

A similar review of practice was conducted by Dr Goddard for
the Easton House team. It will be noted that the Social Services
review was conducted by a manager with no direct line management responsibility for the case in question, and **we recommend**
this this approach is adopted by Health Service Trusts.

In this context it is noted that no review of the placement
breakdown appears to have been completed. The local Social Services Department and Health agencies are addressing this issue at
present. In the course of receiving evidence and at the seminar
convened by us, it was suggested that the kind of case review

conducted by Area Child Protection Committees has much to commend it, and indeed **we recommend** that, given the need for close networking between many agencies and the establishment of supervision registers, some thought could usefully be given by the Department of Health and the professional bodies to drawing on the best practice from child protection in developing an interagency approach to case management for mentally ill patients who are discharged into the community. The Probation Services in Suffolk suggested that such an approach might usefully be extended to a wider range of clients presenting similar problems in the community.

XIII. Psychiatric, Psychological and Multi-disciplinary Assessment

Man consists of body, mind and imagination. His body is faulty, his mind untrustworthy, but his imagination has made him remarkable.
John Masefield, *Shakespeare and Spiritual Life* (1924)

The problem of psychiatric diagnosis in Jason Mitchell's case was approached thoroughly; and there was a range of multi-disciplinary contributions to his care and treatment, as described in Chapters III and IV. There are, however, two aspects of the multi-disciplinary approach to assessment that merit comment.

First, psychological contributions to Jason Mitchell's overall clinical assessment were very meagre. He had been assessed as a result of difficulties at school by the Educational Psychology Service, and at West Park Hospital a standardised intelligence test was administered in response to concerns about his ability to pursue college courses. As noted in Chapter IV, no interpretative report of his variable performance on this test was in evidence in his medical records.

At St Clement's Hospital the clinical psychology post allocated to Easton House had not been filled at the time of Jason Mitchell's admission. Dr Wilson, Jason Mitchell's consultant at Rampton Hospital, and other witnesses attested to the desirability of psychological assessment in this and similar cases. A full assessment by a clinical psychologist might have addressed Jason Mitchell's current social, emotional and interpersonal difficulties, and elucidated cognitive and intellectual deficits. Although we did not take evidence on the matter, a further question for consideration is whether there was a case for more extensive neuro-psychiatric investigations.

A psychological assessment might also have sought to understand Jason Mitchell's world view and explored his thoughts, feelings, aspirations and fantasies. It remains an open question whether he could have engaged in productive psychological work on such areas, but the material resulting from the assessment would have been available to inform the clinical team managing his case.

An alternative and specialised assessment of these areas might have resulted from referral to a psychodynamic psychotherapy service. The level of skill and experience needed in carrying out psychodynamic assessments of patients such as Jason Mitchell is of a high order, as would be provided, for example by a consultant psychotherapist or a forensic psychotherapist at a specialist centre such as the Portman Clinic, London. Such services are scarce.

These remarks do not imply that psychodynamic psychotherapy should have been regarded as an appropriate and effective form of treatment for Jason Mitchell. There are rigorous selection criteria for such treatment, and Jason Mitchell may well have been deemed unsuitable. However the value of an assessment would have been as an aid to clinical understanding of the patient. Assessment might have been helpful in ensuring that deeper aspects of his personality disturbance did not go unrecognised, and might also have enabled a more sophisticated and less judgmental appreciation of the reasons for Jason Mitchell's highly variable presentation to others and the differing reactions to himself he produced within all the services that have dealt with him. Patients with such problems test professional objectivity and teams working with them may benefit from outside support and supervision. **We recommend** that in-patient units whose patients include offenders with disturbed personalities should have access to specialist psychodynamic expertise.

The psychological and psychodynamic assessments referred to above, and any therapeutic interventions they may have prompted, would have had to be done within the context of structure and support provided by a hospital or residential setting. Jason Mitchell probably could not have been consistently or productively helped by counselling in the community, and a counselling model would not have been appropriate for understanding or treating Jason Mitchell's psychological disturbance.

The person who most prominently talked to Jason Mitchell about those areas which would have been of central importance in a psychodynamic assessment was Jackie Leaver. By her own admission she was untrained in this area of work, and, as she honestly acknowledged, was out of her depth, but nonetheless she produced with Jason Mitchell a remarkable report (appended to Chapter IV). As Dr Paul Bowden commented, her report provided:

... a very good developmental history indicating the effects of external events on his emotional development in childhood and adolescence, and I think it is an excellent report.

... It would have made a significant contribution to understanding him as a person.

It does not appear, however, that the report was properly incorporated into the overall clinical appraisal of Jason Mitchell, nor does it appear there was active consideration of how the areas covered in the report should be further explored. Evidence at the Inquiry indicated that Jackie Leaver's relatively peripheral role and low professional status militated against proper weight being given to her reports. In the assessment and management of offender patients, the influences of personality development, early experience and emotional life may need to be taken into account, as well as mental illness. Psychodynamic assessment has an important role to play. Exploration of the areas relevant to psychodynamic assessment requires equivalent rigour, expertise and supervision to other approaches to clinical investigation.

The second aspect of the multi-disciplinary approach at Easton House that merits comment is its emphasis on a behavioural approach. Giving evidence to the Panel of Inquiry, Dr Goddard said of the development of the regime of Easton House:

> We had also developed some expertise in taking patients that the other consultants, not only from within our area but outside, found difficulty in dealing with. And they were often personality disorder patients, very often self-harmers. For these people we felt that we could offer a medium term behavioural, fairly simple sort of period of treatment in Easton House.

Dr Goddard had explained this approach more fully in his report to the Inquiry, written in August 1995:

> An individual behavioural programme was constructed for Jason Mitchell on his first admission and approved by the MDT [multi-disciplinary team] in conference and subject to periodic revisions. The general format of this behavioural programme is common to all similar cases in Easton House and consists of identifying all behaviour which it is aimed to change and organising a clearly identified system whereby the patient can regain personal privileges and resume personal responsibility on demonstrating an improvement. This system of negative reinforcement (i.e. reinforcing adaptive behaviour by removing unwelcome restrictions) was complemented by positive reinforcement in that desired behaviour was reinforced

by attention, compliments and occasional extra privileges. A flexible rather than too rigid an approach was taken when implementing the behaviour programme in line with Jason Mitchell's known ambivalence towards release, rehabilitation and assuming responsibility for himself. The overall aim was to ensure that he attained a level of behaviour which would be acceptable in the community. We were aware that the counsel of perfection would inevitably result in failure and continued institutional care.

Dr Goddard's oral evidence to us suggested that his view of Jason Mitchell's personality disorder was that it was immutable. When asked: 'What would you have been doing for Jason Mitchell as a person as opposed to monitoring?', he replied:

> I find it difficult to forecast whether he would have had any fundamental change in his personality and I somewhat doubt it, given the severity of his personality disorder. He is in the category of the severely personality disordered. It is not just a neurotic boy who has had a hard deal in life and if only his mother had loved him a bit better it would all have been different. There is fundamentally something wrong with this man's central nervous system that would manifest itself as a distorted personality. That is the way I see it.

This appraisal of the likelihood of fundamental change in personality would be widely accepted by psychiatrists. But, in the practical clinical management of a patient who has a disturbed personality, a history of violent offending by an individual and who will be subject to statutory psychiatric supervision, models of clinical understanding have to incorporate an appreciation of the patient's subjective experience, personality and relationships. An approach that focuses on behaviour, and that understands personality disorder only in terms of a brain disorder, carries the danger of shutting off clinical awareness of the patient's inner world and emotional life. Appreciation of them is important in monitoring possible offending risk.

In an inpatient regime focusing too exclusively on a behavioural approach, improvements in disturbed behaviour may lead to inferences that underlying psychological disturbances are reduced and do not need to be inquired into. In the latter part of Jason Mitchell's readmission to Easton House he was relaxed, settled and cheerful. He seemed well when he left the unit on 9 December 1994.

Jason Mitchell's presentation during his stay at Easton House was very variable. It ranged from pleasant compliance to outright hostility and absconding. In this context, there were several occasions when he reported to different members of staff that he had been hearing voices. These reports were intermittent and tentative, and Dr Goddard and his team had moved to a working diagnosis of drug-induced psychosis to account for Jason Mitchell's past psychiatric history. The behavioural approach to his management may have disposed the clinical team to regard the reporting by Jason Mitchell of hearing voices as manipulative behaviour directed towards peripheral or less experienced members of staff.

With reference to the doctor to whom one such report had been made, Dr Goddard said:

> She, to my mind, would have been just the sort of person that Jason Mitchell would have watched and he would have thought: 'Oh, here we go, the thousandth time I have been asked my history, the thousandth time I have been asked these crude mental state examinations and I have read about them in my books anyway. Here goes, she wants to hear about this, that and the other' and quite easily he could have come out with something just to shut her up, play games or whatever.

With reference to the experienced psychiatric nurse, Mr Vincent Lightbody, to whom Jason Mitchell reported voices, Dr Goddard said:

> having come from the day hospital environment, and with all that time off sick, I think he might have been the sort of person Jason Mitchell would have picked on and stirred up.

The Easton House team's deliberations about Jason Mitchell's reports were described as follows:

> We talked about why he might do that, what sort of motives there might be. It was difficult to say. We knew he was bored. We knew he was mischievous. We knew he had a record of telling different people different stories at different times.

When Jason Mitchell was asked about this period by two of us (AG and PG) he could remember telling another member of staff (Ray Sheppard, who was as a Health Care Assistant) that he was hearing voices. Mr Sheppard told the Inquiry, however, that while he could clearly remember discussing with Jason Mitchell the importance of taking medication, he could not remember Jason Mitchell reporting voices to him. Jason Mitchell told us that at various times he had denied hearing voices when he was in fact hearing them, but never the reverse:

> I never faked voices. Look, I've killed two people [*sic*]. I'm not going to pretend. I didn't fake voices.

Dr Goddard told us that he made a positive decision not to explore Jason Mitchell's account of voices for authenticity and did not conduct an interview with him about this. It seems possible, however, that such an interview might have provided an opportunity to test what Jason Mitchell was reporting, and to explore the significance of his report, the motivation behind it, and identify any ambivalence about medication.

Dr Goddard may have believed that such a response from himself or another member of the team would reinforce what was perceived as Jason Mitchell's maladaptive behaviour. An operant conditioning model might be taken to imply that voice reporting behaviour would be positively reinforced by such attention. To use such a model to try to understand what was taking place in this clinical setting was, however, inappropriate. For example, operant conditioning principles require that behaviour is reinforced (rewarded) or extinguished (by ignoring) contingent upon its occurrence – i.e. immediately it occurs, not hours or days later during and after a clinical meeting. Furthermore, if such principles had been operative, what would be taught would be 'not to report voices'. The cardinal principle of therapeutic behavioural treatments is that they should focus much less on the unacceptable, and much more actively upon promoting – in this case – prosocial behaviour.

Behavioural treatment regimes also require careful ethical frameworks and ongoing professional review, as is made clear in the second edition of the 'Code of Practice' for the Mental Health Act 1983, published in August 1993, which states (para 19.1):

> Psychological treatments should be conducted under the supervision of those properly trained in the use of the specific methods employed.

The Code of Practice states, under the heading, 'Behaviour Modification Programmes', pp. 87-8:

> a person with sufficient skills in implementing behaviour modification programmes should be available to monitor procedures as well as the progress of the parties.

We recommend, in respect of behaviour modification programmes and particularly in the absence of valid patient consent, that a locally agreed procedure should be adopted in which the RMO should seek the advice of a suitably qualified person *who is not a member of the clinical team responsible for the patient* [our emphasis]. This will normally be a psychologist, although some medical staff, social workers or nurses may have received special training that equips them to supervise psychological procedures.

The advantage of oversight of psychological treatments by a qualified psychologist is that their training enables consideration of the appropriateness of a number of other models of psychological treatment alongside consideration of the suitability of the behavioural approach. It is regrettable that this did not take place in respect of the behavioural regime used with Jason Mitchell at Easton House.

The behavioural model was also associated with misgivings about individual sessions with Jason Mitchell, and thus may have closed off a means of gaining more personal understanding of him. Beyond the assumption that one-to-one interviews with Jason Mitchell might reinforce maladaptive, manipulative and attention seeking behaviour, there was also a fear of 'splitting' of the team by patients such as Jason Mitchell. Dr Goddard told us:

> One of the things we are very strong on in our multi-disciplinary team in Easton House is that we insist on working together ... we avoid splitting because we work with so many patients who are often very manipulative, at splitting, playing one group off against another.

Mr Graham Stannard, an experienced enrolled nurse who worked on night shifts during the time of Jason Mitchell's admission, told us about his individual contact with Jason Mitchell and explained – quite understandably – that he did not undertake 'one-to-one' work with patients himself. When asked who he would see as the appropriate people for doing such work if it was needed, he said:

> With certain people, depending on their problems, I don't know whether a one-to-one would ever be right, in my opinion. I would certainly think that it needed to be a two-to-one probably. My idea of a one-to-one is being in a room with somebody where nobody else can see what is going on. That is not something that I would like to do.

He went on to confirm that he thought such work should not happen on a unit such as Easton House, and he felt this 'very strongly', because there had been occasions when a patient had got angry or felt trapped or picked on, and lashed out, and staff are also 'open to accusations which again is not a nice sort of thing'.

When asked whether this was an isolated opinion, or one that he thought was widely shared by his colleagues, he said:

> I think we work as a team – I don't think, I know we work as a team and I think we are all of the opinion that really a team should be able to get a rapport with our charges so that we do not need that type of relationship.

We do not know how widespread such attitudes in fact were. It is self-evident that they militate against the possibility of developing an understanding of individual patients.

Exploratory psychological approaches with Jason Mitchell were clearly felt to be precluded. Yvonne Hines, Assistant Ward Manager on Easton 1 Ward, in her evidence, indicated that, while referral to a psychologist had been discussed, it was felt to be inappropriate:

> We would move forward. We were only actually there to place him safely in the community. That really was our role. That is what we felt and we musn't really deviate from it.

Dr Goddard also believed it to be contra-indicated:

> With someone ... we realised could be so manipulative and unreliable, I would not have entrusted that particular type of work to anybody other than someone with considerable experience, and then they would have had to have worked within the team and been supervised. This is because the dangers are too great ... of splitting. And someone like Jason Mitchell, who as I have said his whole persona was to impress, to watch for people's reactions, to find people's weak points and play games ....

It has already been said that attempts to reduce 'manipulative' and 'attention seeking' behaviour should be a minor part of an active regime to promote prosocial behaviour. Even the achievement of more acceptable behaviour is, however, in its turn a minor part of the individual therapeutic needs of a patient, such as Jason Mitchell, with profound disturbances of personality development. Individual work can create an opportunity for monitoring inner life

– a chance for patient and practitioner to try to form a partnership, and to share responsibility when mental health deteriorates.

We recommend that RMOs and clinicians managing offender patients afford such patients regular interviews in private. Assessment and monitoring of inner life cannot reliably be conducted in case conference or clinical meeting settings.

Part G

Transfers

XIV. Surrey to Suffolk

Choosing cannot be anything more than what we feel it to be when
we choose.
Frederick Vivian, *Human Freedom and Responsibility* (1964), p. 62

Dr Yeldham asked the West Park managers to explore the possibility of a transfer to Ipswich on 26 November 1992. On 2 December
1992 they responded that East Suffolk would co-operate in the
transfer subject to a local clinician's approval, and offered to
establish the name of the relevant clinician. Shortly thereafter, Dr
Yeldham contacted Dr Goddard, who immediately requested sight
of the case notes and indicated that he would like to see Jason
Mitchell. It was noted that St Audry's was due to close in March
1993, and that Jason was likely to be admitted to St Clement's. Dr
Yeldham sent a summary of the notes to Dr Goddard on 4 January
1993.

On 15 February 1993 a team from St Audry's visited West Park
to assess Jason Mitchell's suitability for transfer. The team con-
sisted of the Deputy Nurse Manager, Gordon Heffer, Janice Smith,
the Ward Manager, and Ken Dunnett, a specialist adviser on
mental health. They would normally have been accompanied by
either Dr Goddard or his deputy, Dr Hanna. On this occasion Dr
Hanna, who had been scheduled to attend, was unable to do so. The
team met the primary nurse and explored Jason Mitchell's past
problems and further expectations. They also met an Associate
Nurse, the Speech Therapist, an Occupational Therapist, and
Jason Mitchell.

Unfortunately, they were not given the opportunity to meet
Jason Mitchell alone. They ascertained his status under the Mental
Health Act as a restricted patient subject to a deferred conditional
discharge, and that he had had local day leave and enjoyed leave
to go to Suffolk to stay with his family, and had used these periods
well. They noted his medication and that he seemed surprisingly
reliant on his Speech Therapist. They were made aware of the
failed transfer to a rehabilitation ward in the latter part of 1991
following the recommendation of the Mental Health Review Tribu-

nal and were clear that the task on transfer was to finalise his rehabilitation. Their conclusion is set out below:

> We all felt that Jason seemed to be well down the road of rehabilitation but have reservations as to how he will cope once the support of the 'Team' at West Park Hospital is left behind and he embarks upon a more independent life style. Our feelings are that, although he denies this, he will need a considerable amount of support from our team during the initial period with us. He has displayed manipulative behaviour in the past and we also made the observation that his bed space was displayed in a 'shrine like' fashion, very unusual for a person of his age and generation.

Dr Goddard agreed to accept Jason Mitchell as a patient on 24 February 1993. It will be noted that Dr Yeldham was not seen by the visiting team but there were full summary reports, and indeed Dr Goddard met Jason Mitchell, accompanied by his social worker, on 17 March 1993, the day after C3 Division of the Home Office approved his transfer.

Dr Yeldham's request that Jason Mitchell be transferred to Easton House was responded to, promptly and appropriately, by Dr Goddard. He made plain that he was unprepared to offer supervision until he had obtained a good understanding of Jason Mitchell's mental health and had established a working relationship. He conveyed his views clearly in a letter dated 19 March 1993, already quoted in Chapter X (p. 144). Dr Yeldham responded, informing Dr Goddard that the Tribunal had, in fact, been brought forward, that a conditional discharge was already in force, but that Jason Mitchell remained subject to a section 41 restriction order.

On 7 April 1993 Dr Yeldham wrote to Dr Goddard setting out the decision of the Tribunal: a conditional discharge deferred until the following conditions could be met:

1. Residence in a hostel;
2. Acceptance of medication (subject to RMO approval);
3. Submission to ongoing outpatient monitoring as advised by the RMO and Social Worker.

The circumstances of that 'conditional discharge' are discussed fully in Chapter X above.

Dr Goddard accepted the transfer, which was effected on 5 May 1993.

The visiting team appeared to form a view of the index offence as one which was relatively minor (see Chapter VIII) nor was there any evidence that they sought, or were offered a risk assessment by the clinical team at West Park. This view coloured the subsequent understanding, in particular of the nursing and social work staff in Suffolk. The admission notes in the nursing record stated:

> He was being held for attacking a caretaker with a piece of wood in a church ....

and there was evidence from the West Park social worker which supports the view that this is the impression which the visiting team was likely to have received.

Indeed, despite the detailed admission report of Dr Odutoye, which clearly set out the events leading up to the offence and offered some insight into Jason Mitchell's attitude towards it, and indicated his state of mind, it was the lesser interpretation which gained sway.

Nevertheless, the administrative and clinical transfer arrangements were a model of promptness, co-operation, clarity and thoroughness on the part of Dr Goddard, Dr Yeldham and the two purchasing authorities in Surrey and Suffolk.

Patient choice and patient involvement

The issue of patient self-determination was raised on a number of occasions during the Inquiry hearings. Jason Mitchell's wishes that his family should not be contacted; Jason Mitchell's wishes to be discharged to be near his family home; his wishes that he be not so discharged; the choice of placement and his programme within the community; the wishes of staff to receive or not to receive information, unless the patient volunteered it, and the difficulty which the Inquiry experienced in obtaining records without the consent of the patient – all these raised issues about patient self-determination, just as, to a lesser extent, did his wishes in respect of medication.

There is evidence in the records of West Park Hospital, Easton House and the Social Services Department of efforts to involve Jason Mitchell in his treatment programme. Some key documents are co-signed by the worker and the patient, and a number of signed contract documents between Jason Mitchell and Easton House are on file.

Considerable efforts were made by all the professionals and agencies involved to conform to his wishes. Thus staff at West Park first sought placements in Cambridge and then, when Jason Mitchell changed his view, recommended his discharge to Suffolk. Dr Yeldham's report to the Mental Health Review Tribunal in April 1993 stated:

> In August/September last year he (Mr Mitchell) decided he wished to renew contact with his family and return to the Ipswich area. Consequently, the team has helped Mr Mitchell re-establish contact with his family and our Social Worker, Joan Rapaport, has made the appropriate visits and investigations (see separate report). I am of the opinion that this is an appropriate choice as Mr Mitchell's family are his only long-term supporters. In retrospect his leaving the Ipswich area may have been associated with the original onset of his illness. Mr Mitchell has made initial visits to his family and spent the Christmas period with his father. It would seem most appropriate to rehabilitate him to an area where he wished to live and where he has family support.

This recommendation was supported by the Social Work report.

It is interesting to note that when Dr Yeldham requested a home visit from the social worker in September 1992 she received the following reply:

> I have been very concerned about our lack of first hand information regarding Jason's home circumstances, Jason's relationship with his father and family and Mr Mitchell's lack of information about his son's general well-being and circumstances. I have at various times discussed the position with Jason. However, he has made it clear that he does not want me to make contact. In view of the restriction order, my hands are somewhat tied. As you know nearest relatives in respect of Part III of the Act have somewhat limited rights, especially if the patient objects. I verified on 10.9.92 with my team manager that I cannot proceed without Jason's permission.

In fact, such a visit was made on 31 October 1992.

When questioned on this issue Joan Rapaport stated that she had an obligation to the Mental Health Review Tribunal to try to contact the nearest relatives, and it was this which enabled her to over-ride the patient's wishes that she should not contact his family. She said: 'I see it as constituting a bar, but a bar I have to work with. But the bar was lifted at the time of statutory input.'

When asked, 'Do you regard patient choice as being an absolute priority in that kind of situation?' Dr Yeldham responded: 'Not necessarily. I mean if there had been major contra-indication to that happening then one would have looked at it and talked about it with the patient.'

Jane Barnett was asked about the issue of patient consent when making the placement at Larkhill Way, rather than continuing to seek a therapeutic placement for Jason Mitchell. She was asked:

Q. How important do you regard patient choice in that context?
A. I think it has to be important because in order to supervise him effectively, I mean you hope with powers of persuasion you might be able to dissuade him from a place that is not at all suitable but if they do not agree you are unlikely to get the co-operation you would get if you attended to their wishes. So I think it's a balancing act really.

When further pressed, she added:

You can only treat it with each individual case.

This echoes Dr Yeldham's views. The guidance on care management issued by the Trust contains the following statement as para 14:

All of the legislation and guidelines around after care and care in the community makes it quite clear that the person who is the subject of the care programme has the right to refuse any service at any time. Until clarified by further guidance/legislation, persons registered as being in need of supervision still have the right to refuse services offered.

Clearly, obtaining a patient's willing consent to a treatment plan will tend to promote a successful outcome; particularly where (as in the case of a therapeutic community) the programme can proceed only with the patient's willing co-operation. In this case it appears not inappropriate to have responded supportively to Jason Mitchell's clear view that he did not wish his family to be contacted and to work towards an achievement of an agreement. When Jason began, however, to express the wish to return to Ipswich, family contact was made, albeit using the powers of the report to the Mental Health Review Tribunal and subsequently agreement from Jason Mitchell to visit his father. Jane Barnett too attempted to work towards obtaining agreement but nevertheless, despite Jason

Mitchell's reservations, established contact with Mr Mitchell senior and attempted to renew contact between Jason Mitchell and his elder sister.

We have in the course of this report placed considerable weight on the need for carers and treaters to obtain a clearer understanding of the family relationships and their meaning for Jason Mitchell. We readily acknowledge the difficulties of undertaking such work from the base of West Park Hospital. Thus the logistical appeal of the discharge proposal for transfer to Suffolk is only too evident. The poverty of the quality of the family relationships, the clearly identified unsuitability of a placement with father, father's ambivalence towards Jason Mitchell and Jason Mitchell's own negative experiences while living in the Ipswich area must, however, all have begged the question about the level of support which Jason Mitchell was likely to receive from his family on transfer. It should, however, be remembered that Jason Mitchell absconded on two occasions from West Park Hospital to see his father in Ipswich. This might suggest that, even had Jason Mitchell been rehabilitated in Cambridge, he might well still have returned to the Ipswich area.

Once transferred, and again in the face of some opposition from Jason Mitchell, efforts were made by Dr Odutoye, staff from the Linkways ward and the social worker to establish some family support.

The grounds for supporting Jason Mitchell's wishes in respect of the placement at Greenwoods were very strong. When his interest waned, and he expressed a preference for the placement at Larkhill Way and to avoid a placement in Ipswich, his wishes were respected.

We accept the assertion that the degree of respect to be paid to patient's choice is always a fine balance. The need to subordinate patient choice, when risk to self or others is in issue, was not called into question in this case. It should have been more actively canvassed by those involved in the discharge of Jason Mitchell to his home environment. At the very least the apparent lack of family support should have led to more concentrated attention being paid to community support for Jason Mitchell.

XV. Larkhill: Placement and Displacement

> In the public mind, the aspirations of reformers are transmuted, by
> the touch of a phrase [such as 'community care'] into hard-won
> reality …. All kinds of wild unlovely weeds are changed, by statutory
> magic and comforting appellation, into the most attractive flowers
> that bloom not just in the spring but all the year round.
> Richard Titmuss, 'Community Care: Fact or Fiction?'
> from *Commitment to Welfare* (1961), ch. IX, p. 104

Thus in 1961 wisely wrote Professor Titmuss, the doyen of academic thinking about social policy. In 1987 Dr Goddard was employed to participate in turning that aspiration into a reality by
means of closing the old St Audry's 200 bed asylum and reproviding
services within the community, and on the site of St Clement's
Hospital. Supported by a good working relationship between the
then Health Authority and the Social Services Department, with
support from Housing Authorities and Housing Associations, and
in partnership with voluntary bodies, an impressive range of services was developed. The target closure date of 1993, moreover, was
achieved. Dr Goddard described the task well:

> There were patients of all varieties … a great many of them were
> severely enduringly mentally ill … schizophrenic patients, manic
> depressive psychoses and severe personality disordered types. We
> did a very thorough job of assessing and reassessing these patients
> and I think we did a job without sounding too conceited of which I
> am still very proud. So at the end of the period we had a good variety
> in East Suffolk of supported after-care accommodation.

It was into this network of mental health services that Jason
Mitchell was to be discharged in August 1994 from the rehabilitative unit at Easton House, St Clement's Hospital, to shared accommodation, run by East Suffolk MIND.

Planning for discharge

The Easton House policy document states: 'The ESLH(NHS) Trust policies on discharge and after-care and the provisions of the Mental Health Act (1983) and the Code of Practice will be adhered to.' Appended to the policy document are the Discharge Policy Statements issued in May 1994, at the precise time of Jason Mitchell's trial period of authorised leave of absence from hospital and his subsequent discharge to Larkhill.

The statement said: 'Discharge planning should commence on or before the day of admission and should involve the individual, relatives and carers, and other agencies and services that may be required.' It goes on to list eleven other requirements. All these requirements appear to have been complied with, although we have not seen the documentation required to be raised following an 'unsatisfactory' discharge consequent upon a placement break-down.

While Jason Mitchell's placement at Easton House was properly coloured by the expectation of discharge, once appropriate accommodation had been found, we have already seen that the Easton House team was determined to form its own view of his condition before preparing for discharge. Thus, while Jason Mitchell was admitted on 4 May 1993, the first discussion about placement on discharge is recorded at a case conference held on 4 August 1993, when the social worker was asked to begin investigations into placement options. The exploration of these options is consistently recorded in medical, nursing and case conference notes throughout the period.

Options

The discharge options varied over time. Initially (September 1993) the Hawthorns and Eastwood Terrace were considered. These are described as 'medium term rehab/therapeutic support' and 'supported accommodation with rehab', respectively both having sleep-in staff cover. Jason Mitchell's expressed preference not to be housed in Ipswich was respected. By October Eastwood was the preferred option. By November, when a transfer to Linkways, a rehabilitation ward within St Clement's was imminent, a request was made to social services for a 'hostel placement'. Social Services records show this to have been a referral for a place at Greenwoods, a therapeutic community in Essex. Jason Mitchell visited the project in November and, according to the social worker's records, his view was 'very favourable'. The formal application was not made until February 1994, possibly because the hostel had not achieved accredited status, i.e. an approval from the Social Services Department that social workers could purchase places there. Very shortly thereafter, however, on 24 February, Greenwoods wrote declining to accept Jason Mitchell, saying: 'We consider that our community would not offer enough security and that our therapeutic approach would not meet his needs.' It suggested another therapeutic community which might be able to meet his needs. The case conference on 16 February had supported a twin-track approach, looking at Hawthorns as well as Greenwoods.

Perhaps unsurprisingly, Jason Mitchell began to lose interest in pursuing further therapeutic placements, and was expressing a preference for a local resource. It also appeared, according to Social Services records, that an out-county placement 'might incur additional costs'. 'So it was decided in consultation with Mr Fifield (Supervisor) that I [Jane Barnett, Jason Mitchell's social worker] should explore local alternatives.' In March the medical records noted: 'Should be discharged as soon as possible.'

During April, visits were made to the Hawthorns and Gyppeswyck projects, both in Ipswich, the latter offering rehab/support with sleep-in staff, and to Larkhill Way, Felixstowe, which offered rehab/support accommodation without sleep-in staff.

Dr Goddard, who had been involved in setting up the accommodation, was familiar with the residents living at Larkhill Way, and had made previous successful placements in such accommodation of patients with considerably more serious histories of actual harm and mental illness than that displayed by Jason Mitchell. (It should be remembered that a very strong recommendation against a placement with Jason Mitchell's father had been made by the social worker from West Park.)

The nursing records of 19 April 1994 show that 'Jason Mitchell said that Larkhill Way was very impressive and he would certainly like to go there'. Indeed the record shows that 'Jason Mitchell has phoned the MIND organisation and has fixed himself an interview for possible placement at Larkhill'. On 27 April, arrangements were made for a trial at Larkhill on 3 May 1994 and 6-9 May 1994. On 18 May 1994 he started a month's leave at Larkhill and remained there until his re-admission to Easton House on 8 November 1994 on the breakdown of the placement.

Larkhill Way procedures

Larkhill Way is managed by East Suffolk MIND. The Health Authority and Social Services Department have a joint contract with the organisation to manage a number of care establishments. The admission policy requires a referral from an approved agency, in this instance from the Social Services Department, to a project manager. At the time of Jason Mitchell's admission there was no policy requirement that project managers should refer the question of the admission of a client who was a restricted patient subject to section 41 of the Mental Health Act 1983 to a more senior manager. The prospective tenant patient was required to complete a self-assessment form. A three-cornered discussion would take place between the Project Manager, the prospective tenant and the referring agencies representative, at which the needs of the candidate, the purpose of the project and the information supplied by the referring agency would be canvassed. If the candidate was acceptable, an overnight stay would be arranged to enable the candidate and the other residents to form a view; and, if favourable, an assured shorthold tenancy of six months would be agreed. It would have been the expectation that a copy of the Community Care plan would be made available, from which the Project Workers would develop a shared action plan with the tenant. MIND operates a policy of keeping records secure, but they are open to the resident.

There was some dispute between the project manager and the social worker about the quantity of information supplied to the project at the time of admission. Miss Jane Barnett (social worker) in her statement reported that Fiona Gilmour (the project manager) had indicated that 'she preferred not to receive detailed written social histories of potential residents, but rather let them choose what they divulged about themselves'. Miss Barnett states that she made Miss Gilmour aware of Jason Mitchell's status under the Mental Health Act and the restrictions he was subject to. She was not aware of his contact with the psychiatric services after the index offence but was aware of the diagnoses at West Park Hospital and St Clement's Hospital. In her written statement Miss Gilmour said, 'I did not particularly require social histories but that did not mean that I did not want to know anything that was relevant.' She confirms that MIND were represented at the case conference on 8 June 1994 and 'We therefore did know of his status'.

Jason Mitchell at Larkhill

While there is some suggestion from one of Jason Mitchell's fellow residents at the shared accommodation of a degree of reluctance to share with him, there was general agreement that they were prepared to give it a go. Jason Mitchell returned to the ward in good spirits on the evening of 9 May 1994, having enjoyed his stay at Larkhill. Lawrence Markwell from the hostel called the ward at Easton House to say that the leave period had been successful.

During the early period of his stay, staff and residents and visitors saw the pleasant, compliant side of Jason Mitchell's character of which we have heard. A fellow resident said: 'That weekend he seemed OK.' Staff said that they 'found Jason Mitchell on the whole to be amiable. Generally, people found Mitchell OK and quite friendly. He certainly looked different from our other residents and his behaviour was that of a charming softly spoken young man.' The mother of one of the residents, on meeting him for the first time, said: 'I was horrified because I thought he looked rather like a bovver boy. I said hello to Jason Mitchell and he smiled. I thought that he had a lovely smile and very nice blue eyes and a soft gentle voice.' All were unanimous in the view that Jason Mitchell did not present as a mentally ill person.

During June and July, conference reports were positive. 'At present the placement at Larkhill going well. No problems at present' (8 June 1994). 'Appear to be no concerns or complaints and is doing well' (20 July 1994).

Concerns about the placement *were*, however, beginning to be expressed. On 17 July the mother of a resident had complained about Jason Mitchell's threatening behaviour towards herself and her husband. On a visit to her son she had picked up some mail and asked Jason Mitchell and her son 'Why don't you pick your papers up?' Jason Mitchell, who had been drawing a picture, leapt up and stood at the bottom of the stairs displaying ugly looks to the parents of his fellow resident. He forbade the parents to come into the house without first ringing the bell. The resident's mother said, 'I did not say anything because Jason Mitchell looked so nasty, his eyes were very odd-looking.' She and her husband left the house, but needed to return, at which point Jason Mitchell said: 'How dare you come in; you did not knock. How dare you come in, get out.' She said, 'he waved his arms at me and was very threatening. I was very frightened.' She concluded her statement by saying 'Jason Mitchell had a strong personality. At first he was polite and courteous and nice. He was also very articulate. I think that Jason Mitchell had behavioural problems and could bamboozle someone into doing whatever he wanted them to.'

In early July the social worker was recording that Jason Mitchell was being awkward, upsetting the other residents and finding it hard to get on with a staff member, although at the case review in August everything was going well. By mid-August Jason Mitchell was telling his social worker that he wanted to move on to more independent accommodation. He was wanting to normalise his existence and found the idiosyncrasies of his fellow residents difficult to take. This was reported at a case review on 17 August. By the end of August he was less insistent in his view that he wanted to move on.

Staff too were finding Jason Mitchell less likeable. The staff member who had the best rapport with him said: 'Towards the end of his stay he became very difficult to talk to ... there was a marked difference in the way that Jason Mitchell was behaving. One minute he would be very charming, the next he would just shut off .... I would not say that he presented as being bizarre, although sometimes he would say one thing, and when we joined in the conversation he would claim that we had said something which we had not.' This behaviour was reflected in his relationship with the other project worker who said: 'His behaviour was unpredictable. One minute he was very friendly and he would then clam up and in the next minute he would be rude. He was not a very nice person to know.'

Residents describe exactly similar behaviour, and by August/September one resident was saying: 'I became more and more frightened and complained to [the staff] who suggested that I turn my room into a bedsit and lock myself in. This is what I did. I became too frightened even to leave the room and was afraid even to go to the bathroom upstairs and adjacent to my room.' This resident, when we met him privately with another resident, said: 'I was deeply frightened, fear, deep in my guts.' It seems that this was not fear of physical violence. It was nevertheless a deep fear, inspired by Jason Mitchell's unpredictable and intimidating behaviour.

The project worker was also feeling intimidated. She shared her feelings with her supervisor, and with Jason Mitchell's social worker. The Housing Services Manager also discussed these concerns prompted by a further letter from a resident's mother complaining that Jason Mitchell had persuaded her son to accept responsibility for the payments for a guitar which Jason Mitchell had purchased and a letter from the other resident who was frightened. Since Jason Mitchell was also expressing the desire to move on, it was decided not to renew his tenancy, since 'we did not feel that the Larkhill Way project was the most ideal placement for him and that he would be better placed in a more independent, probably self-contained situation where it was not necessary for him to share with other people who were vulnerable'. Jason Mitchell was informed by letter on 20 September, although it was made clear that he would not have to move out until he had somewhere else to go.

In early September Jason Mitchell visited the local police station at Felixstowe ostensibly to confess to a crime but did not pursue his undisclosed purpose. The police found no reason to pursue it. His motivation remains obscure.

During October the social worker was focusing on finding an alternative placement for Jason Mitchell and was expressing concern about the potential isolation which independent living arrangements could cause. This concern was communicated to, and shared by Dr Goddard.

On 2 November 1994 the project worker rang the social worker, saying that the situation in the house was very worrying, Jason Mitchell was intimidating the residents who understandably were frightened. The project worker did not want these concerns to be shared with Jason Mitchell. The social worker visited with the project worker. Jason Mitchell did not acknowledge any problems and it was difficult to confront him with the fact in the light of the project worker's wishes.

On 4 November, an incident occurred where, following an argument Jason Mitchell 'tapped' (the resident's word) another resident lightly on the head with a small hammer. We have seen the hammer. It was in fact not as fearsome an instrument as its name implies. It was the kind used for striking a bell, or for piano-tuning. The resident went to his room, but the project worker was very concerned and contacted the project manager. They sought to contact the social worker who, as a part-time worker, was not available, but established contact with both the out-of-hours social worker and the psychiatrist (Dr Hanna) responsible for offering support to the project, on duty in Dr Goddard's absence. Both advised contacting the GP, but the project workers felt that Jason Mitchell would present his reasonable self. They felt that they did not have evidence to support a hospital admission. Ultimately, since the other residents were not at the project they decided, reluctantly, to leave the matter over the weekend. When contacted, Dr Goddard immediately agreed to see Jason Mitchell and arranged his re-admission to Easton House for social reasons and not on clinical grounds.

Conclusions

Given the facilities for housing accommodation available in East Suffolk, the MIND shared accommodation at Larkhill (which we have visited) was not ideal, but it was as good as could conceivably be found at the time. Efforts had been made, but had failed to find a place for Jason Mitchell in a therapeutic environment. Other options had been sought, unavailingly. Larkhill was the next best alternative. We do not think that there was a lack of information exchanged between the relevant workers. Once the decision had been made that Jason Mitchell was suitable for the shared accommodation, we do not think that there was any shortfall in the degree of support for the residents. Everyone from whom we have heard spoke favourably of the MIND project. There was nothing untoward in the placement. Prompt and appropriate action was taken when it became clear that Jason Mitchell was not fitting in.

XVI. Return to Easton House, November 1994

How dull it is to pause, to make an end,
To rust unburnished, not to shine in use!
as tho' to breathe were life.
            Tennyson, *Ulysses*

Dr Goddard arranged for Jason Mitchell's re-admission to Easton House on 8 November 1994 as an informal patient. He noted that

> Jason has fallen out with the other two residents such that they have moved out. Project leader very worried about the situation and possibly intimidated (like everyone else in the Project) by Jason.

Jason Mitchell's status on re-admission to the secure unit was that of a voluntary patient. He was seen to have been admitted solely on social grounds but was expected to conform to the house rules. He remained a conditionally discharged restricted patient.

It is interesting to note this was the third occasion on which Jason Mitchell had been returned from a less secure to a more secure setting because of disagreeable behaviour towards staff or other residents and that on two occasions the reason for re-admission had not been openly addressed with Jason Mitchell.

In Chapter III, Dr Yeldham is quoted as listing symptoms which emerged when Jason Mitchell was medication free which she took to be indicative of psychotic illness. Some of these were evident in Jason Mitchell's behaviour at Larkhill Way. For example, his very disturbed sleep pattern, meditating, a deterioration in his behaviour and communication pattern with staff, preoccupation with religious matters and talking about religious themes including devils (the reference at Larkhill Way was to witchcraft). She also referred to a distinct change in the way he dressed and the care with which he dressed. These two features were not observed at Larkhill Way. These behaviours had also been present to some extent at Easton House and were not interpreted in the same way. Jane Barnett had indicated in evidence that she would have found it helpful to have had some advice about symptoms of recurring mental illness. Given the Easton House view of his condition, a list like Dr Yeldham's would not have been available to her, but it does support the view that such advice would be of assistance to social supervisors.

The admitting doctor said that Jason Mitchell was unco-operative and in a reactive silly mood. Jason Mitchell claimed not to know why he had returned and could not say anything about it. Indeed, the doctor records, 'Patient is very resistant to disclose what happened between him and these 2 residents – last admitted in 3/93 because of threatening behaviour towards someone(?) since then patient says he was able to control himself.' A drug screen was arranged and he was admitted for observation. The nursing staff too found him visibly hostile and uncommunicative. The following day staff noted that he had settled well on the ward.

There is little evidence of any analysis of the reasons behind the breakdown of the placement. The reason given for his admission as set out in the Admission Assessment is: 'Admitted so that we may find more suitable accommodation', and notes that he was admitted 'informally following an altercation with two other residents such that they moved out'. The Emergency Care Plan set out three tasks:

a) discreet observation;
b) contractual rules to be observed;
c) adherence to house rules, e.g. times for getting up, attending meals, telling staff of whereabouts (drug screen to be done tomorrow).

No link is established with the problematic final Care Plan, nor is there a breakdown review meeting, as set out in the Discharge and Care Programme Approach Policy Statement which at 11 states, 'where a discharge is deemed "unsatisfactory" a copy of all documents will be forwarded to the Quality Co-ordinator who will compile separate reports for the Management Team'. In June 1994, a jointly signed policy on the discharge of persons from psychiatric hospitals had been published by the Suffolk Social Services Department and the East Suffolk Local Health Services Trust. This commendable document, which deals thoroughly with the withdrawal or cessation of the Care Programme states: 'in the event of the person concerned being re-admitted to hospital, the multi-professional team must decide if this requires a temporary suspension of the Care Programme or the end of the programme on the grounds that the person is no longer in need of the services provided.'

The case conference record of 30 November states simply 'Problem Rehousing: Both agencies are aware that clearer guidance is needed on the analysis of breakdowns and we are pleased to note that this work is well in hand.'

Dr Hanna noted on 11 November that Jason Mitchell was claiming to be able to control himself. He was 'calm, cooperative, but prefers to keep certain issues for himself esp. his family relationships'. The nursing notes say, 'He remained very anti staff.' During the next week Jason Mitchell was referred to as, 'his usual contrary, arrogant, self centred self' and on 15 November staff remarked that he was using the place like a hotel.

Jason Mitchell had discussions with his social worker and the housing officer about accommodation on 16 November and he also requested a move to Linkways, the rehabilitation ward.

Suffolk Housing had been approached around the beginning of November by one of the other residents at Larkhill Way who was seeking help as he felt threatened by Jason Mitchell. The housing officer visited Larkhill Way and asked the staff to arrange for Jason Mitchell to get in touch with her. She next heard from Jason Mitchell's social worker requesting housing for Jason Mitchell.

After the discussions on 16 November and after thorough exploration as to why Jason Mitchell had left Larkhill Way and about details of the level of support which Social Services could offer, the housing officer made an offer of a one bedroomed house on 24 November. A detailed discussion took place at a case conference on 30 November. Jason Mitchell was offered the one bedroomed house or a one bedroomed flat. He preferred the latter. A further property was located in a more suitable area and this too was offered, but by then Jason Mitchell had gone missing.

The housing authority staff behaved with commendable speed and thoroughness and with practical offers of assistance which it would be hard to match in any of the authorities known to us.

We asked how such accommodation could have been considered appropriate given the starting point of a therapeutic community. Jane Barnett's notes confirm that she was anxious that Jason Mitchell should not be moved on from Larkhill Way until the right package of care had been found to meet his needs. She discussed with Jason Mitchell the potential isolation, a concern which she and Dr Goddard, shared and Jason Mitchell agreed that he would need support. The conference which was held on 30 November agreed that no move would take place until a support arrangement which would supply daily cover to meet Jason Mitchell's needs for emotional, psychological and social support from a male support worker was in place. This had already been set out as an objective in the earlier Social Services Care Plan dated 2 November 1994.

Towards the end of November staff were noting that Jason Mitchell was polite but he was also disruptive towards other patients. On 2 December Dr Hanna saw him as he was complaining of hot flushes and cold sweating. Jason Mitchell said that he had suffered these attacks on and off since 1988, about five or six times a month and that they lasted for about half an hour. Dr Hanna stated in evidence that he eliminated panic attacks and anxiety, thyrotoxicosis and drugs as possible causes. He recommended that Jason Mitchell be kept under observation. Nursing records note that Jason Mitchell had not complained of his attacks, indeed that evening he appeared very relaxed.

There was some concern about Jason Mitchell's association with another patient who was known to have access to drugs, and at Dr Goddard's suggestion Jason Mitchell was told of the danger that this presented to his conditional discharge and the possibility of recall.

In their evidence nursing staff remembered Jason Mitchell being helpful and pleasant while decorating the ward for Christmas. The last person to see Jason Mitchell at Easton House was a staff nurse who wrote on 12 December, 'he looked very smart when he came to the office door that evening and I commented on this. He smiled warmly and thanked me. He looked as if he was ready for a party or some other festive social gathering of which there were various going on at the time in the days leading up to Christmas. He then said "I'm just going out for a while for a short walk, is that OK?" That was the last time I saw Jason Mitchell.'

Jason Mitchell then left the ward, as he was entitled to do.

Part H

Miscellany

XVII. Missing Patients Procedure and Police Activity

And if we do but watch the hour,
There never yet was human power
Which could evade, if unforgiven,
The patient search and vigil long
Of him who treasures up a wrong.
                              Byron, *Mazeppa*, stanza 10

For more than 20 years there has been in place at St Clement's Hospital a policy and procedure for dealing with patients who leave the hospital grounds without leave of absence. Through their established and regular relationship with the local police force, the managers of the hospital have operated a system of alerting the police who in turn undertake to search for, and, where the legal power exists, to return to hospital, any missing patient. East Suffolk Local Health Services NHS Trust's Missing Patient Policy of April 1995 (a revised version of an earlier policy document, itself revised in August 1995) states:

The Missing Patient

All patients are our direct responsibility and a high degree of care must be exercised in order to ensure their safety and welfare.

At all times the whereabouts of all patients should be known to the nurse in charge and the care team. In the case of patients on an outing the person in charge of the group takes responsibility.

Meal-times, medicine-rounds, and hand-over periods must be used as times to check patients' whereabouts.

Absent patients may be considered under two categories as follows:

Category A
Any patient considered a risk to self; a danger to others; and those formally detained under the Mental Health Act 1983. This includes young persons under the age of sixteen years.

Category B
Any patient of Informal status, but not considered at risk to self or a danger to others.

All members of staff must report to the Nurse in charge of the ward immediately they believe that a patient is missing.

Any request for publicity to be referred to the on-call Senior Manager.

Action to be taken by Nurse in Charge of Ward

1. Determine when and where patient was last seen.

2. Ensure that patient is really absent without consent and has not, for example, been given permission to leave the ward.

3. Search ward and annexes, enquire of other wards and departments.

4. Discuss with Duty Doctor – consider physical and mental condition of the patient (age, gender, confused, frail, suicidal, danger to self or others, etc.).

5. Take into consideration the prevailing weather conditions.

6. Take into consideration the time of day or night.

7. Inform Duty Directorate Manager of relevant details.

8. Commence Missing Patient Action Record (Form MP1).

9. Complete Missing Patient Forms: Personal Details & Description (Form MP2); Other Details (Form MP3).

10. Ensure that full details are communicated to incoming staff at hand-over times.

11. Ensure that the completed record documents are placed in the patient's record.

12. Ensure that copies of the completed record are sent to Medical Records Officer & Quality Co-ordinator.

Action to be taken by Duty Directorate Manager

1. Discuss situation with Nurse in Charge of Ward.

2. Delegate staff to search immediate ward precincts and establish that the patient is not on another ward, or in other internal areas, or in hospital grounds.

3. If patient is not found, agree with Nurse in Charge of Ward that missing patient process be continued, and under which Category (A or B), and ensure regular reviews.

4. Ensure that full details are communicated at hand-over times.

5. If the situation appears serious to the degree that senior managers may need to be involved in the decision-making process, the on-call Duty Senior Manager must be informed as soon as possible. In less urgent situations, and in all cases, the Operational Services Manager must be informed at the earliest convenience during normal working hours.

Patients missing when on outings

1. The person in charge of the group should arrange a search of the immediate area.
2. Contact base for advice.
3. Contact the Police for assistance.
4. Ensure the safety of the remaining patients.

Action to be taken on return of patient

1. Patient should be examined by Medical Officer as soon as possible after return.
2. Action Record (Form MP1) must be concluded by Nurse in Charge of Ward.
3. All relevant parties must be informed of outcomes.
4. All records including Nursing and Medical Notes, Day/Night Reports, must be completed. A review of the incident must take place involving all relevant disciplines as soon as practicably possible.

The missing patient procedure was initiated by Staff Nurse Angelina Cracknell, on night duty, together with the acting Clinical Night Manager for St Clement's Hospital, Mrs P. Pitcher, within a few hours of Jason Mitchell leaving Easton House on the night of 9/10 December. The police response, in accordance with agreed procedures, was immediate. The circumstances under which the absence of Jason Mitchell was communicated to the two police officers who arrived to take particulars that night will be described fully hereafter.

Earlier absconding: before 9 December 1994

As a young offender, Jason Mitchell was well known to police officers in Ipswich. Detective Constable Paul Royal, the officer who finally arrested and charged Jason Mitchell with the three murders, described how over the early 1980s he had seen Jason Mitchell climb the ladder of juvenile offending, beginning with truancy from school and progressing through petty theft and burglary to robbery. But from 1988 onwards Jason Mitchell was either in institutions of one sort or another, or away from his home area.

From May 1993, however, when Jason Mitchell transferred to his home area, from West Park Hospital, Epsom, to Easton House, St Clement's Hospital, Ipswich, until the third week of December 1994, he came to the notice of the Suffolk Police, reported as a missing patient from St Clement's, but not in connection with any criminal investigation.

On three separate occasions the procedure for tracing Jason Mitchell when missing from the hospital was put into play. Each time, a member of the hospital staff telephoned Ipswich Police Station, and officers put into effect their own missing persons procedure. This requires the police to attend the hospital and obtain full details for circulation on a form which includes a detailed description, the circumstances under which the patient went missing, any likely addresses which may be visited, and any other information which might assist in tracing the missing person.

Jason Mitchell was first reported missing on *29 December 1993* at 7.46 am, having last been seen at 1.15 am. In the initial call to police Jason Mitchell was described as 'on Section 37/41, arrestable ... may be heading for 11 Acton Road, Bramford, his father's home where he had been brought up as a child'. The police acted swiftly. By 8.09 am an officer had called at Robert Mitchell's home at 11 Acton Road, but there was no reply. On the form which an officer completed at the hospital at about 9 am, both Jason Mitchell's father's address and that of a girlfriend were shown as places Jason Mitchell might be likely to visit. Shortly after 10 am Jason Mitchell returned of his own accord to the hospital ward.

The second absence was lengthier. On *17 February 1994* at 7 am Ipswich police were told that Jason Mitchell was missing, having been seen last by staff at 4 am. That original message mentioned 11 Acton Road, but the reference was noted, 'unlikely to visit'. The subsequently completed form mentioned 'potentially violent, drugs, solvent abuse'. 'PNC' (Police National Computer) showed 'violent, escaper, drugs, mental'. Again, Jason Mitchell's father and girlfriend were shown as contact addresses. The progress report on which the enquiry was updated showed that several attempts were made by the police to see Robert Mitchell, but it was not until 2 March 1994 that an officer finally spoke to him. Jason Mitchell's father said that he had not seen his son recently, but that if Jason Mitchell did appear he would persuade him to return to the hospital and inform the police.

The progress report also showed that on 19 February the police were told by Easton House staff that 'Mitchell is a Category A patient under sections 37 & 41 [of the Mental Health Act 1983]. If found, return to Easton House.' This mention of Category A caused some confusion, to which we shall allude hereafter. At Easton

House it merely indicated that, if found, the patient should be brought back (as distinct from Category B, when patients should be asked to return voluntarily). To the police this categorisation indicated a dangerous escaper who would resort to extreme violence to maintain his liberty. It has been in constant use by the penal system in respect of prisoners, ever since the escape of George Blake in 1966, the initial categorisation being made by the police when the prisoner is first taken into custody on arrest.

At about 5 pm on 4 March 1994, Jason Mitchell was arrested by Cheshire police officers, who found him attempting to hitch-hike at a service area on the M6 motorway near Warrington. Apart from saying that he had been visiting friends, he declined to discuss the events of the past two weeks. He presented no obstacle to being returned to St Clement's by ambulance on the following day. He gave no explanation to hospital staff why he had absconded.

Eight days later, on *12 March 1994*, Jason Mitchell again absented himself from Easton House, just after 2 pm. Much of the information subsequently obtained by the police was identical to the details shown on the two earlier forms, but on this occasion, although 11 Acton Road was shown as the address of Jason Mitchell's father, it was omitted from the section on 'likely to be visited'. In fact, during the ten days which ensued before Jason Mitchell voluntarily returned to the ward (at 10.30 pm on 22 March 1994) police officers did not call there. The officers were doubtless influenced by a report on the enquiry progress form, which stated that Robert Mitchell had told police on a previous occasion that he had not seen his son for eight or nine years. If Jason Mitchell is to be believed, he had in fact spent his entire period of absence living with his father. This is what he told hospital staff. On none of the three occasions was Jason Mitchell ever interviewed by the police following these periods of absence. Police forces might contemplate adopting a procedure for inquiring about the circumstances of repeated abscondings by detained patients and in particular restricted patients. **We so recommend**.

9/10 December 1994

Shortly before midnight on Friday 9 December 1994, the night staff nurse on duty noted that she had been instructed by the nurse in charge to take action if Jason Mitchell did not return by 11.30 pm. Jason Mitchell had not returned to Easton House. She alerted the acting clinical night manager, Mrs Pitcher, and together they decided to implement the missing patients procedure. Since they were unaware of Jason Mitchell's whereabouts, of his lack of accommodation and of his history of illicit drug/alcohol abuse and glue-sniffing activities, they placed him in Category A – a patient considered to be a risk to himself or a danger to others. The log sheet for that night discloses as much.

LOG SHEET ... Friday   DATE 9th-10th
                                                DEC 1994

SITE MANAGER	FIRE OFFICER	PATIENTS A.W.O.L	WARD
		Jason Mitchell Cat 'A' Easton I	

NIGHT: P. Pitcher N. Duf

WARD	PROBLEMS OF NOTE, ADMISSIONS, UNTOWARD OCCURRENCES

Easton I Jason Mitchell – Inf – failed to return from evening out. Cat A missing patient implemented at 12 mn. No further news at present. Please inform Admin this am.

The log sheet for the following day (Saturday 10 December) again recorded Jason Mitchell as being absent without leave, 'Cat A' and noted 'Easton I: J. Mitchell. Remains A.W.O.L. Cat A. No further information available.' The log sheets for Sunday 11/12 December and for Monday 12/13 December still recorded Jason Mitchell as a Category A missing patient. Thereafter, until he was noted on 20/21 December as being 'in police custody', Jason Mitchell was recorded as being 'A.W.O.L.', uncategorised. Nowhere in the hospital records was he ever recorded as Category B ('not considered at risk to self or a danger to others').

Just after 1 am on 10 December two police officers came to Easton House. Mrs Cracknell recalls the officers commenting to the effect that the risk element in Jason Mitchell's case would not have been present had it not been for his illicit drug-taking, to which Staff Nurse Cracknell insisted that there was more to it than that, given Jason Mitchell's record of violence in the past and his unpredictable behavioural problems. She had no doubt that his was a Category A case, and that there was no question of any down-grading within the Missing Patients Procedure. Mrs Pitcher, in a written statement to the Inquiry, does not remember any discussion or indeed mention of treating Jason Mitchell as Category B status.

Superintendent Worobec told the Inquiry that the under-standing of the police officers who relayed the information back to their colleagues was that Jason Mitchell was in effect a Category B missing patient because he was not a restricted patient under sections 37 and 41 of the Mental Health Act 1983. Hence, in the minds of the police, there may have been a lessening in the urgency to find Jason Mitchell as a missing patient than if he had been treated as a restricted patient. At least that was the police attitude until Jason Mitchell became a suspect in the criminal investigation of the homicides of Mr and Mrs Wilson on or shortly after 14 December.

It is clear that Staff Nurse Cracknell and Mrs Pitcher told the officer who took the initial report on the night of 9/10 December that Jason Mitchell was, in the unfortunate terminology of the hospital categorisation, in Category A. The police report, however, subsequently noted that 'Mitchell is not Cat A as suggested by staff when they initially called. He is lodging at Easton House awaiting a placing to a community home.' In the space on the form for 'Any other information' the word 'INFORMAL' has been inserted. How and when this information came to be written on the form we do not know and have not sought to ascertain. It seemed to us to be an idle exercise since the misunderstanding (if there was one) of Jason Mitchell's status mattered not at all. There was in fact an immediate police search for him. That the police did not discover Jason Mitchell's whereabouts is, with hindsight, a matter of deep regret. Why the police did not find him at his father's house in the hours and days following the alert of 9/10 December is a matter to which we now turn. The misunderstanding may have arisen because the Missing Patients Procedure inadequately provided for co-ordinated documentation between hospital and police. We think the provisions for tracing patients absent without leave need reviewing and possible revision. We comment on this in Chapter XXII.

The police search, 10 December 1994 and after

Within hours of the information that Jason Mitchell was a missing patient the police took steps to trace him, calling on his former girlfriend at 10.30 am on 10 December. She told the police what she had told them on two previous occasions when they had called on her looking for Jason Mitchell, that she had not seen him for six months, and had no desire to do so.

For the next five days police action in the missing patient enquiry was confined to briefing various officers at the start of their shifts, and responding to an updating enquiry from St Clement's. By mid-week Jason Mitchell was being mentioned in a more intensive police investigation. The interest in Jason Mitchell had switched from assistance to mental health services to investigation of a major homicide.

At 1.35 am on Wednesday 14 December 1994 police officers, who had been alerted by worried friends and relatives, broke into 112 The Street, Bramford. They found the dead bodies of the owners, Arthur and Shirley Wilson. A murder enquiry under Detective Superintendent Peter Worobec was established, which initially concentrated on a meticulous forensic examination of the Wilsons' home. As information began to come into the enquiry team, actions were allocated to officers and various lines of enquiry pursued.

Acton Road, Bramford is adjacent to The Street, a short distance from number 112. Although the former was Jason Mitchell's 'home address', he did not become a suspect in the enquiry at this stage, even when a local resident who had known Jason Mitchell since early school-days heard of the killings and considered the fact that she had seen him on 13 December in Bramford with 'a silly smirk on his face', worth reporting to the police. Her statement was taken on 14 December, one of the first in the murder enquiry.

On 15 December Detective Constable Paul Royal and another officer called on Robert Mitchell at 11 Acton Road. They took a written statement from him, which showed that Jason Mitchell had come straight to his father's home after leaving Easton House on the night of 9/10 December, and that father and son had spent the weekend together. Jason Mitchell had left home around noon on Monday 12 December, saying that he was returning to Easton

House. His father was aware that Jason Mitchell had no money with him. DC Royal told us that Robert Mitchell assured the officers that if Jason Mitchell returned he would contact the police. Mr Mitchell handed the officer two Red Band cigarettes, a highly significant piece of forensic evidence. A Red Band cigarette stub had been found in the Wilsons' bungalow; neither of them smoked. The stub was forwarded to a specialist laboratory, but DNA examination eventually proved inconclusive.

The call at 11 Acton Road was logged by DC Royal on the Missing Person progress report sheet. On the same day his colleague PC Humphreys telephoned Easton House to ask staff to notify police if there was any news of Jason Mitchell. On 16 December, a nurse on the staff of Easton House saw Jason Mitchell in Argyle Street, close to the centre of Ipswich, and telephoned Easton House. According to the police progress report, it was an hour later that they were notified. The progress sheet also shows 'murder incident room updated' and there is a reference to 'CID checking public houses in area'. Jason Mitchell remained untraced. At 2.20 pm on the same day, police telephoned Easton House and requested that, if Jason Mitchell returned, they be notified immediately. Shortly afterwards they again telephoned and asked that Jason Mitchell should not be informed of the 'police interest'. The officers making these enquiries were shown in the nursing notes as DC Royal and PC Humphreys.

What the police did not do at this stage was to give any publicity to their wish to interview Jason Mitchell. DC Royal asserted that 'there was nothing to put to him' at this point, but it is clear that the police were trying to find him in order, as Superintendent Worobec put it, 'to implicate or eliminate' Jason Mitchell from the murder investigation. After Jason Mitchell had been charged, an artist's impression appeared in a local newspaper and was immediately identified by the owner of a local guest-house where Jason Mitchell had unsuccessfully sought lodging on the afternoon of 14 December. With striking tattoos of a snake on his cheek and a crucifix on his forehead, this thin six feet three inches tall man could reasonably be expected to have been quickly identified. Indeed, the mere mention of his name would have led to him being traced, when he was seen by several people in Bramford who knew him well.

After the mention of the sighting in Argyle Street, the progress report for the Missing Person enquiry showed an updated description and various briefings for officers coming on duty, with a record of an unproductive visit to his sister. The final entry is for 18 December and records, 'late shift reminded'.

If the police were by now seeking to interview Jason Mitchell as actively as records would indicate, it is surprising that they did not consider it necessary to revisit Robert Mitchell, although his home was only about one hundred yards from where the police mobile incident vehicle was parked, opposite the Wilsons' bungalow. Jason Mitchell had returned there by Saturday 17 December. A witness subsequently told police he had seen Jason Mitchell and his father in Acton Road.

Whatever was being done by the murder enquiry team, since 14 December there had been a continuing and painstaking search of the Wilson home, including the garden and their car, for forensic evidence, particularly latent fingerprint impressions. The two Scenes of Crime Officers principally concerned used a variety of techniques to make some impressions which they found suitable for photographing and hence for comparison. These included some found on 14 December which could not be photographed until 19 December, after chemical treatments had been effective.

All the marks found were compared by an expert in the Suffolk Police fingerprint bureau on 20 December. At about 3 pm a number were identified as having been made by Jason Mitchell. This information was passed to Superintendent Worobec. A decision was taken to release publicly Jason Mitchell's name and description as being someone whom the police urgently wanted to interview in connection with the deaths of Arthur and Shirley Wilson. A press release was given out.

After 5 pm police officers were sent to 11 Acton Road, Bramford. It was DC Royal who broke in with other officers to find Jason Mitchell sitting in the darkened house, with his father's dismembered torso in the bedroom.

Conclusion

It has been no part of the Inquiry's remit or task to look at anything relative to the criminal investigations into the triple homicide that began with the discovery of the bodies of Mr and Mrs Wilson in the early hours of Wednesday 14 December. The Inquiry's task was to examine the functioning of the Missing Patients Procedure at St Clement's Hospital and to determine the relationship of mental health services to police responsibility for mentally disordered persons in the Community.

Nothing that the Inquiry has heard indicates anything other than full compliance with existing procedures by hospital authorities and police force for effecting a ready return to hospital of those who should not be allowed to be in the community and, if and where necessary, returned to detention in hospital. That is not to say that the present procedures do not need tightening. Clearly, the respective roles of hospital management and chief officers of police need to be clearly defined, understood and properly implemented. To that issue we shall return in Chapter XXII.

ANNEX TO CHAPTER XVII

Jason Mitchell's known movements, 9-20 December 1994

Fri. 9.12.94	Leaves Easton House by 7.30 pm. Reported missing as a Cat 'A' to police at 00.10, 10.12.94. Police telex shows 'Objection to publicity – Y'. Missing Persons Form shows 'Drugs – Violent'.
	Jason Mitchell arrives at father's home, 11 Acton Road at 'about 7 pm'.
Sat. 10.12.94	Stays at 11 Acton Road.
Sun. 11.12.94	– ditto –
	Trip out 7.15 pm for 15 mins to buy Old Holborn tobacco. Ran after 2 girls briefly.
Mon. 12.12.94	Leaves home at noon. Had no money. Father gave him 2 'Red Band' cigarettes.
	Between 4.30 pm and 5.15 pm kills the Wilsons.
	5.15 pm seen to run from their address.
	5.30 pm – 6.30 pm arrives at Bosmere Guest House, Ipswich. Pays.
Tues. 13.12.94	Leaves Guest House before 5.45 am.
	About 8.25 am seen in Paper Mill Lane, Bramford, near father's address. Smiling unnaturally.
	About 12.30 pm seen in River Hill, Bramford. 'Silly smile.'
Wed. 14.12.94	1.35 am police force entry to the Wilsons' address, 112 The Street, Bramford and find them dead. Red Band cigarette found.
	About 7.15 am seen in Whitton Layers, Bramford.
	About 8.30 am seen walking from Whitton Layers.
	10.00 am –10.15 am seen on Whitton Layers.
	10.25 am possible sighting in Paper Mill Lane, Bramford. Witness's house subsequently burgled. £60 cash stolen.

	About 12 noon, called at The Beeches Guest House, Ipswich (no vacancies).
	About 12 noon. Books room for one male at Bosmere Hotel, Norwich Road, Ipswich. Pays £15.
Thurs. 15.12.94	Robert Mitchell seen. Statement taken.
	7.45 am, 9.30 am, 3.00 pm, 4.30 pm. In the Bosemere Hotel. Paid further £15. Puts something in a rubbish bin. Very restless, could not sit still. Stays overnight but does not have breakfast.
Fri. 16.12.94	No longer in Bosmere Hotel. 1.00 pm and 1.20 pm seen in Woodbridge Road, Ipswich by Staff Nurse. Missing Person's Report states that Davis reported this to police 1 hour later. Shows 'Murder incident room updated', 'Late shift reminded'.
Sat. 17.12.94	Seen with father at 2.30 pm in Acton Road, Bramford.
Sun. 18.12.94	Jason Mitchell kills his father.
Mon. 19.12.94	5.30-5.40 pm seen to leave the house, but otherwise apparently stays inside.
Tues. 20.12.94	1.00-2.00pm noises like furniture moving heard from 11 Acton Road.
	5.30 pm police force entry to 11 Acton Road and arrest Jason Mitchell.

XVIII. Appropriate Adult in Action

– if it be established that a man's mind is such that he would be incapable of understanding the nature of the proceedings, he should not be put on his trial and convicted for the offence: such a conviction could not stand – it is not merely defects of the mind which may bring about that result. Defects of the senses, whether or not combined with some defect of the mind, may bring about that result ....

Mr Justice (later Lord) Devlin in
R v. *Roberts* [1954] 2 QB 329

When Dr Paul Bowden reported on 21 June 1995 to the Crown Court on the mental state of Jason Mitchell (he had examined him at Norwich Prison on 1 June 1995) he wrote:

I am concerned at Mr Mitchell's fitness to plead but believe this aspect should be addressed shortly before the trial .... I believe that Mr Mitchell's illness affects his mind in all its activities including his judgment.

The trial effectively took place at the pre-trial hearing on 7 July 1995 when Jason Mitchell pleaded guilty to manslaughter on the grounds of his diminished responsibility. He was given three life sentences and passed into the prison system. Within four days he was transferred to Rampton Special Hospital, where he has remained. Should Jason Mitchell have been diverted from the criminal process before 7 July and hospitalised as being unfit to plead?

The question whether a person is unfit to plead is usually determined (if at all) on arraignment, i.e. the moment when he is asked to plead to the indictment. But it can be raised at any time by the prosecution, defence or the court. Where the question arises whether the accused is under a disability which would be a bar to his being tried, under the law since 1991 the court may have regard to the nature of the supposed disability and may postpone the question of fitness to plead until any time up to the opening of the defence. There was no need to postpone the issue in Jason Mitchell's case since his guilty plea concluded the trial. If Jason Mitchell's fitness to plead was 'addressed' by any of the three actors in the criminal process, it does not appear to have emerged as a

matter to be considered by the court. An accused's solicitor potentially can raise the issue. The Royal Commission on Criminal
Justice (the Runciman Commission) states that duty solicitors
should be involved as far as possible in consultations between police
surgeons, suspects, and the psychiatrist (CM2263, 8 July 1993,
para 92 p. 45), but it said nothing about how any issue relating to
fitness to plead should be raised. It may be that an accused,
misperceiving his own fitness, gives his legal representatives instructions not to raise the matter, for good or bad reasons. In which
case the legal representative is probably bound to obey the client's
instructions, whatever may be his own thinking. If the defence is
content not to raise the issue of fitness to plead, why should the
prosecution raise the matter? A guilty plea to manslaughter would
more than adequately ensure a disposal, whether to prison or to
hospital, that would provide the public safety. Given muteness
from the Bar, the judge would feel justified in accepting the fact
that there was no bar to a trial on the grounds of the accused's
fitness to plead. In the adversarial system of criminal justice there
could be no quarrel with that attitude and outcome. But is it a
satisfactory way of dealing with a mentally disordered offender?

From the moment that Jason Mitchell was taken into police
custody it was obvious that he was mentally disordered. Within
three hours of his arrival at Ipswich Police Station the Custody
Officer had called for the presence of an Appropriate Adult. Mr
Jonathan Eckersley, an Approved Social Worker, arrived at the
Police Station, qualifying to assist Jason Mitchell as 'someone who
has experience of dealing with mentally disordered or mentally
handicapped persons but is not a police officer employed by the
police'.

The requirement for an Appropriate Adult is to ensure that
vulnerable individuals do not make admissions which are inher-
ently false. The Code of Practice under the Police and Criminal
Evidence Act 1984 (PACE) requires that the Appropriate Adult
should be told by the police that he or she is not acting simply as
an observer. The Code provides:

> The purposes of his presence are, first, to advise the person being
> questioned and to observe whether or not the interview is being
> conducted properly and fairly, and secondly, to facilitate communi-
> cation with the person being interviewed.

It is important that those who act as an Appropriate Adult are fully aware of their responsibilities. Mr Eckersley, who attended from a quarter to nine in the evening on 20 December until a quarter to one in the morning of 21 December, was present during an interview which Jason Mitchell had with his solicitor, Mr Craig Marchant; a medical examination conducted by Dr Goddard; a police inspector's review of the case; and an interview by detective officers lasting only three minutes at which Jason Mitchell made no comment. Mr Eckersley well understood his role, including, if necessary, intervening in the process. He said he found no cause at any time to intervene. He was asked specifically whether, if there was a question in his mind of the unfitness of a suspect to be questioned, he would intervene in that situation. To which he replied:

> I would. I think that would certainly be a matter that I would be discussing with the doctor – since at that stage Jason Mitchell appeared in the course of the psychiatric assessment to be calm and polite and answered the questions put to him there was nothing to arouse suspicion of any incapacity on Jason Mitchell's part to under- stand what was being said to him and to suspend appropriately. Dr Goddard, moreover, was not diagnosing any mental disorder.

At midday on 21 December 1994 Mr Robert Buxton, another Approved Social Worker, was present at Ipswich Police Station to act as the Appropriate Adult. He attended a further medical exami- nation by the police surgeon and later two reviews of the case by a police superintendent and an inspector. He also attended a half- hour interview at which Jason Mitchell made no comment. Whether or not it was Mr Buxton's function to be present as the Appropriate Adult, he remained throughout the psychiatric exami- nation conducted by Dr Ball, a forensic psychiatrist from the Norvic Clinic at Norwich, who was called in by Jason Mitchell's solicitor. Mr Buxton took no part in that process, but remained silently as an observer. No question arose at that stage of Jason Mitchell's fitness to plead, although Dr Ball was concluding that Jason Mitchell was exhibiting psychotic symptoms.

Since Dr Ball was carrying out his examination at the behest of the defence solicitor and was, therefore, not observing whether or not an interview with police officers was being conducted properly or fairly, Mr Buxton was strictly acting outside his prescribed functions. But the fact that Mr Buxton felt that his presence might be helpful in protecting the rights and interests of Jason Mitchell discloses perhaps the need for a wider role to be accorded the Appropriate Adult. May it not be that in the case of mentally disordered persons, a person neutral to the criminal process and independent of both the police and defence could perform the function of acting whenever there is a question of fitness to plead?

The Appropriate Adult system is conceived within the context of police questioning of a suspect in the short period of detention in police custody between arrest and charge (or release from custody). There seems no good reason why the Appropriate Adult's role should be so narrowly confined. If it be a part of the Appropriate Adult's function to intervene whenever there is a suspicion that the mentally disordered detainee is incapable of understanding what is taking place, or cannot communicate reliably with his legal representative, why should that function cease the moment that police custody ends? We see great merit in the Appropriate Adult being to hand at any stage of the criminal process pre-trial.

When Dr Bowden pointed up his worries about Jason Mitchell's fitness to plead in June 1995 (less than three weeks before the hearing at Ipswich Crown Court on 7 July 1995) an Appropriate Adult, if in play, could have objectively assessed the desirability of raising the issue before the court. When the matter was put to Dr Bowden as a possible solution to the problem of setting before the court an accused's fitness to plead, he answered:

> It is a very important issue which I have never had expressed to me before but is exactly paralleled by a person who is manifestly mentally ill who wishes to plead not guilty and will not enter a plea of diminished responsibility which would be acceptable to the court and where the issue of fitness to plead is used to manipulate the situation, that is if they would plead guilty to manslaughter on the grounds of diminished responsibility, it goes through as manslaughter on the grounds of diminished responsibility but because they want to plead not guilty, the court then raises the issue of fitness to plead as a means of entrapping them but it is the reverse of what your are proposing – that an amicus is appointed before the court as a guardian to advise the court and that also would serve the function of the example that I put to you with regard to diminished responsibility.

We recommend that the Appropriate Adult system in criminal justice should be re-examined with a view to extending its role.

APPENDIX TO CHAPTER XVIII

CHRONOLOGY OF POLICE ACTIVITY

JASON MITCHELL: 5.25 PM ON 20 DECEMBER 1995 (APPROX) TO
12.30 PM ON 22 DECEMBER 1995

Date	*Time*	*Occurrence*	*Officer/Witness*
20.12	5.25 pm	Arrest and conveyance to Ipswich Police Station.	DC ROYAL D/SGT CUSHNAHAN DC STOCKBRIDGE P/SGT CORBLE WPC HUMPHRIES PC BRIGHT
20.12	5.45 pm	Arrived at Ipswich and seen by Custody Officer.	P/SGT SQUIRRELL
20.12	6.16 pm	Search and seizure of clothing.	DC RADFORD Mr CUSWORTH
20.12	6.36 pm	To cells under constant supervision by various officers while medical staff, solicitor and social worker called out.	PC ARTHUR PC JAMES PC STARK PC HARRISON
20.12	8.35 pm	To doctor's room for examination to determine fitness for detention and interview (suspended 8.46 pm).	Dr GODDARD (JM's RMO) Dr KNIGHT (police surgeon) Mrs CORNFORTH
20.12	8.47 pm	To interview with solicitor and appropriate adult.	Mr MARCHANT (JM's Solicitor) Mr ECKERSLEY (Appropriate Adult)
20.12	10.30 pm	Continuation of medical examination.	As 8.35 plus Mr ECKERSLEY
20.12	10.55 pm	Declared fit for detention and fit for interview.	Dr GODDARD
21.12	1.00 pm	Due to comments made by MITCHELL, written log commenced by officers involved in constant supervision.	PC CASSIDY PC TAYLOR PC MORGAN PC STROM
21.12	3.10 pm	Superintendent's Review (PACE).	SUPT JONES (In presence of Mr BUXTON & Mr MARCHANT)

		Continuation of constant supervision.	PC TAYLOR PC ROOT PC TAYLOR PC KENT
21.12	6.00 pm	Inspector's Review (PACE).	INSP BENNEWORTH (In presence of Mr BUXTON & Mr MARCHANT)
		Continuation of constant supervision.	PC IVES PC WARNER
21.12	6.44 pm	Examined by Dr BALL at request of defence.	Dr BALL (independent forensic psychiatrist from Norvic Clinic) Mr BUXTON
		Continuation of constant supervision.	PC WARREN PC HAWKINS
21.12	8.10 pm	Examined by Police Surgeon Dr McCARTHY. Certified fit for detention and interview.	No statement
21.12	9.04 pm	Interview. No comment. Concluded 9.31 pm.	DC ROYAL DC FOSTER Mr BUXTON Mr MARCHANT

XIX. Bereavement

No worst, there is none. Pitched past pitch of grief.
More pangs will, schooled at forepangs, wilder wring.
Comforter, where, where is your comforting?
                                        Gerard Manley Hopkins,
                                        'Spring and Fall'

The killings of Mr and Mrs Wilson and Mr Mitchell in a small close-knit community, by a young man well-known to many people in the area where he grew up, affected many lives. Foremost among the victims' families, friends and associates were the son and two daughters of Mr and Mrs Wilson and Jason Mitchell's brothers, sisters and mother.

We were anxious to discover what support had been offered to these victims and what ongoing support was needed during the process of the Inquiry, during which many painful issues would be explored. We were also concerned to discover what support had been offered to the wider community of Bramford, in whose village the killings had occurred and where many people had actually seen Jason Mitchell around at the time.

Finally, we wished to ascertain what support had been offered to staff who had been clearly stunned by the killings and who faced the additional trauma generated by the Inquiry itself.

We were impressed by the response of the Social Services Department and the voluntary sector to the wider community, by the prompt, substantial and much appreciated support offered to the son and daughter of Mr and Mrs Wilson by Victim Support in Suffolk, and by the contact which it established and help which it offered through Jason Mitchell's mother to his family members. The extended network of Victim Support services also established contact with Mr and Mrs Wilson's other daughter who lived far away from Suffolk.

Suffolk Social Services Department co-ordinates three multi-agency Crisis Care Support Teams. A detailed description of the work of the teams was provided by Janet Dillaway (Assistant Director of Social Services). The teams include staff from the social service and probation services, the emergency services, the health service and local voluntary organisations many of which receive some financial support from Suffolk County Council. All the team members have been trained in psychological de-briefing techniques, and the focus of the service is to offer people who have been exposed to traumatic experiences the opportunity to share their experiences, to normalise their reactions and to help them devise coping strategies.

A public meeting was held in Bramford on the evening of 19 December 1994 and was attended by 75 residents. A further meeting was held on 23 December 1994. On this occasion the meeting was held in the afternoon, since some concern had been expressed about people, especially older people, leaving their homes after dark. This meeting was attended by only a handful of people. A further meeting was requested and this was held on 6 February 1995, but only one person attended. A separate meeting, which attracted 29 participants, was held in a sheltered housing complex for older people in Bramford. The intention had been to consider holding a further meeting around the anniversary, but on reflection the Social Services team decided not to go ahead with this. The *East Anglian Daily Times* published a feature marking the anniversary aimed at demonstrating just how positively, and how well the villagers were coping one year on.

At all events copies of a leaflet 'Coping with a Personal Crisis' were distributed and information was given about Victim Support and the Samaritans. People were informed that, should they experience any difficulties, they should contact either the support team or one of the individual agencies.

Individuals who were more closely affected, victim's family members for example, were channelled to Victim Support which is considered to be better able to offer one-to-one extended contact.

Victim Support, which is also represented on the Crisis Support teams, offered direct and continuing help to Mr and Mrs Wilson's son and daughter in Suffolk. They felt they had been well supported and informed by Victim Support, SAMM (Support after Murder and Manslaughter), their solicitor, our secretary Mr Brian Morden and, above all, by the police. The Wilsons felt they were kept reasonably well-informed about the unfolding events as they happened. The support offered to the other daughter was also appreciated, but she commented that it would have been helpful to have been assisted by a volunteer who had had personal experience of losing a family member in similar circumstances.

In our view the response of the Social Services Department, the multi-agency Crisis teams and of Victim Support was impressive.

Employers too have a responsibility, and in this instance Mr Wilson made special mention of the support offered by his employer both at the time of the killings and in allowing him time to attend the Inquiry. Mr and Mrs Wilson's daughter, employed by the Ipswich Hospital NHS Trust, considered its response to be adequate but less forthcoming than that afforded to her brother.

The employers of the staff in Social Services and in the Health Trust, whose employees had been responsible for Jason Mitchell's care, offered counselling and, where appropriate, leave of absence was granted. Counselling support was also extended by the Trust to the staff of MIND.

Both families would have valued a direct approach from the East Suffolk Local Health Services NHS Trust itself. Mr and Mrs Wilson's relatives greatly appreciated the way in which the police supported them, by giving the maximum information possible and by attending the funeral. They noted that the staff of the Trust did not react in a similar way. The absence of contact between the staff of the Trust and the families of the victims and of the perpetrator is, however, not unusual in the public services. Such staff often face a real difficulty in expressing normal human responses at such times. They want to say how sorry they are to the victims, not as an admission of liability, but for the sorrow which the events have caused. If they do so, they are often faced with a barrage of questions which they may be unable to answer and where ill-considered responses merely serve to add to, rather than alleviate, the feelings of the families. Not infrequently, they will have been expressly forbidden to establish contact by managers acting on the advice of insurers or lawyers who are seeking to protect the employer's position in the face of potential litigation. Staff themselves may feel that expressions of sympathy, or attendance at funerals, would be regarded as intrusive or unwelcome. This was not so in this case.

A careful, sensitive, proactive and, above all, human approach should be adopted in such cases. **We recommend** that employers, their legal advisers and insurers should find ways of helping their staff make direct personal contact with bereaved families – unless families do not wish for this.

The Inquiry itself can be an ordeal for relatives and staff. Through our secretariat, we established early contact with Mr and Mrs Wilson's family and with a member of Jason Mitchell's family, and offered contact with counselling services. All the family members were invited to meet with us as well as attend the Inquiry. They were invited to let the secretariat know of issues, questions or concerns which they wished us to explore. They took advantage of that offer, often to good effect.

Christopher Wilson's consistent attendance, his evidence and his remarkable generosity of spirit were striking in the extreme. It appears that his attendance was found helpful by all members of his family.

It was in part a concern for victim families which led us, with the assistance of Suffolk Health Authority, to mount a one-day seminar which included a review of the effects of such happenings on the families of victims, and considered their role in the Inquiry process.

Professor Paul Rock presented a moving and substantial analysis of the views of victims on the process of Inquiries and on the impact of the experience of homicides on their lives. He noted that families recognise the opportunity which an Inquiry presents to explore issues and raise questions not available to them at a criminal trial particularly where there has been a plea of guilty and hence limited disclosure of the homicidal event. In the case of Jason Mitchell his plea and sentence, with evidence only from forensic psychiatrists dealing with the offender's mental state, lasted only half a day of court time.

Mr and Mrs Wilson's children were not interested in blaming individuals but in tracing flaws in the system that had been responsible for the release of Jason Mitchell. Indeed in his statement at the close of the Inquiry, Chris Wilson had the astonishing detachment and objectivity to say: 'Every Agency has gone into great detail to explain their role in the care and control of Jason Mitchell and their aspirations for him. We must not forget that he is now locked away for a long, long time. He is also a victim and I say to those agencies, you have all failed him.' The family told Paul Rock that they 'wanted to say our piece and say what we thought .... It is not about our parents, it is about Jason Mitchell, but it has had an impact on the family. It has affected the whole of the family. People should be aware that it has effects.' Paul Rock points out that a public inquiry 'may be the one, final opportunity which families have to comprehend how and "why" the victims were killed'.

It is our firm view that the families of victims have a most central public concern, and are key representatives of the wider community whose interests Inquiries such as ours are established to serve. In our view they should be given the opportunity to be present at any inquiry into homicides, whether that Inquiry be held in public or in private. Such opportunity might usefully be provided by the sponsoring authority in the terms of reference it gives to the independent panel of inquiry. **We recommend** that all authorities mandated to set up inquiries under NHS Executive Guidance HSG (94) 27 of 10 May 1994 should actively consider including such direction in its terms of reference.

The crisis care contact was felt to have been made with Jason Mitchell's family via the Victim Support Team who visited his mother and offered help via her to the extended family. This offer did not reach them. Consideration should be given by Social Services and Victim Support to making direct offers of help to all members of victims' families individually. The normal practice of the helping agencies is to respond to requests for advice and assistance, but in circumstances such as these the department in Suffolk had already adopted a more proactive outreach stance to the wider community. **We recommend** that a more direct, proactive and individual approach to the members of victims' families should be adopted by all agencies engaged in crisis support work.

Part I

Selected Topics

XX. Deferred Conditional Discharge

It has been observed that those who most loudly clamour for liberty
do not most liberally grant it.
Dr Johnson, *The Lives of the Poets*, ed. Cunningham
(1854), vol. I, p. 135

When the Mental Health Review Tribunal sat on 3 September 1991
to consider Jason Mitchell's application for discharge from detention in hospital, it concluded that he was still suffering from a
mental illness – namely, schizophrenia – but that the illness was
no longer of a nature or degree which made it appropriate for him
to be detained in hospital for medical treatment. Since the Tribunal
went on to consider, however, that it was appropriate for Jason
Mitchell to remain liable to recall in the event of a relapse, it was
bound to discharge him, but only conditionally. The conditional
discharge was, moreover, to be deferred until such arrangements,
acceptable to the Tribunal, were in place. The main condition was
'residence in a hostel approved by the RMO'. The confirmation of
the conditional discharge came eventually in August 1994. It thus
took nearly three years for suitable accommodation to be found for
Jason Mitchell. In the meantime his loss of liberty continued. The
effect of the deferment of his conditional discharge was for the
system to speak with a forked tongue. The good news in September
1991 was for the patient to be told of his conditional discharge and
the expectancy of early release from detention. The bad news was
his continuing – indeed, long-continuing – detention.

The power to defer a conditional discharge does not allow the
Tribunal to defer deciding the case either to see how the patient's
health improves or worsens or to reconsider its decision in the light
of later developments. (That arises from the House of Lords Decision in *R* v. *Oxford Regional Mental Health Review Tribunal, ex
parte Secretary of State for the Home Department*, to which we
referred in Chapter X.)

Conditional discharge is a confusing concept even without the
added confusion of deferment. If the patient has surmounted the
difficult burden of proving that he is not ill and does not need to be
in hospital for his own or anyone else's sake, what case can there

be for keeping him in hospital at all? And on what basis should he be subject to supervision in the community and recall to hospital? It would be logical, and make for sound practice, if the tribunal was empowered simply to decide that the patient is fit for discharge provided that the conditions are met.

The protracted delay in finding suitable accommodation so as to perfect the conditional discharge is, unhappily, not uncommon. Judge Anwyl QC told us that she had known cases to be deferred for 'over a year, going on for two years' and she did not demur from the view that some deferments lasted over four years. Judge Uziell-Hamilton, who presided over the 1993 Tribunal, said that she had 'rarely ever deferred a conditional discharge', but we are aware that contemporaneously deferred conditional discharges constitute a major concern of the Tribunals. Judge Henry Palmer, whom we called as an expert on Mental Health Review Tribunals, described the status of a patient who has been given a deferred conditional discharge as 'highly unsatisfactory'.

The point can be put simply. Where a Tribunal decides on a deferred conditional discharge, it is declaring that a detained patient should enjoy his or her freedom and is sufficiently well to enjoy that liberty, contingent only on arrangements for accommodation being made; the contingency should be met promptly in order not to frustrate the right to liberty. Both the Annual Reports of the Mental Health Review Tribunals for 1993 and 1994 (paras 10.14 and 9.12, pp. 28 and 25, respectively) referred to two Broadmoor Joint Study Days in 1993 and 1994 addressed to the twin problems of preparing and planning the patient's discharge and of risk assessment in the context of deferred conditional discharges.

Is a patient's dischargeability inconsistent with his or her remaining detained? Even if the law under the Mental Health Act 1983 (and any residual common law provision) permits prolonged detention under a deferred conditional discharge, there is a serious risk that it falls foul of the European Convention of Human Rights (we include in Annex 3 the main international legislation and principles in relation to mental disorder). Article 5(1)(e) of that Convention states that a 'person of unsound mind' deprived of his liberty by arrest or detention is entitled to take proceedings 'by which the lawfulness of his detention shall be decided speedily by a court and his release ordered if the detention is not lawful' (Article 5(4)). The European Court of Human Rights decided in *X* v. *United Kingdom* (1981) 4 EHRR 181 that anybody detained because he or she was 'of unsound mind' was entitled to a periodic judicial consideration of the merits of continued detention. This was so even if the detention was ordered by a criminal court. Hence all restricted and unrestricted patients under hospital orders have the procedural safeguard of European Human Rights law.

Whether a protracted deferment of a conditional discharge constitutes a violation of Article 5 has not been tested at Strasbourg, but a case is pending before the European Commission of Human Rights. We assume, quite apart from any possible ruling from Strasbourg of unlawfulness in a case such as Jason Mitchell's, that the position is profoundly disturbing and calls for some remedial action. Those who proclaim a mental health patient's rights to liberty must ensure that liberty is a reality. But what action can be taken to remedy the defect?

If the *Oxford* decision (mentioned above) were to be reversed by statute, tribunals which gave a deferred conditional discharge could alter the patient's status adversely in the case of a relapse in the patient's mental condition. At present the deferred conditional discharge can be extinguished by a further application on a reference by the Home Secretary; the latter took place in March 1993 (eighteen months after the 1991 Tribunal hearing) but its nullifying effect was misunderstood by the Tribunal (see Chapter X).

But where the patient remains well, or is not so ill as to make it appropriate for him or her to be detained in hospital for medical treatment, the door to freedom remains shut so long as arrangements for accommodation in the community are wanting. Once the conditional discharge is deferred there can be no reason, other than setting in place the arrangements, to hinder the patient's conditional discharge.

Judge Palmer expressed the view that the responsible health authority and the patient's RMO are under an immediate and continuing obligation to meet the condition of the deferred conditional discharge, and to that end to do everything reasonable to achieve that objective. This poses a dilemma for the patient's RMO. If the latter, pending arrangements for accommodation in the community, thinks it clinically wise to stop the patient's medication in order to test the effect on the mental condition, he will not pursue enthusiastically hostel accommodation and would not readily contemplate the patient leaving the hospital at least in the short term. The 'drug holiday' might indicate a need for prolonged detention: yet the obligation is to promote instant discharge from hospital.

The issue boils down to the provision of accommodation for such patients in the community. Should tribunals have the power, within a reasonable time-scale, to order the responsible authorities to provide accommodation so as to facilitate the confirmation of a conditional discharge? Mr David Long, the Chief Executive of East Suffolk Local Health Services NHS Trust, told us that any power to try and force the provision of accommodation would be wholly unreasonable if the facility had to be in the health service provider's locality. He implied that if there was a possibility to go beyond the provider's area some such power might be tolerable. We believe the problem will remain so long as there is a paucity of specialised accommodation for discharged patients.

One way out of the problem of shortages in suitable accommodation would be for tribunals to be released from the stark choice whether to discharge, either absolute or conditional (and deferred), or not. Judge Palmer noted the fact that tribunals have no powers to authorise trial leave for patients or to order transfer to another hospital – for example, transfer from a special hospital to a regional secure unit or to conditions of lesser security.

Whatever is proposed to remedy an ongoing defect in the present law and practice, there are a large number of problems affecting many agencies and professional bodies. Judge Palmer stated firmly that he would like to see an in-depth review of not just the deferred conditional discharge procedure under section 73(7) of the Mental Health Act 1983, but the whole of Part V of the Act: Mental Health Review Tribunals: sections 65 to 79. **We recommend** that the Secretary of State for Health set in train a review of the Mental Health Review Tribunal system. In the foreword to the Annual Report for 1994, Sir John Wood, the Regional Chairman for Trent, referred (p. 3) to the recommendation in *The Falling Shadow* that the work of tribunals should be thoroughly reconsidered. Sir John added:

> It is a point that the Council on Tribunals has also expressed in its recent Annual Reports. Such a review is likely to be welcomed by the Tribunals themselves.

In the last two years there have been calls for a review of the Mental Health Act 1983, to which the Minister of State for Health, Mr John Bowis, MP, responded that, 'sooner or later', a review will be needed. Any review of Part V of the Act should be undertaken only in the context of a review of the whole Act.

XXI. Controlling and Testing for Illicit Drugs

The authorised cure for all forms of psychosis
Is pills, or quinine in occasional doses.
Couplet composed by an anonymous inmate
at Broadmoor, *c.* 1926, cited in Partridge,
Broadmoor (1953) p. 103

The Mental Health Act Commission, in its most recent 6th biennial report has highlighted the widespread problem of illicit drug use in psychiatric settings:

> The misuse of drugs appears to be a growing problem in all types of mental health services. Drug misuse poses particularly acute problems for inpatient services. In a recent survey by the Royal College of Nursing for the BBC, 70% of respondents (187), from both urban and rural areas, said that the misuse of illicit drugs was a problem on their unit. Only half of these units had a policy in relation to patients who use illicit drugs.
>
> Members of the Mental Health Act Commission ... report general concern about the limited specialist services available to patients who have these problems. There are also widespread concerns about the integration of patients who abuse drugs (both illicit drugs and alcohol) with other mentally ill patients. (Mental Health Act Commission, 1995, Sixth Biennial Report 1993-95. London: HMSO, para 9.6, p. 105)

Services for problem drug users in Suffolk were recently reviewed in a report by the NHS Drug Advisory Service (June 1995) (HAS(95)D2.P). The report noted 'evidence of widespread and growing drug misuse of all kinds across Suffolk' (p. 1), and the report concluded that there was a pressing need in the health district to develop a coherent, purchaser-led and needs-led strategy for drug misuse services. There was no consultant for substance misuse and such an appointment was 'imperative in contributing specialist clinical advice which would guide purchasing strategies, offer clinical guidance to service providers and develop overall guidelines and policies' (p. 1). In this context it is not surprising that approaches to controlling and testing for drugs are variable and lacking in guidance.

The primary means of investigating evidence of drug misuse (apart from enquiring of the patient and others) is by urine testing. Dr Christie Brown helpfully tabulated information from the Maudsley Hospital's laboratory about the time for which drugs are detectable in the urine after ingestion:

Morphine	Three days
Amphetamine	One to two days
Methadone	Typically three days (up to nine has been recorded)
Barbiturates	
long acting	Up to two weeks
short acting	Two to three days
Benzodiazepines	
therapeutic doses	One to two weeks
high dose (abuse)	Typically one month, up to four weeks
Cocaine	Typically one to three days
Cannabis	
'naïve' users	Two days
regular users	One to two weeks

Most drugs are undetectable within a few days of cessation of use, and therefore urine drug misuse screens may need to be carried out repeatedly on individuals whose symptoms are thought to be exacerbated or caused by illicit drugs.

Difficulties arise when patients decline requests for urine samples, but clinical staff consider them essential – for example, if it is suspected that symptoms are drug-induced. Dr Christie Brown suggested that the decisions made by staff about the restrictions on a patient following his refusal to give a urine sample should perhaps be the same as if a sample tested positive. For example, if certain freedoms were contingent on negative tests, and restrictions followed positive tests, refusal of a test would lead to the latter response.

Practices vary, however, at different hospitals. Dr Yeldham observed that, in a specialised drug treatment service, clinicians can set expectations that samples will be provided under supervision, and this is part of the 'contract' which patients in such services have to accept. In a general psychiatric unit, a desirable approach would be to explain the adverse effects of drugs and obtain the patient's co-operation and acceptance that testing has to be part of their treatment programme.

There are difficulties in devising policies that use incentives or loss of privileges in inpatient settings. At Easton House, no particular restrictions followed Jason Mitchell's refusal to provide a specimen. Even in a special hospital, refusals to provide specimens may have to be accepted. Dr Wilson told us that at Rampton, patients suspected of taking illicit drugs are informed of the suspicion and asked to provide a urine sample. If the patient refuses, he cannot be compelled to provide a specimen. The practice of isolating the patient in a room until he complied would not be followed.

There is a need for guidance and consistency. The Mental Health Act Commission has suggested that special consideration now ought to be given to considering the complex legal, ethical and medical issues raised by the misuse of drugs in psychiatric services:

> There is a pressing need for research to determine the extent and nature of the problem and into effective solutions, as well as a more immediate need for guidance in producing a framework for the development of local policies (*ibid.*, p. 106).

The Commission also advised that it would be helpful if the Department of Health provided some input,

> ... so that hospitals can develop policies which not only alleviate the problem but do so in a manner which conforms to current ethics and standards (*ibid.*, p. 106).

We concur with the Commission's views. In the Department of Health's Press Release (95/554) outlining the response of the Health Minister, Mr John Bowis, MP, to the Commission's Report, he is quoted as saying:

> I share the Commission's concern about drugs misuse and we are considering what part we can most usefully play in supporting the development of agreed local policies to tackle on-site drug misuse. Local Drug Action Teams, which are being set up as part of the Government's anti-drugs strategy, should be able to support this work.

XXII. Role of the Police

> The police service cannot be held solely responsible for community
> safety ... the factors which lead to offending are not within their
> direct control. Nor can any other single agency or organisation be
> held solely responsible. The growing complexity of society requires
> a multi-faceted approach .... The case for the partnership approach
> stands virtually unchallenged but also hardly tested.
>
> Report of the Standing Committee on Crime Prevention
> through Safer Communities, August 1991

The Morgan Report, from which this quotation is taken, was a
watershed in the partnership approach to crime prevention and
provided the catalyst for a different approach to crime reduction
which had been gathering momentum for a decade.

Soaring statistics of recorded crime had previously given birth
to the Home Office Working Group on Crime Prevention and
another on the Fear of Crime in 1990, of which our Chairman was
a member. In January 1984, Circular 8/84 was jointly issued by five
government departments, displaying central government's support. This was followed by Circular 44/90 and the booklet 'Partnership in Crime Prevention' which provided guidelines by way of
examples of best practice. In addition, there were numerous initiatives at local and national level, including the Safer Cities Programme and Crime Concern.

The Morgan Report produced a number of significant recommendations, although not all of these (in particular those involving
substantial expenditure) have been accepted by government. What
the Morgan Report did help to accentuate and encourage was the
growing acceptance, even among police officers, that 'policing was
too important to be left to the police'.

There was also a slight but important change in emphasis,
established in the Morgan Report, from the narrow focus on crime
prevention to the wider and all embracing 'community safety'.

A plethora of professionals, working groups, committees, crime
watches and local initiatives have based their work on the Morgan
Report. The partnership approach continues to flourish. Despite
the accent on community safety rather than basic crime prevention,

it is clear, however, that the emphasis remains on preventing and dealing with crime in the publicly-understood sense of the word.

In relation to dealing with mentally ill people, and in particular the growth in numbers of patients in the community as a result of the government's Community Care Programme, there has been so far little consideration given to the particular problems which affect community safety. One exception is the Clunis Report, which found fault with all the agencies concerned, with particular criticism for the lack of co-operation between them. It is not immediately apparent to us that those findings have been everywhere regarded as important.

The importance of carefully-established protocols between the various agencies who deal with mentally ill people is surely self-evident. It is not sufficient – for example, as in the case of Jason Mitchell – for a hospital to have a detailed policy for reporting missing patients to the police if that system contains ambiguities which are confusing to the police, and if the police have no written policy of their own. It is crucially important for police and hospitals to have established joint policies for dealing with section 136 cases (to which we allude below), missing patients, the transport of patients, access to each other's records and other matters of mutual interest and responsibility.

It is also important that each agency is aware of the core functions and responsibilities of the other, with appreciation of the restrictions and limitations which influence each other's work. This can be properly achieved only by joint training and discussions, with the strong support of senior management.

There are undoubtedly many excellent local initiatives in various parts of the country. Nationwide, however, the picture is patchy. If the partnership approach is to have any influence on the way in which society deals with the increasing number of mentally ill people in the community, then there will have to be a voluntary and marked enhancement of inter-agency liaison at local level. Otherwise the recommendations of the Morgan Report, which envisaged a statutory responsibility for the local authority and funding for local co-ordinators in community safety, will need to be actively reconsidered.

Mental health responsibilities

It is the police who bear the initial brunt of dealing with mentally ill people in the community who commit offences ranging from inappropriate behaviour in the street to the most serious crimes. In the course of examining the role of the police in relation to the tracing of Jason Mitchell after he absented himself from Easton House on 9/10 December 1994, we became aware of the importance which different police forces give to preparing their officers to deal with this growing operational commitment. For many years initial police training for dealing with the mentally ill has been relatively brief and centred on police powers under sections 136 and 137 of the Mental Health Act 1983. These two sections provide:

136. (1) If a constable finds in a place to which the public have access a person who appears to him to be suffering from mental disorder and to be in immediate need of care or control, the constable may, if he thinks it necessary to do so in the interests of that person or for the protection of other persons, remove that person to a place of safety within the meaning of section 135 above.

(2) A person removed to a place of safety under this section may be detained there for a period not exceeding 72 hours for the purpose of enabling him to be examined by a registered medical practitioner and to be interviewed by an approved social worker and of making any necessary arrangements for his treatment or care.

137. (1) Any person required or authorised by or by virtue of this Act to be conveyed to any place or to be kept in custody or detained in a place of safety or at any place to which he is taken under section 42(6) above shall, while being so conveyed, detained or kept, as the case may be, be deemed to be in legal custody.

(2) A constable or any other person required or authorised by or by virtue of this Act to take any person into custody, or to convey or detain any person shall, for the purposes of taking him into custody or conveying or detaining him, have all the powers, authorities, protection and privileges which a constable has within the area for which he acts as constable.

(3) In this section 'convey' includes any other expression denoting removal from one place to another.

The Code of Practice, made under the Mental Health Act 1983, proclaims that good practice depends on the local Social Services Authority, District Health Authority, NHS Trust and the Chief Officer of Police establishing a clear policy for implementation of section 136 (para 10.1a). The policy should define the responsibilities of the police officer to remain in attendance, where the patient's health or safety or the protection of others so require when the patient is taken to a place of safety (other than a police station) (para 10.3a). It also states that police officers have a responsibility, with other agencies, for the satisfactory returning to the community of a person assessed under section 136 who is not admitted to hospital or immediately placed in accommodation. Apart from these directions in relation to the specific statutory power to deal with the mentally disordered who are found in public places needing care or control, the police are not otherwise under prescription about their responsibilities generally in relation to the mental health system.

Police officers have had to rely on practical experience in developing any expertise in this sensitive aspect of their work. Many have developed sound professional skills and displayed considerable compassion in dealing with mentally-ill people, and in several areas there have been excellent local initiatives, but it is now patently clear that compassion, experience and minimal training are not enough.

The Clunis Report (1993) highlighted the shortcomings of the police and other agencies in this difficult and sensitive area, particularly regarding inter-agency co-operation. The Home Office issued Circular 66/90 (which has now been followed by Circular 12/95) which has been sent to Judges, Court Administrators, Chief Constables, Chief Probation Officers and Prison Governors, dealing with mentally disordered offenders and inter-agency working. Chief Constables are asked, inter alia:

(a) to develop arrangements for examination by psychiatrists or other mental health professionals of detained persons, including Sec. 136 cases;
(b) to consider setting up mental health assessment schemes at selected police stations;
(c) to appoint force co-ordinators to develop policy and practice (including effective contacts with other local services and agencies);
(d) to contribute to any strategic discussion of local arrangements for mentally disordered offenders and to co-operate with any local inter-agency schemes such as those based on courts to ensure that force policy on deciding when to charge reflects the need to safeguard the public as well as to meet the health and social care needs of individuals.

What the Home Office Circular has not addressed is the pressing need for a higher degree of training for operational police officers in dealing with a variety of mental disorder situations in their daily work. It is, of course, entirely a matter for individual Chief Constables to decide the degree of emphasis which should be placed on this aspect of training in accordance with perceived local needs. We commend to any police force, which has not already done so, the current training and policies in place within the Metropolitan Police. These include, *inter alia*:

    (a) training to be provided for all operational staff up to and including the rank of Inspector, in recognising the various aspects of mental illness and in dealing with sufferers from mental ill-health;

    (b) a liaison officer of supervisory rank on each Division to be provided to supply a greater degree of specialist knowledge and to ensure co-operation with local hospitals, social services and other related agencies;

    (c) the existence of formal local protocols with hospitals and other agencies;

    (d) a straightforward guide 'Policing Mental Disorder' at each Division available to all staff; and

    (e) guidelines for custody officers in deciding when charging a mentally disordered offender, or taking other appropriate action.

It is our understanding that similar training and policies have been taken up by a number of police forces, and received consideration by the Home Office Central Training Unit. It would be a considerable step forward if this degree of commitment was to be formally provided nation-wide. **We so recommend.**

XXIII. Training and Education

> Education is what survives when what has been learnt has been forgotten.
>
> B.F. Skinner, 'Education in 1984', *New Scientist*,
> 21 May 1964, p. 484

Arising out of the Reed Committee's Report in November 1992 – *The Department of Health/Home Office Review of Health and Social Services for Mentally Disordered Offenders and others with similar needs* – there have been a number of initiatives to promote and enhance all the various services for mentally disordered offenders, by focusing attention on training and education in the forensic field. NACRO (National Association for the Care and Resettlement of Offenders) produced in 1994 a training pack, *Working with Mentally Disordered Offenders*, and CCETSW (Central Council for Education and Training of Social Workers) in 1993 surveyed existing training provision for qualified staff in the probation service and in local authority social services: *Training for Work with Mentally Disordered Offenders*; more recently (November 1995) CCETSW has published *Training Guidance* for employers, practitioners and trainers in social work as a companion volume to *Forensic Social Work: Competence and Social Work Data*. H.M. Inspectorate of Probation in September 1995 produced an impressive report of a thematic inspection on *Dealing with Dangerous People: The Probation Service and Public Protection*. This is due to be followed up in March 1996 with a comprehensive 'Good Practice Guide' for the Probation Service. From our limited perspective of the work undertaken by probation officers in 1987-89 in Jason Mitchell's case we recognise that there is a need to reinforce and improve the training of probation officers working with dangerous offenders, both while they are in custody pending discharge and in the community on supervision. The social work emphasis now on forensic work, and the element of training in such work, is of great importance when social workers and probation officers are dealing with offenders who are simultaneously cared for and treated within criminal justice and mental health systems. It seems to us that the Home Secretary's statutory instrument (which, at the time of writing, is the subject of a judicial review) to reduce the status of probation officer training, by removing the necessity of the social work qualification, is misguided. If the Care in the Community policy is to be effective, the needs of the mentally disordered met, and the security of the community safeguarded, much greater emphasis will need to be placed on providing those staff who carry the responsibility for delivering the service with the necessary skills.

We contribute our own few thoughts on how best education and training can be provided in four specialist areas of public services for mentally disordered offenders – social work, clinical psychology, psychiatry and mental health review tribunals.

Social work

Neither of the social workers allocated to Jason Mitchell's case were Approved Social Workers at the time of allocation though both were pursuing training and both were well qualified and experienced. Jane Barnett appropriately used her knowledge of working with troubled adolescents to model her work with Jason Mitchell but was clear that she needed the guidance which should have been available to her from the clinicians in her role as social supervisor in order to spot deteriorations in Jason Mitchell's mental health.

The Probation Officer who managed Jason Mitchell's discharge from Feltham perceptively and persistently pursued a placement in a Richmond Fellowship hostel for him despite the fact that such a course was unusual. Nevertheless she stated that she considered that she had no experience of mental health issues.

We are pleased to note the initiative undertaken by CCETSW in developing competencies in forensic social work. Care in the Community policies demand workers who are skilled in working at the interface between the health, criminal justice, housing and personal social services systems and this development is welcomed.

We were struck by the information supplied in the CCETSW survey that within the existing caseloads of staff working in this field, only 19.7 per cent of the time was spent in direct work with clients and that only 6.1 per cent in treatment interventions. **We recommend** that purchasers of social care should seek to ensure that an adequate supply of forensic social work is available in their areas.

We recommend that any social services worker assigned the task of social supervisor of a restricted patient should be an Approved Social Worker. **We further recommend** that the relevant Government departments should set a target date by which all social supervisors of restricted patients will have acquired the competencies in forensic social work set out by CCETSW.

Clinical psychology

It was recognised by those giving evidence to the Inquiry that the perspective and contribution of clinical psychology to the assessment and management of Jason Mitchell would have been highly desirable. Witnesses indicated that there is a continuing difficulty in the recruiting and retention of qualified psychologists. This reflects the severe national shortage of qualified clinical psychologists.

Clinical psychology training in the UK is postgraduate, of three years duration and leads to a doctoral degree conferring eligibility for inclusion in the British Psychological Society Register of Chartered Psychologists.

There are currently twenty-three courses in the UK, with a total of 220 training places funded by the Department of Health through Regional Education Purchasers. Almost all trainee clinical psychologists are salaried, full-time employees of the National Health Service.

Of the approximately 3,500 clinical psychology posts in the UK around 550 are known to be currently vacant. This vacancy rate of probably 16 to 20 per cent is a matter of serious concern to the profession, National Health Service Trusts, health purchasers and the Department of Health. In short, the development of community and hospital mental health services is seriously compromised.

The problem is a continuing failure of the Department of Health to fund an adequate number of training places. As long ago as 1990 a Department of Health-funded project, commissioned from the MAS (an independent organisation) identified a training need of 300 commissions per year. Last year – 1995 – was the first year in which commissions exceeded 200.

In a report prepared by the profession at the request of the Department of Health, published in November of this year (Turpin 1995), it is clear that existing courses are operating below optimum capacity and could readily cope with an additional 50/60 trainees, with minimal additional resources training approximately 340 per annum.

The impact on services in general, and forensic services in particular, is that posts are very difficult to fill. In a market context, salaries are driven up, even if they are filled. From the training point of view, the forensic speciality interests trainees. But finding training places and experienced tutors and supervisors is extremely frustrating for course organisers.

We recommend that the Department of Health should ensure the funding of adequate numbers of training places.

Psychiatry

The quality of psychiatric care and attention given to Jason Mitchell was generally good. In particular, the two consultants mainly responsible for Jason Mitchell's treatment before the killings, Dr Yeldham and Dr Goddard, impressed us as conscientious, thorough clinicians. Their commitment to Jason Mitchell's care, and the quality of their medical documentation, were excellent. Patients like Jason Mitchell who have histories of serious offending, drug taking and personality difficulties do not always receive such committed, long-term care from general psychiatry services.

Any detailed retrospective review of a case will nonetheless highlight areas in which the professional training and education might generally be enhanced. In relation to psychiatric training the two areas of importance in this case are forensic psychiatry and psychodynamic assessment.

There has been an increasing emphasis during recent years on the need to develop better services for mentally disordered offenders. As a matter of policy their care is the responsibility of health and social services. There has also been an increasing emphasis on the importance of assessment and containment of risk, and the maintenance of long-term supervision in the community. In many districts liaison between mental health services and criminal justice agencies has been strengthened and there is a slow growth in the number of local secure psychiatric beds. The services in Ipswich exemplify these developments. The care and management of offender patients is an integral part of much general psychiatry practice, and is not confined to specialists in forensic psychiatry.

There is therefore a sense in which general psychiatrists also need to be good forensic psychiatrists.

Three aspects of the clinical assessment and management in Jason Mitchell's case might have been given more prominence within a specialist forensic psychiatry service: first, consideration of future offending risk; secondly, seeking understanding of his emotional and fantasy life; and thirdly, monitoring the possible recurrence of thoughts of violence. Consideration of all three aspects was relatively sparse in the West Park and St Clement's case notes. Following the offence in 1990 there are no recorded instances of specific enquiry of whether Jason Mitchell had further hallucinations, thoughts or fantasies with violent or homicidal content. None of the psychiatrists who gave oral evidence to the Inquiry could recall asking about this specific area in their interviews and assessments of Jason Mitchell's mental state. At Easton House such enquiries may even have been deliberately avoided. In giving oral evidence to the Inquiry, Dr Goddard acknowledged that it was a possibility that Jason Mitchell may have had homicidal thoughts for some time before he committed the killings. When asked to comment on Jason Mitchell's claim that no one had asked him about his thoughts, Dr Goddard replied:

> With somebody like Jason Mitchell, it has to be taken with a certain amount of salt. His proof is so unreliable and ... he has given such various accounts of his treatment elsewhere that you could not say that it was necessarily reliable or truthful. But it is possible that there was some truth behind it in that perhaps he was not particularly subject to very timetabled routine, rigorous discussions about his thoughts, about violence and homicide.
>
> I think [during] the time with us, there certainly have been conversations about the index offence and violence, and so on, but it would probably have been done in a fairly indirect way rather than a structured interview looking particularly at those issues.

When asked how he thought Jason Mitchell might have responded to direct questioning on such matters, Dr Goddard continued:

> I think he would have delighted at the opportunity of being engaged in such conversations. They would have perhaps titillated him. He would have enjoyed watching, as I have often said before, for reactions and how he was having an effect on people .... He purposely presented a persona of menace and would have delighted in that being talked about and elaborated upon ....

I think a lot of the people working with him felt that might have been counter-productive.

In response to being questioned whether this led the team actively to avoid asking about such matters, Dr Goddard agreed:

I think certainly in conference there was some discussion about a policy on trying to avoid rewarding maladaptive behaviour, including conversations, but there was no veto on any individual discussing anything they liked with him, but there was that underlying joint plan, if you like ....

While we agree with Dr Goddard that such enquiries might not necessarily have resulted in a different outcome, it is nonetheless generally important that careful enquiries about further thoughts of violence should be part of the routine monitoring of any psychiatric patient who has previously exhibited significant violence. The offending history should always be in the foreground rather than the background of the clinician's thinking.

The skills and expertise of general and forensic psychiatrists do not differ fundamentally. The two specialisms may differ, however, in the sets of attitudes and the focus of clinical interests of their practitioners. While even the most optimal range of psychiatric training will not prevent unforeseen and serious offences being committed by patients, we believe that the elements of forensic work in contemporary mental health services are such that all trainees in general psychiatry should spend a period of training in a forensic psychiatry service under the supervision of a forensic psychiatrist. **We recommend** this. It would help ensure that they become equipped to practise general psychiatry with the perspective and sense of priorities needed in the management of patients who have offended or shown serious violence. In addition it is desirable that general psychiatrists taking up consultant posts with responsibility for secure beds should have had a period of training in forensic psychiatry.

Psychiatrists managing offender patients also need skills in psychodynamic assessment. The clinical knowledge on which the management of patients like Jason Mitchell is based should include as far as possible an understanding of their personality development, self-image, and emotional life. The need for psychodynamic assessment is not confined to the relatively small group of patients who are suitable for psychodynamic psychotherapy. Psychodynamic assessment is needed for the wider purpose of contributing to an understanding of the patient's inner world, and the nature of their personal relationships with others, including clinical staff. Adequate training in this area of practice is essential, both for general and forensic psychiatrists. The need to include this aspect of clinical assessment did not appear to be fully appreciated in Jason Mitchell's case.

We recommend that arrangements for psychiatric training, both nationally and locally in Suffolk and in the Anglia and Oxford region should be reviewed and if necessary enhanced, so as to ensure that all trainees in general psychiatry receive adequate clinical training and experience in psychodynamic and forensic aspects of psychiatry.

The specialist services are also necessary to provide second opinions, advice, and treatment and follow-up when necessary. Specialist opinions in these areas should be readily available to senior psychiatrists in permanent posts. We would observe that despite its substantial size – with a population of 650,000 and the major conurbation of Ipswich – there are no forensic psychiatrists within Suffolk. **We recommend** that the new Suffolk Health Authority should review whether the availability of forensic psychiatry services is sufficient.

Mental Health Review Tribunals

The first Annual Report of Mental Health Review Tribunals (1993) stated (para 10.3, p. 27) that 'four years ago it was decided to form a very small group to produce ideas on training for tribunal members'. After some modest developments on a local basis it was decided in 1993 to extend training on a national basis. The Training Group, which included all tribunal clerks together with a number of Regional Chairmen and representatives from the Department of Health, decided to make arrangements for two induction meetings a year for new tribunal members. Ultimately two induction courses took place in 1995 at Dorking and Stockport. The Annual (1994) Report heralded this enterprise and went on to say that the Training Group had drawn up 'a full programme ... and eminent and experienced guest speakers have been invited and have agreed to talk on subjects affecting the work of Mental Health Review Tribunals'. This excessively modest programme of training has not so far extended beyond the newly-appointed members. Judge Palmer was hardly exhibiting judicial boldness in asserting to us that 'training provision at the moment is wholly inadequate and could be hugely improved and would be improved if the funds were available to do it'.

It appears that the Judicial Studies Board, which is responsible for the 'training' of judges has offered its assistance in developing training for members. The Board runs training courses for administrative tribunals generally, of which there are 70 different types. Judge Palmer told us that the Board has used video material as part of its training sessions for tribunal members. Judge Palmer described to us, to much hilarity, a Board video all about a dog called Toby.

> It is some simulated tribunal carried out by actors and the law which they apply is invented law about the destruction of dogs. And so you have on video three members of the tribunal and the clerk and the witnesses, and the training material there enables one to comment on the way the tribunal is conducted.

To which Judge Palmer sardonically added:

> But, of course, as it applies to 70 different tribunals, it is not of very great help to Mental Health Review Tribunal members. We need a specific video relating to our tribunals and our problems.

While we acknowledge that there is no point in calling for training without having a clear idea of what it is designed to do – what sorts of knowledge and skills tribunal members need – it is to us wholly unacceptable that training should be so inadequate for members of a judicial body carrying such a heavy burden of decision making, particularly when that decision making concerns the liberty of the subject and the safety of the public.

We recommend that attention is given to identifying and meeting more thoroughly the training needs of existing as well as new tribunal members. We also believe it would be helpful educationally if tribunal members were informed about the clinical outcomes for patients following discharge decisions. Confidential retrospective reviews might also be of value in the small number of cases in which patients re-offend seriously following discharge. Although the decision-making of the tribunal is legal and not clinical, the legal decisions are made on complex clinical cases. In medical practice, clinical audit is now universally recognised as an integral and valuable means of gaining knowledge and improving decision making. A similar approach could usefully be adopted by mental health review tribunals.

XXIV. Inquiries after Homicide: Some Procedural Issues

On doit des égards aux vivants; on ne doit aux morts que la verité.
(We owe respect to the living; to the dead we owe only truth.)
Voltaire, *Oeuvres* 1785, vol. I, p. 15n

The irreversibility of death is a psychological problem with which human beings have wrestled since the beginning of time. It has given rise to an infinite variety of complex philosophical and religious beliefs, many of which have the function of preparing men and women for the only event in their lives for which there is absolute certainty, and of consoling the bereaved in their loss. Few of us are able confidently and sensitively to talk of death, least of all sudden and unexpected death. And when the death is at the hands of a murderer who survives to be held criminally responsible, the bereavement of the victim's families, friends and the community in which the homicidal event took place takes on heightened significance. As Professor Paul Rock told us at the private seminar held on 3 November 1995, bereavement is often described by sociologists as an example of 'anomic terror'. He added:

> Meaning is lost, and the secondary victims of homicide can retreat into a private grief so deep and ineffable that they risk estrangement even from those close to them, from others who are also grieving, endangering the very fabric of their close social world. Bereavement after homicide can be corrosive and isolating, throwing members of families and social networks in on themselves in a kind of implosion of anguish. At its core, there is a mass of confusing, frightening and tumultuous sensations which propel people step by step and often blindly.

NHS Guidance

Given the special human reactions to violent and unnatural deaths, it is little wonder that society's response has been to make provision for public investigation. The coroner system has been for at least eight centuries a distinctive Anglo-Saxon system for judicial inquiry where a deceased person dies violently, unnaturally or unexpectedly, or where the cause of death is unknown. Since the jurisdiction of the Coroner's Court is extremely limited in scope, confined to determining the cause of death there has always been a need in some homicide cases to investigate more widely and to that end to establish an inquiry about the circumstances leading up to and surrounding a violent and unnatural death. Inquiries after homicides involving mental health patients, previously set up, *ad hoc*, by central or local government, were mandated by the NHS Executive Guidance to Health Authorities dated 10 May 1994 (NHS Executive HSG (94)27). Likewise a circular was sent to local authority's social services. The key sections of the Guidance read:

> 33. If a violent incident occurs, it is important not only to respond to the immediate needs of the patient and others involved, but in serious cases also to learn lessons for the future ...
>
> 34. Additionally, after the completion of any legal proceedings , it may be necessary to hold an independent inquiry. In cases of homicide, it will always be necessary to hold an inquiry which is independent of the providers involved.
>
> 36. In setting up an independent inquiry the following points should be taken into account:
>> i. the remit of the inquiry should encompass at least:
>> - the care the patient was receiving at the time of the incident;
>> - the suitability of that care in view of the patient's history and assessed health and social care needs;
>> - the extent to which that care corresponded with statutory obligations, relevant guidance from the Department of Health, and local operational policies;
>> - the exercise of the care plan and its monitoring by the key worker.

The procedure for inquiry panels is not prescribed. Inquiries frequently reveal significant variations of approach.

Statutory/non statutory

The Guidance reflects central government policy to place the responsibility for public inquiries squarely on health services and social services. Even where the public disquiet is expressed nationally, the responsibility will rest with the directly relevant authority. In the case of the deaths and injuries on the children's ward at Grantham and Western General Hospital during the period February to April 1991 (the Beverley Allitt case) the Secretary of State for Health instructed the three members (Sir Cecil Clothier KCB, QC, Miss Anne MacDonald RGN RSCN and Professor David Shaw CBE, FRCP, FRCP (Edin)) to conduct the Inquiry 'on behalf of Trent Regional Health Authority'. While the report was made to the Secretary of State and published by HMSO, it was strictly non-statutory and therefore had no power to compel witnesses to give evidence or to disclose relevant documents. The only instance of a statutory inquiry, with powers of compulsion, in this area in modern times was the Ashworth Hospital Inquiry. There, a non-statutory inquiry set up by the Department of Health in conjunction with the Special Hospitals Service Authority was converted into a statutory inquiry (under section 125 of the Mental Health Act 1983) after the Prison Officers' Association had walked out of the Inquiry and threatened to advise its members not to co-operate.

Where an inquiry is established, exceptionally, under section 125 of the Mental Health Act 1983 (or any other statutory power), the inquiry is equipped with powers set out in section 250 of the Local Government Act 1972. These powers enable the Inquiry to request any person to attend to give evidence or to produce any documents in his custody or control. There is also a power to administer the oath, though this is not obligatory. The non-statutory inquiries generally regard themselves informal and do not treat witnesses as if they were in the courtroom. Surprisingly, the Independent Review Panel to East London and the City Health Authority and Newham Council (the Woodley team) asked 'witnesses of fact before us that they would speak the truth' (part 10, p. 166 of the Report).

By section 250(4) of the Local Government Act 1972 the relevant Minister can order that any costs incurred be paid by the local authority; and orders for costs can be made against parties. This provision proceeds upon the assumption that, ordinarily, the Minister is liable for the costs of the inquiry. In the case of inquiries under police legislation the police fund will bear the costs of any party to the inquiry. The threat of not getting one's costs may ensure that a party conducts its case properly. In Lord Scarman's inquiry into the Brixton Disorders 10-12 April 1981 his report stated (Cmd 8427, Appendix A, paras 15 and 16, p. 141):

Costs
15. Under Section 32(5) of the Police Act 1964, the Home Secretary may direct that the whole or part of the costs incurred by any person for the purposes of a local inquiry shall be defrayed out of the

police fund, subject to taxation. The Home Office invited Lord Scarman to make recommendations to the Home Secretary on the exercise of this power at the conclusion of the Inquiry.

16. Lord Scarman informed the parties concerned at the preliminary hearing that he intended to recommend to the Home Secretary that the reasonable costs taxed on the common fund basis of any party granted leave to be represented be met from the police fund, except where he considered that the person representing the party had wasted the time of the Inquiry. He would expect and hope to be able to give a warning if and when he considered that point was about to be reached and would not make any adverse recommendation as to costs without giving the party concerned an opportunity to make representations to him.

A flexibility in apportioning the costs of an inquiry among the sponsoring authorities and parties is thus within the realms of statutory possibility.

Obtaining documents

When we started out on the Inquiry in the summer of 1995 we experienced some difficulty in obtaining all the relevant documentation, for the simple reason that an initial approach to Jason Mitchell for his consent to waive confidentiality in his medical and social services records was stoutly rebuffed. Fortunately, once the criminal trial proceedings were concluded, his consent was forthcoming. Indeed later on in the Inquiry Jason Mitchell gave his consent (a) to the waiver of legal privilege to his solicitor's personal notes of conferences conducted in the days immediately following arrest on 20 December 1995; and (b) to some paintings and drawings, held by the Art Therapist at St Clement's Hospital, which Jason Mitchell had done during September – December 1993.

At the time of the rebuff, we approached the Chairman of Suffolk Health Authority with a view to seeking from the Secretary of State for Health a statutory authorisation. The response was not unhelpful. Further efforts, we were instructed, should be made to obtain the required consent, failing which the Minister would consider the matter sympathetically. In the event the only adverse effect to the Inquiry was some delay in gathering in the documentation and analysing the contents.

Obtaining the requisite documentation will inevitably be the first organisational step facing any Inquiry. If the sponsoring authority can itself supply the entire documentation, the Inquiry's task is made that much easier. But this will be rare. More commonly, the patient may have received care from, or crossed the jurisdictional boundaries of, health authorities, general practitioners, the special hospital system, social work departments, the prison service, and probation departments. While key reports and discharge summaries may have travelled with the patient, no Inquiry which sets itself appropriate goals of thoroughness can readily assume that such summaries are sufficient. Assessment of the adequacy of communication between different agencies over time is almost inevitably an issue which the Inquiry has to address.

Unless the Department of Health equips an Inquiry with statutory powers, it is difficult, if not impossible, to obtain all relevant documents without obtaining the patient's consent. Agencies other than the sponsoring authority frequently condition release of documents on the patient's formal written consent. Individual doctors risk disciplinary proceedings before the General Medical Council if the patient does not release them from their obligation of confidence.

Perhaps surprisingly, patients, or where the patient has died, his/her relatives, can usually be persuaded to co-operate. If the violent event has led to criminal proceedings the support of the patient's defence lawyers can often be crucial. They may have secured a trusting relationship with the patient. If they can be persuaded to advise the patient to co-operate, the necessary consent can more readily be obtained.

If the violent event occurred when the patient was unmedicated, and medication is restored after arrest, the patient's attitude to the prospect of an Inquiry, in addition to other factors, may change over time. There are therefore delicate issues of timing involved in making the approach. The importance of success is critical. Delay in obtaining consent will delay the assembly of documents, and without the documents the Inquiry will be unable to see with clarity what the key issues are.

Although no Inquiry, so far, has reported that it was unable to discharge its terms of reference by reason of inability to obtain crucial documents or evidence, it is quite possible to imagine that this could happen. A refusal by the patient to give consent, or, equally problematic, a revocation by the patient of consent previously given, could place an Inquiry in grave difficulties. A decision to equip the Inquiry with statutory powers could then be unavoidable.

Confidentiality and disclosure

Consent removes any barrier to disclosure based upon principles of confidentiality. That is explicitly recognised, for example, in the Department of Health's 1988 Guidance 'Personal Social Services: Confidentiality of Personal Information' (LAC(88)17, HN(88)24, HN(FP)(88)22):

> Nothing in this guidance prevents the disclosure of personal information for whatever purpose with the consent, expressly or by necessary implication, of the subject.

The Guidance recognises that for the consent of a mentally ill or mentally handicapped person to be valid, he must be capable of managing his own affairs (para 45). If the patient is subject to the Court of Protection, or if there is an Attorney with an Enduring Power, their interests must be taken into account. In other cases consent may be validly obtained through an agent.

The same principle would apply with respect to a medical obligation of confidence. Lawyer-client privilege, which vests in the client and not the lawyer, can likewise be waived by the patient/ client, and in those circumstances documents otherwise falling within the scope of the privilege can be obtained. Indeed, more generally, it can be suggested that the patient's consent should be sufficient to obtain disclosure to an Inquiry of records from any agency, subject only to valid resistance on grounds of public interest immunity.

The medical records on a patient held by the sponsoring authority are, in principle, subject to an obligation of confidence. That they may be disclosed without the patient's consent can be based on two grounds: first, to enable the authority the better to perform its own statutory function, and secondly, in the public interest. The public interest is always capable of justifying or excusing, or even mandating disclosure of confidential material.

Disclosure of documents without the consent of the subject is far more problematic. For example, the Department of Health Guidance cites only two justifications: for 'social work purposes' or 'in strictly limited and exceptional cases, where the law or the public interest may override the subject's right to confidentiality' (para 16). Under the former, in the context of a department or another organisation discharging its statutory function, the Guidance says that disclosure can be made where a 'committee of inquiry may need to have personal information in considering a case'. Under the latter there is, perhaps regrettably, no explicit reference to disclosure to a public inquiry. Although this can be read as permitting disclosure, this is not the invariable interpretation placed on the Guidance by authorities and departments. Greater clarity and explicitness would undoubtedly be welcome. **We so recommend**.

Guidance to doctors from the General Medical Council does not at present enunciate in clear terms any right or duty to breach confidence in the cause of co-operating with an Inquiry. The only exception to the obligation of confidence to which the Inquiry can point is contained in Rule 81(g) of the GMC's 'Blue Book' on Professional Conduct and Discipline, that the public interest 'might override the doctor's duty to maintain confidentiality'. Yet for the doctor concerned the choice is unenviable. Faced with a complaint to the GMC from his erstwhile patient, he/she might be able to persuade the Council that Rule 81(g) was in point, but there appears to be no precedent to reassure. There is no system, moreover, whereby the doctor can obtain an advisory ruling. After consultation with his medical defence society, a general practitioner, who was approached by the Inquiry set up by South Devon Healthcare Trust, declined to take the risk.

If it is desired that Inquiries should continue to be set up on a non-statutory basis, we see advantage in clarifying circular guidance to ensure that co-operation and disclosure is explicitly stated to be proper. It might also assist if the GMC and UKCC, and any other professional bodies, were asked to clarify their disciplinary codes, stating whether the giving of evidence to a Public Inquiry constitutes grounds for overriding confidentiality.

There is an arguable case for saying that the High Court may be available to require the attendance of witnesses or the production of documentary evidence. There is a rule in the Rules of the Supreme Court – Order 38, rule 19(1) – which authorises the Crown Office to issue a subpoena 'in aid of an inferior court or tribunal'. To qualify as an 'inferior tribunal' the Public Inquiry would need to be recognised by law and in its functioning be acting judicially or quasi-judicially. In a case involving a police disciplinary inquiry – *Currie* v. *Chief Constable of Surrey* [1982] 1WLR215 – the court said that the tribunal need not be statutory. In that case the disciplinary body was created by regulations made pursuant to statute. An Inquiry after homicide, set up under the compelling Guidance from the Department of Health ('it will always be necessary to hold an independent inquiry, in cases of homicide') may on the face of it not be legally recognised or acting quasi-judicially. But both prerequisites for the issue of a subpoena may flow from the fact that Public Inquiries are nowadays clearly susceptible to judicial review. Twice in recent times non-statutory Public Inquiries have been the subject of challenge in the courts. In the Ashworth Hospital Inquiry the Prison Officers Association sought to prevent the Secretary of State for Health from converting the Committee of Inquiry into a statutory body. Mr Justice (Now Lord Justice) Kennedy said (Report of the Committee of Inquiry into complaints about Ashworth Hospital, Cmd 2028-I, Appendix 6E, p. 316):

> ... in considering the criticisms now being made it is important to bear in mind that this Inquiry, whether with or without statutory powers, is like others that have gone before it – for example, Lord Scarman's Red Lion Square statutory inquiry and the non-statutory Strangeways inquiry conducted by Woolf LJ – just an Inquiry. It is by nature inquisitorial, not adversarial. No one is on trial even if at times certain individuals feel tempted to suggest otherwise. So decisions such as which documents are seen, which witnesses are called and how the witnesses are handled in terms of how much evidence is led, what cross-examination is allowed and to what extent attention is paid to rules governing the admissibility of evidence are all matters for the Committee subject only to the over-riding requirement that the proceedings shall be fair. Fairness may require some witnesses to be protected more than others, but what cannot be done is to say that the proceedings of an inquiry are fundamentally flawed just because, for example, formal discovery or cross-examination has not been permitted to go as far as it would normally go in a trial.

Public Inquiries, while remaining substantially free from legal rules and technicalities of the legal process, are nevertheless subject to judicial scrutiny which renders them like tribunals. If central government is unwilling to endow Public Inquiries with all the powers necessary to perform their inquisitorial function, it should ensure that no procedural obstacle is placed in their way. Since Public Inquiries will nearly always require access to disparate documentation from a variety of sources, the speedy assembly of documents can be the most important and difficult aspect of an efficient and effective Inquiry. The difficulty may in turn lead to a delay of a comprehensive understanding of the contents of documents, thus frustrating the process of early warning to witnesses of what they will be asked to give evidence about. There is no identifiable gain – indeed, there is clear disadvantage – from denying Inquiries statutory powers to require production of documents and the ability to compel witnesses. If it is the fear of central government having to bear incalculable costs of Public Inquiries with aspects of local government administration that precludes the benefits of unforeseeable powers, there should be at least the alternative method of obtaining such powers via the processes in the High Court. **We recommend** that the Rules Committee be invited to consider amending Order 38, rule 19, to make it clear that non-statutory Public Inquiries set up by central or local government qualify for subpoena powers.

XXV. Prisons and Mental Health Services: Interplay of Documentation

Reconciling the requirements of patient confidentiality and public safety can present problems throughout the [mental health] system.
Hale, *Mental Health Law*, 4th ed. (1996), p. 161

Jason Mitchell spent 18 months, from December 1987 to May 1989, in prison on remand and serving a two-year Youth Custody Order. During the period August 1988 to March 1989, he underwent 31 sessions with a visiting consulting psychiatrist at Feltham YOI, the medical records of which disclose symptoms tending to show the onset of schizophrenia. From the moment of discharge from custody in May 1989 into a hostel under supervision, the records of the penal system lay dormant, undiscovered and undisclosed to all those in the mental health system who had responsibility for Jason Mitchell's care and treatment from April 1990 onwards. The 'lost' records were also denied to probation officers and social workers who intermittently became responsible for Jason Mitchell's care and supervision in the community. How could it happen that one arm of government (the prison service) failed to inform another arm (the mental health services) of documentation relevant to their respective responsibilities?

It was not as if the first entrants on the mental health system had not tried to uncover the records relating to the earlier custodial period of 1988/9. Shortly after Jason Mitchell was remanded in custody to Feltham Remand Centre on 8 February 1990, Dr Dexter, the locum Senior Medical Officer, asked the psychiatrists at West Park Hospital to assess Jason Mitchell with a view to the Crown Court remanding him to hospital for treatment under section 36 of the Mental Health Act 1983. On 23 March 1990 Dr Richard Penrose, together with a staff nurse from West Park Hospital, visited Feltham. They asked to see any medical records, but nothing was forthcoming. The visitors were untroubled by the absence of records, either in support of the Youth Custody period in 1988 and 1989 or the six-week period of remand immediately preceding their

visit, simply because it was manifest to them that Jason Mitchell
was seriously mentally ill and required treatment in a secure
setting. Hence they did not, understandably, persist in their request. When preparing the psychiatric report of 10 August 1990 for
the impending hearing at the Central Criminal Court, Dr Pugh
wrote, on 23 July 1990, asking for copies of any medical notes. Mr
G.B. Robinson, a hospital principal officer at Feltham YOI, wrote
on 30 July that, after a thorough search had been made, he was
unable to locate any case notes for the years 1987 to 1989. No one
appeared to appreciate at that time that a search among the records
at Hollesley Bay YOI might have revealed the fact that that
establishment had been Jason Mitchell's last port of call before
discharge, and that authorisation of records might not have been
effective to transfer pre-1990 records from individual penal establishments. The transitional period of warehousing records no doubt
produced its own confusion.

When the Inquiry made its own request in the Autumn of 1995
to Hollesley Bay YOI, Jason Mitchell's IMR was recovered from
their archives. Fortunately the six-year rule for destroying records
had not been put into operation. (We describe the sequence of
events that led to the uncovering of the records in Annex 1 to this
Report.)

The impact of the records, post-1995

It was represented to us, mainly by Dr Goddard and his team at
Easton House, that our desire to canvass the reflections of clinicians and others, having been deprived of the knowledge obtainable
from Jason Mitchell's IMR of 1988-89, was to indulge in a hypothetical exercise. Dr Goddard told us:

> I wonder about the value of these hypothetical questions. If I may be
> so bold just for the moment to say again that I think they have very
> little value. I would have thought that the purpose of the Inquiry
> should be more concerned with what people did, how they performed
> in the light of the circumstances they found themselves in at the time
> and with the information that they had, and not too much in the
> 'would-have-beens', 'could-have-beens', 'should-have-beens' and the
> speculative, the conjectural, because, after all, how much weight can
> you put on these? They are responses that are going to be given with
> the light of hindsight and be coloured by the position people feel
> themselves in.

We do not think that a Public Inquiry is so restricted in its investigation. It must look into the events as they were circumstanced. Omissions from the events under scrutiny can be as revealing as admissions. Dr Goddard conceded that he could not disagree with the proposition that, if he had in fact been diagnosing and treating Jason Mitchell based on wholly inadequate information, he would have been protesting that it was outrageous that the mental health and penal systems had deprived him of vital information for him to carry out his responsibilities fully. Hence we did canvass with the relevant witnesses what impact, if any, the records might have had on their care and treatment of Jason Mitchell. Predictably, Dr Goddard said that, with the qualification of impermissible indulgence in the hypothetical, he would have been better informed of Jason Mitchell's medical history but thought it would not have deflected him from a diagnosis of drug-induced psychosis. It might have caused him to pause, but not to alter his assessment. Dr Yeldham, for her part, also denouncing resort to hypothesising, regarded the 'lost' records as strongly confirmatory of her diagnosis of schizophrenia. Dr Christie Brown, while not revising his view that the decision to give Jason Mitchell his conditional discharge was not necessarily wrong, did think that good practice would demand that *all* available information should be made use of in reaching any assessment.

We believe that records such as those compiled by Dr Latif are potentially of great clinical significance, and the importance of their transmission must be recognised by the Prison Service and its medical staff. The records in this case contained detailed descriptions of symptomatology arising from 31 interviews over a period of seven months when Jason Mitchell was 18, a vulnerable age for the onset of schizophrenia. They may have represented the starting point of his history of mental illness, and they would have affected how his subsequent presentations were evaluated and treated. From a clinical point of view it is of fundamental importance that such records are passed on to those subsequently involved in the patient's care.

This was also the reaction of other professionals who became in 1989 and 1994 responsible for Jason Mitchell's supervision and care in the community. Both Miss Christine Turnbull and Miss Jane Barnett told us forcefully that knowledge of Jason Mitchell's earlier psychiatric history of 1988/89 would have informed them in such a way that they would have put in place some psychiatric input to support Jason Mitchell in hostel or other accommodation, or have sought a placement in a therapeutic community out of hospital. It would also have led them to pass on the critical information to those voluntary agencies which were responsible for managing the accommodation.

It seems clear to us that the absence of knowledge about Jason Mitchell's mental health history was a handicap – even possibly a serious handicap – to Miss Turnbull in providing for post-discharge placement in May 1989. Had she known of the psychiatric problems evidenced by Jason Mitchell's sessions with Dr Latif she would almost certainly have arranged for some psychiatric input in the supervision of Jason Mitchell at the Richmond Fellowship hostel in Cambridge. Furthermore, she would have advised the hostel managers as to Jason Mitchell's mental health, quite apart from any psychiatric element in the supervision. It was one thing for all members of the medical profession, within and without the prison system, to have sight of a patient's medical records while in prison. It is another dimension to the problem of supervising mentally disordered offenders in the community. Those, whether in the statutory or voluntary agencies, who have the care of the mentally disordered in the community, must likewise be appraised of documentation indicating mental health problems. We deal with the issue of medical confidentiality hereafter. Before we do that, we describe the situation with regard to the keeping of medical records within the prison system.

The system of prison documentation

The origin of the single Inmate Medical Record (IMR) came in a 'Dear Doctor' letter of December 1986 from the Director of Prison Medical Services, Dr John Kilgour CB. The idea behind the change was two-fold: first, that an inmate medical record would be raised for every prisoner and the record would move around the prison system with the prisoner's transfer from prison to prison; and secondly, that the medical confidentiality for the IMRs should mirror the confidentiality principle within the NHS. Thus prisoners would retain their right to confidentiality of their medical records despite the loss of liberty involved in imprisonment. These two aims relating to medical care and treatment in prison have generally survived subsequent changes. Dr Kilgour issued a second 'Dear Doctor' letter in June 1987 which gave details of the documentation. The following year the Home Office issued to all prison governors and prison doctors a Circular Instruction (No 34/88) setting out what was called the Prison Medical Documentation Document. The new approach to medical records was in place when Jason Mitchell was serving his sentence of two years' Youth Custody. His IMR, raised in December 1987 when he was remanded in custody to Norwich Prison, circulated around the penal establishments until his release from Hollesley Bay YOI in May 1989.

In 1990 a fresh Circular Instruction (No 23/90) altered the storage arrangements for the IMRs. From December 1990 the IMR, on the prisoner's discharge from prison, went into central storage for retention. It was clearly envisaged that the centralisation of IMRs would include previous records. Jason Mitchell's IMR that was held by Hollesley Bay should strictly have gone to central storage. That it failed to make the journey remains, and must remain, an unexplained mystery.

Prison records have not yet been computerised. But Dr Rosemary Wool, Director of Health Care for Prisoners, told us that computerisation is under way. Plans have been made over the last two years but implementation has been dependent upon getting some pump-priming money. She expects that finance will become available for the next financial year. We add our voice of expectation that the existence of all prison records will be on computer by the end of 1996. Until there is a central database it will not be possible instantly to identify the location of medical records. It is apparent that considerable progress has been made since 1987/88 to ensure that IMRs remain with a prisoner's 'core' records and follow the individual prisoner through the prison system. It appears, however, that this system does not extend to remand prisoners. This is a defect that needs attention. It is important that mentally disordered offenders who, on sentencing, do not come into the penal system, but move from a remand situation to hospital or some community facility, are assessed on information acquired on remand. The more ill the offender, the more likely it is that there will be evidence to assist the courts and subsequently the clinicians. If it is claimed that what happened to Jason Mitchell's IMR in 1990 is unlikely to be repeated, all we can say is that when Jason Mitchell was arrested in December 1994 and sentenced to three terms of life imprisonment on 7 July 1995 the system did not access the IMR from his previous period of custody. The Prison Service is in urgent need of an electronic system for cataloguing and tracking prisoners' custody histories and the records, both administrative and medical, relating to these periods.

We recommend that the Prison Service should ensure that by the end of 1996 it has in place a database and a fully effective system whereby prisoners' IMRs follow them – including, importantly, those of remand prisoners – wherever they may be in the penal system.

The distribution of IMRs outside the prison system

Circular 34/88 requires relevant information from a prisoner's IMR to be communicated on the prisoner's discharge from custody to relevant medical practitioners in the National Health Service. There is general agreement that a prisoner's medical records should be treated no differently from a patient's records within the NHS. As soon as a person is registered with a GP the latter will have sent to him or her the records held by the patient's previous GP. The problem arises out of the fact that many discharged prisoners do not get themselves registered. The guidance in Circular 34/88, however, does not extend to the prison medical service sharing information with probation officers or social workers, although we heard some evidence that a prison medical officer, if requested, might give some inkling to a probation officer or social worker of some medical or psychiatric problem which the prisoner presents.

Dr Rosemary Wool, the Director of Health Care for Prisoners, referred us to the health care standards laid down in 1983 which included multi-disciplinary case-working. She pointed to a specific document, *Mental Health Services in Local Prisons* (1994), regarding multi-disciplinary care regimes and the need to establish good working relationships with local health and social services in the prison's catchment area. While this provides a broad indication of the forward thinking of the prison directorate, it falls short of inculcating into medical practitioners the need to share with probation officers who are preparing prisoners for supervised discharge all information about the prisoner's physical and mental health. The evidence which we received does not inspire confidence in thinking that the medical profession is receptive to a weakening, let alone an abandonment of the principle of confidentiality for medical records, although we detect a desire on the part of prison administrators to find a way of furthering the safeguards for public safety without jeopardising the precepts of the doctor-patient relationship.

In the handling of Jason Mitchell's case there was evidence, both contemporary and in retrospect, to indicate that there is even today a stout resistance to the disclosure of medical records outside the circle of fellow medical professionals. The medical actors of 1988/89 would not contemplate acting any differently today. Dr Latif told us that he had not prepared a report in 1989 for the probation service because he was never asked to do so. Mr Clarke, the current Governor of Hollesley Bay, informed the Inquiry that information from an IMR would be disclosed to a probation officer only with the prisoner's consent. Mr Strong, Health Care Manager at Feltham at the relevant time (and now the Governor of Huntercombe YOI), informed us that some prison medical officers who did feel able to alert a probation officer to the existence of relevant information on an IMR, were prepared to inform the probation officer only that there was relevant information on an IMR, the details of which would be passed to a GP on release. While this would, post-release, alert the GP to any past or current mental health (or general health) issues which might exist, it would not assist a probation officer at the time of preparing a prisoner for release to a hostel or other form of supported accommodation. The probation officer (and any receiving hostel) would be ill-informed and thus be in an insecure position about the propriety of any placement. And, as we have observed, many prisoners do not have GPs. Given the Probation Service's supervision responsibilities, probation officers are crucially placed to act as a link between the prison medical service and community health and social services. If mentally disordered offenders who are discharged from prison are to be supervised successfully, so as to avoid re-offending, it is vital that the supervision is fully effective. Where an IMR contains relevant information as to a prisoner's mental health, or to a potential risk of self-harm, such information should be made available to the prisoner's probation officer or social supervisor.

There can be little doubt that some way must be found to circumvent the civil libertarian argument (which we fully recognise as a primary consideration) that a prisoner should possess all the rights of a citizen (including confidentiality in the doctor-patient relationship) except those expressly or by implication taken away by the law. There is no express exception in the law that removes the right. Indeed, if anything, since December 1986 there has been an enhancement of such right by the separation of medical records from prison administrative records. Is there, by implication, any derogation or diminution of the right?

The prisoner who is seen by a prison doctor does not always do so voluntarily, unlike the ordinary citizen's visit to his GP or the outpatient clinic of a hospital. The prisoner will frequently undergo a medical examination against his will. On reception into prison, for example, the doctor is under a duty to examine the prisoner and note any ailment or medical factor. On other occasions – for example, certifying a prisoner as fit for removal from association, under the well-known Rule 43 of the Prison Rules, or fit to undergo any disciplinary process – the doctor will examine the prisoner. Furthermore, there will be matters communicated in the course of the doctor-patient relationship of which the prison doctor will be bound to inform the governor of the prison. Supposing a prisoner, in the course of seeking medical advice and treatment about his medication, informs the doctor of illicit drugs concealed in the prison. Confidentiality may be outweighed by the demands of prison security. So too, the argument might run that the probation officer or the social supervisor must be in possession of information about the discharged prisoner's physical and mental health, both for the sake of the ex-prisoner as well as of the community to which the prisoner is returning. Those who might have future contact with a discharged mentally disordered offender do have civil liberties to be protected.

In its impressive report on dangerousness, entitled *Dealing with Dangerous People: The Probation Service and Public Protection* (1995), the HM Inspectorate of Probation stated (p. 61):

> *Medical confidentiality*: Reference has been made to the importance of sharing information, albeit within clear boundaries imposed by protocols. There are important ethical issues surrounding patient confidentiality. This issue was beginning to create dilemmas for some doctors and probation staff, where medical information might have helped inform risk assessment or decision-making during supervision.

The report goes on to observe that the needs of victims were not always taken into account. It states that 'victims, particularly where a violent offence was involved, often wanted protection, reassurance and information at all stages of the criminal justice process'. We think that there are real differences between the citizen going to his GP and the prisoner receiving medical advice and care and treatment from the prison medical service. And we conclude that this justifies at least a modification, but not necessarily abolition of the principle of confidentiality in respect of all prison medical records. We would wish to preserve the principle but carve out a limitation which would safeguard public security. We offer suggestions that provide a field for choice.

We were initially most attracted by an ingenious suggestion from our Counsel, Mr Thorold. He observed that, since the Access to Health Records Act 1990, a patient is entitled to possession of his or her own medical records and thus the status of medical records has changed significantly. That is so, but the patient's right is not very different from a consent from the patient for disclosure to others, which has the effect of waiving any confidentiality. It has always been the medical profession's advice to doctors that medical records will be handed over if the patient consents to such action. Mr Thorold's proposal is that on reception into a penal establishment the prisoner should be asked to sign a document allowing the sharing between key professional workers of essential medical information. We do not feel confident that this would work. We think it is likely that many prisoners would refuse to sign any such document. We remind ourselves that when we first approached Jason Mitchell to waive confidentiality in respect of his medical records at West Park Hospital for the purposes of our Inquiry he was obdurate in refusing his consent. It was only a few weeks later when he was able to reflect on his position, that he readily acquiesced. And we feel uncertain about the reaction of the civil liberties lobby, which will regard the routine obtaining of prisoners' waivers on a proforma as being extracted compulsorily under the cloak of coercive powers intrinsic to the prison situation, in much the same way as the provisions in the Civil Justice and Public Order Act 1994 (sections 33 to 38) allowing courts to draw adverse inferences from an accused's silence are regarded as compelling an accused to incriminate himself or herself, and hence as unfair and a violation of international law on human rights. Mr Strong told us that when HIV was becoming a real concern the Prison Service adopted a 'need-to-know' policy on the disclosure of HIV status of prisoners. The policy was interpreted by some prisons as telling every Tom, Dick and Harry when X was discovered to be HIV positive. The memory of that is a distinct disincentive to operating a waiver system on reception. But we would not rule it out as an option. Mr de Frisching came up with an alternative proposal. Given the desirability of preserving medical confidentiality for prisoners, there is a need within the prison itself for some departure from the strict application of the principle. Key medical information may often have a direct impact on the management of a prisoner within the institutional setting. Suicide risk is one such situation. Prison staff will want to know in sufficient detail of the health aspects in order to make sensible management decisions. Once it becomes accepted that key medical information, short of disclosure of medical records, would be communicated through a system of case conference and joint working in the context of parole decisions and aftercare provisions, it would not be sensible or feasible to exclude the members of the probation service, working in prison and outside in the community in health and social services, from such information. That was Mr de Frisching's preferred route, and he was optimistic that it could be achieved, consistent with maintaining medical confidentiality. But he acknowledged that his preferred option required a level of sophistication and good communication that were too aspirational to command acceptance. And, in any event, who is to evaluate the 'keyness' of the medical information? Dr Latif in 1989 would have merely said that Jason Mitchell exhibited no psychotic symptoms, let alone a schizophrenic illness. Yet the notes disclosed Jason Mitchell hearing voices talking to him suggestive of an embryonic mental illness. It is the person who has direct responsibility at the time of the discharged prisoner's placement in the community who must assess the material in the medical records. That means nothing less than a direct line between the prison medical service inside and the health and social services outside. That is the third option.

Our chairman's preference, shared among the other four of us with greater or less enthusiasm, would be for Parliament to amend the prison and mental health legislation to provide, with suitable safeguards, that probation officers and social supervisors exercising statutory obligations in respect of mentally disordered offenders discharged from prison on supervision in the community should have access to prison medical records. It was a feature of the Mental Health Act 1959 that it provided that where a prisoner who had been receiving psychiatric treatment in prison but was not sectionable under the mental health legislation, there was a requirement on the prison service to send a report to the medical officer of the home area to which the prisoner was being discharged. That report would be forwarded to the GP once the prisoner had re-registered with a general practitioner. That statutory provision was not re-enacted in the Mental Health Act 1983. A variant on those proposals which would relate only to restricted patients would be useful, if limited in scope. Suffolk County Council submitted that whenever a Restriction Order is made by a criminal court the receiving hospital should, on request, be provided with a copy of the patient's IMR, assuming of course that the patient had been in the prison system. That could be achieved by a simple amendment to section 41, empowering the criminal court on making the Restriction Order, to authorise the availability of any prison medical records of the restricted patient. Alternatively, it could be the function of C3 Division of the Home Office to obtain from the Prison Service copies of any prison medical records.

We recommend that the question of confidentiality of prison medical records should be fully reviewed. As a first step towards such review we recommend that the General Medical Council and other professional bodies should be asked for their views.

XXVI. Inter-agency Information

All knowledge is of itself of some value. There is nothing so minute
or inconsiderable, that I would not rather know it than not.
                              Dr Johnson, quoted in Boswell's
                              Life of Johnson, vol. 2, p. 357

Suffolk County Council, in its helpful written submissions to us of
14 December 1995, acknowledges that relevant information regarding Jason Mitchell was not available to professionals and
others working in the multi-disciplinary teams of both West Park
Hospital and St Clement's Hospital. It comments:

> It is sadly a common finding of mental health inquiry reports (and
> child protection reports) that relevant information has not been
> recorded; has been misrecorded (or its significance diminished); or
> has not been sought, been made available to, or been known to those
> who are working with the relevant individuals.

We would unreservedly echo the concise statement of the present
position about the nature, volume and flow of information between
all those responsible for the care and treatment of patients and
others within the scope of mental health and Social Services. Our
Inquiry has disclosed one major area of deficiency in personal and
documentary communications, the failure to transmit information
contained within the Inmate Medical Record. Failures to share
information appear throughout our report and add nothing to the
insistent calls of earlier and, no doubt, contemporaneous inquiries.

Rather than tread the path of other inquiry reports, we content
ourselves with one observation. It is manifest from what we have
learnt in this Inquiry and from our knowledge of reports in other
mental health inquiries in the 1990s (Ashworth, Clunis, Robinson
et al.) and in child abuse inquiries in the late 1980s (Beckford,
Carlile, Cleveland, Orkneys *et al.*) that there is a tedious repetition
of the deficiencies and a deafening silence by way of governmental
response beyond exhortation in departmental circulars. While we
do not doubt that there have been improvements in recent years,
the failures still recur. We think that this is the result of a lack of
any overall review of a highly complex structure in which informa-

tion technology inevitably has a larger part to play. The question of communication between the providers of services, moreover, does not begin and end within mental health services. Education, housing, civil and criminal justice are all relevant services in this regard. This leads us to recognise that the topic is far beyond our expertise.

Our view, however, is that the time has come – if it has not already passed – for a thorough review of the whole subject of the supply and dissemination of information within the interlocking services to all those persons in need of treatment, care and control. **We recommend** that the government urgently considers establishing an independent committee (it does not need to be a Royal Commission, although that would indicate the high importance of the subject-matter) to review the subject.

Part J

Conclusions and Recommendations

XXVII. Conclusions: The Wider Perspective

We must make community care work if we are to avoid slipping yet further back to the pre-Dickensian era of neglect. The vision of real community care needs a united effort to push it back on to the political agenda. Better mental health services are clearly within our grasp now.

> Professor Elaine Murphy, *After the Asylums:*
> *Community Care for People with*
> *Mental Illness* (1991) p. 236

We have said at the outset of this report (Chapter II) that the killings in the village of Bramford in December 1994 were unpredictable and, in any meaningful sense, not preventable. In short, no one was to blame for the deaths of Mr and Mrs Wilson or Mr Mitchell, save for the perpetrator, Jason Mitchell. But it is possible to see ways in which, if the management of Jason Mitchell's case had taken a different course, the deaths of three people might have been avoided. In this concluding chapter we highlight a number of significant features of the present systems of criminal justice, the penal system and the mental health system in coping with mentally disordered offenders. Training for all those involved is essential.

First and foremost, we are advocating the use of a wider range of therapeutic regimes and methods of clinical assessment to encompass not just those who are diagnostically suffering from a recognisable psychiatric illness, but also those whose psychotic symptoms and gross emotional and behavioural maladjusments do not fit easily into psychiatric categories of primary mental illness. We ended Chapter II by noting that Dr Goddard had deliberately not adopted the psychodynamic approach to exploring and understanding Jason Mitchell's case because his clinical view of personality disorder would imply unresponsiveness to psychological approaches. The disciplines of psychiatry and psychology need to be much more clearly harmonised in their approach to this area of work.

Lack of teamwork between the medical and non-medical professional was never more evident than during Jason Mitchell's period in Youth Custody in 1988/89. Even if Dr Latif had been right not to diagnose schizophrenia, the 31 sessions he had with Jason Mitchell, which he copiously recorded in the medical records, should have suggested referral of Jason Mitchell's case to clinical colleagues and his aftercare needs to other professionals. Everything which Jason Mitchell was communicating indicated a strange young man who might at that stage be diverted from a depressingly predictable downward move into illness and more criminality. The rescue may have been possible then; it became increasingly an uphill and unfulfilling task. There are lessons, we think, to be drawn by the prison system in developing much more sophisticated regimes for young adult offenders. What we heard from Mr de Frisching about the Bittern unit at Feltham YOI would appear to provide a base for the development of psychological techniques, exploring the social backgrounds of these under-achievers of the educational system who find no compensation in stable family life. Containment of such disordered young people in prison without active constructive treatment, education and rehabilitation is a dereliction of duty to society as well as to those individuals.

The prison system is wholly dependent upon the activities of criminal justice. The adversarial principle of prosecution and trial militates against the widest dissemination of the circumstances leading up to and surrounding the criminal event. Early identification of the offender's mental disorder and diversion from criminal justice could profitably play a more prominent part in the management of offenders. The specialist needs of mentally disordered offenders call for precise assessment and for the provision of specialist services. General psychiatry cannot provide such services without the aid and assistance of forensic expertise and services. Where appropriate, criminal justice can provide the forum for a coming-together of the disparate professionals. And it is not just the professionals whose voices must be heard and heeded. The contribution from non-professionals who have so much more direct contact with hospital patients is often invaluable.

Once the mentally disordered offender becomes a restricted patient within the mental health system, it is the institutions of that system that bear the burden of safeguarding patient rights, including the Mental Health Review Tribunals. These are ripe for review (see Chapters IX and X).

The difficulties of adjudicating on applications for discharge must also confront the Discretionary Life Panels set up under the Criminal Justice Act 1991 to deal with the release and recall of discretionary lifers. The distinguishing feature is that the latter system apparently contains no power to defer release. The two parallel systems should be brought into alignment. Mentally disordered offenders may fortuitously pitch up in either system, with different release results.

Our penultimate Chapter (XXVI) exposes a perennial chestnut. The free flow of information among all those, present and future, who will be required to take responsibility for the care and treatment of mentally disordered offenders, is vital – and the most vital is the precise information available to those supervising in the context of community care. The responses of health and social services to the Secretary of State's recent (December 1995) pronouncement on the need to improve community care for the mentally disordered could usefully include consideration of our conclusions and recommendations.

XXVIII. Recommendations

The recommendations are presented in page order and are categorised as follows:

Category A: comprising those recommendations directed to Purchasers and Providers of health and social services in Suffolk.

Category B: comprising those of general application in the field of mental health.

A Suffolk Health invites the members of the Inquiry Panel to – reconvene, in private, within six months of publication of this report, to consider the responses, both official and unofficial, to the recommendations; and to report activity to Suffolk Health early in 1997.

B Significant contributions to clinical assessments by profes- **42** sional staff in disciplines other than psychiatry and nursing should be captured systematically, e.g. in the compilation of reports for case conferences, other reviews and hospital transfers.

B Social Services Departments which transfer case responsi- **46** bility for restricted patients should also transfer the case records.

B In any case where the criminal event involving a mentally **120** disordered person is serious or dangerous, it should be the responsibility of the Crown Prosecution Service to prepare a full account of the criminal event before criminal proceedings have been finalised. The CPS should also ensure that this account is transmitted, after the criminal process has run its course, to all those involved in the criminal proceedings, to clinicians subsequently responsible for the care of the patient, and to C3 Division of the Home Office in respect of restricted cases. The account should become an established part of the patient's clinical record.

B The Crown Prosecution Service should review its procedures **121** in relation to the prosecution of mentally disordered offenders destined to be routed into the mental health system through a Hospital Order.

B The Royal College of Psychiatrists, the Royal College of **125** Nursing and other relevant professional bodies, should issue guidance to their respective members not to rest content with information about the 'index offence' but to inquire thoroughly into the criminal events.

B Efforts should be made to ensure that the medical members **136** of tribunals dealing with restricted patients are forensic psychiatrists.

B The third category member of the Mental Health Review **137** Tribunal should be named 'other relevant discipline' and the Lord Chancellor's list should include a number of psychologists.

B The medical member of the tribunal should expect the **139** hospital to provide a set of summary documents with reports from the professionals involved in the multi-disciplinary teams responsible for the patient's care and treatment.

B The House of Lords' decision in *Secretary of State for the* **143** *Home Department v. Oxford Regional Mental Health Review Tribunal [1988] A.C. 120* should be reversed by law so as to allow a tribunal to adjourn an application in order to give time for a further examination of the patient's mental health before any decision to discharge is made.

B Four general measures in respect of restricted patients should be considered by the Home Office:

1. C3 Division of the Home Office should act as a repository **151** of information about the patient's index offence(s);
2. The procedures and practices of C3 Division could use- **151** fully be compared with Home Office practice in relation to Discretionary Lifer Panels;
3. The notes for the Guidance of Social Supervisors should **167** be reviewed and revised to take account of potential conflicts in the roles of social workers arising from changes in the Community Care, Mental Health and Criminal Justice legislation;
4. The Case Worker Guide should be updated to require **154** information not just from the RMO but from others who will bear responsibility for the after-care of the patient.

A Case conferences should be recorded more fully. **163**

A Where a breakdown in a community placement occurs, the **164** existing review systems should be implemented.

A Health and Social Service Purchasers should review the **165** balance of expenditure to see if a more specialised focus could be developed within the range of community-based residential services in order to provide a locally-based therapeutic service.

A The Purchasing Authority should consider developing qual- **165** ity standards applicable to the care of patients with histories of violent offending. Such standards might include requiring Providers to ensure that a full range of assessment approaches, including access to forensic psychiatry services, is available to such patients.

A An externally facilitated multi-disciplinary review should **165** be undertaken of the balance between behavioural and psychodynamic approaches at Easton House and the skills available to develop a greater degree of flexibility.

A External, peer group audit should be incorporated into the **166** Trust's quality assurance programme; and the Purchasers, perhaps in concert with the Department of Health, should develop contract monitoring measures more finely tuned to the needs of services for people with mental health problems.

A Purchasers should ensure that there is clinical audit of **166** hospital psychiatric teams to examine multi-disciplinary working and the representation of varied and possibly contradictory perspectives in clinical records.

B The Department of Health should draw together the existing **167** fragmented policy guidance on the role of Local Authority and Health Services staff in the care and after-care of mentally ill people in an integrated document of guidance.

B Internal reviews of practice following major untoward **167** events should be conducted by a manager with no direct line management responsibility for the case in question.

B Given the need for close networking between many agencies **168** and the establishment of supervision registers, some thought should be given by the Department of Health and the professional bodies to drawing on the best practice from child protection in developing an interagency approach to case management for mentally ill patients who are discharged into the community.

B In-patient units whose patients include offenders with dis- **170** turbed personalities should have access to specialist psychodynamic expertise.

B In respect of behaviour modification programmes and par- **175** ticularly in the absence of valid patient consent, a locally agreed procedure should be adopted in which the RMO should seek the advice of a suitably qualified person who is not a member of the clinical team responsible for the patient. This will normally be a psychologist, although some medical staff, social workers and nurses have received special training that equips them to supervise psychological procedures.

B RMOs and clinicians managing offender patients should **177** afford such patients regular interviews in private.

B All Police Forces should have formal Missing Patients **205** Procedures agreed with local hospitals and Social Services, and within these a system for inquiring into the circumstances of repeated absconding by detained patients, particularly those subject to restriction orders.

B The 'Appropriate Adult' system in criminal justice should be **216** re-examined with a view to extending its role.

B Employers, their legal advisers and insurers should find **221** ways of helping their staff make direct personal contact with bereaved families, unless the families do not wish for this.

B All authorities mandated to set up inquiries under NHS **223** Executive Guidance HSG(94)27 of 10 May 1994 should actively consider including in their Terms of Reference directions that families of victims should be given the opportunity to be present at any Inquiry into homicide, whether the Inquiry is held in public or private.

B A more direct, proactive and individual approach to the **223** members of victims' families should be adopted by all agencies engaged in crisis support work following homicides and similar events.

B The Secretary of State for Health should set in train a review **230** of the Mental Health Review Tribunal system in the context of a review of the Mental Health Act 1983.

B Police Forces nation-wide should commit themselves to **238** adopting the training and policies for dealing with mentally ill people, as currently practised within the Metropolitan Police.

A Purchasers of social care should ensure that an adequate **240** supply of forensic social work is available in their area.

B Any social services worker assigned the task of social super- **240** visor of a restricted patient should be an Approved Social Worker.

B The relevant Government departments should set a target **241** date by which time all social supervisors of restricted patients will have acquired the competencies in forensic social work set out by CCETSW.

B The Department of Health should ensure the funding of **242** adequate numbers of training places for Clinical Psychologists.

B All trainees in General Psychiatry should spend a period of **244** training in a forensic psychiatric service under the supervision of a Forensic Psychiatrist.

B General Psychiatrists taking up consultant posts with re- **244** sponsibility for secure beds should have had a period of training in forensic psychiatry.

B Arrangements for psychiatric training both nationally and **245** locally in Suffolk and in the Anglia and Oxford Region, should be reviewed and, if necessary, enhanced so as to ensure that all trainees in general psychiatry receive adequate clinical training, and experience in psychodynamic and forensic aspects of psychiatry.

A The new Suffolk Health Authority should review whether **245** the availability of forensic psychiatry services is sufficient.

B Attention should be given to identifying and meeting more **246** thoroughly the training needs of existing, as well as new Mental Health Review Tribunal members.

B Tribunal members should be informed about the clinical **246** outcomes for patients following discharge decisions, and confidential retrospective reviews should be held in cases where patients re-offend seriously after discharge.

B There should be greater clarity and explicitness in the **254** guidance concerning the disclosure of documents to public inquiries.

B The Rules of the Supreme Court – Order 38, rule 19(1) – **256** which authorise the Crown Office to issue a subpoena 'in aid of an inferior court or tribunal' should be reviewed by the Rules Committee to make it clear that non-statutory public inquiries, set up by central or local Government, qualify for subpoena powers.

B The Prison Service should ensure, by the end of 1996, that **262** it has in place a database and a fully effective system whereby prisoners' IMRs, including those of remand prisoners, follow them wherever they may be in the system. The provision should encompass access to the system for all those involved in the penal system.

B The question of confidentiality of prison medical records **267** should be fully reviewed. As a first step towards such review, the General Medical Council and other professional bodies should be asked for their views.

B The Government should consider establishing an inde- **269** pendent committee to review the subject of the supply and dissemination of information within the services dealing with people in need of treatment, care and control.

Annexes

1. Inquiry Procedure, Terms of Reference and List of Witnesses

Inquiry procedure

The Panel of Inquiry was announced by Suffolk Health Authority on 22 May 1995, with the following terms of reference:

1. To examine and assess the quality of treatment and continuing care of Jason Mitchell, leading up to his absence from Easton House, St Clement's Hospital, Ipswich on 9 December 1994, in particular the appropriateness of such care and treatment, having regard to:

    i. his socio-medical history, including any previous psychiatric treatment;

    ii. the index offence of 8 February 1990 leading up to the conviction at the Central Criminal Court on 10 September 1990 and any other relevant criminal events;

    iii. the deferred conditional discharge by the Mental Health Review Tribunal in September 1991 plus the similar order made by the Mental Health Review Tribunal on 6 April 1993;

    iv. his mental health while at West Park Hospital, 1991-93;

    v. assessments from time to time of risk of harm to himself and others;

    vi. any indications of deterioration in mental health immediately prior to 9 December 1994;

    vii. any behaviour of an unusual nature during the period of conditional discharge in 1991 and after care supervision, 1991-94;

    viii. the extent to which Jason Mitchell's mental health care matched the statutory obligation, relevant guidance from the Department of Health (including the Care Programme Approach. (HC(90)23/LASSL/(90)11) discharge guidance and local operational policies;

    ix. the extent to which any prescribed Care Plan for Jason Mitchell was effectively delivered to, and complied with by Jason Mitchell;

    x. the history both of prescribed medication and of the use of illegal drugs.

2. To inquire into the circumstances leading up to and surrounding Jason Mitchell's continued absence from Easton House, from

9-20 December 1994, in particular, to examine the adequacy of local
arrangements for dealing with patients who absent themselves
from hospital, the effectiveness and efficacy of such arrangements
and the exercise of individual responsibilities, including a review
of the aftermath of Jason Mitchell's absconding in February/March
1994.

    3.To examine the adequacy and appropriateness of inter-agency
arrangements for collaboration among, and communication be-
tween the relevant agencies – Suffolk Health Authority; East
Suffolk Local Health Services NHS Trust; Suffolk Police Authority;
C3 Division of the Home Office; Suffolk County Council Social
Services Department; Suffolk Coastal District Council Housing
Department; and East Suffolk MIND – in the provision of care or
control of Jason Mitchell, or of other services.

And to report to the Suffolk Health Authority not later than 31
January 1996 (or such later date as the Authority shall at any time
indicate) with such recommendations as the independent Panel of
Inquiry shall think fit to make. The Suffolk Health Authority
undertakes to publish the report in due course.

    The inquiry is to be held in such place(s) within the county of
Suffolk, as the Panel may determine.

    The Inquiry is to be held in public but the Panel may, if it thinks
fit, hold any part of it in private.

*

The composition of the Panel was as follows:

Sir Louis Blom-Cooper QC (Chairman).

Dr Adrian Grounds, University Lecturer in Forensic Psychiatry,
Institute of Criminology and Department of Psychiatry, University of Cambridge.

Mrs Pat Guinan, Consultant Clinical Psychologist, Psychology
Services Manager, CommuniCare NHS Trust, Blackburn.

Mrs Anne Parker, Simon Fellow, Manchester University (former
Director of Social Services, Berkshire).

Mr Michael Taylor, former Deputy Asst Commissioner, Metropolitan Police.

Mr Oliver Thorold, Counsel to the Panel of Inquiry.

Mr Brian Morden, Secretary to the Inquiry.

The Panel held a preliminary hearing in Ipswich on 2 August 1995 at which it set out its procedure. It granted legal representation to Dr Ray Goddard and to East Suffolk Local Health Services NHS Trust who were represented by Mr John Taylor (Solicitor, Hempsons) and Mr Howard Weston (Solicitor, Mills & Reeve) respectively. At the opening of the oral hearings at Thingoe House, Bury St Edmunds, on 25 September 1995, Mr David Mylan (Solicitor, T.V. Edwards) applied for legal representation on behalf of Mr Jason Mitchell. This application was refused, but the Panel indicated that two of its members (Dr Adrian Grounds and Mrs Pat Guinan) would visit Rampton Hospital to see Jason Mitchell, which visit Mr Mylan was invited to attend. The visit took place at Rampton Hospital on Sunday 1 October 1995. Dr Grounds and Mrs Guinan revisited Rampton on Wednesday 11 October 1995 and interviewed Jason Mitchell. Notes of the two interviews were circulated to the parties. Subsequent to the oral hearings Dr Grounds met Jason Mitchell's elder sister, Ms Fiona Mitchell. During the course of the hearings, legal representation was granted to Suffolk Health (Mr Colin Brown, Solicitor, Le Brasseur J. Tickle) and Suffolk County Council (Mr David White and Mr Christopher Jackson, Solicitors).

The oral hearings were scheduled to take place over a three-week period commencing Monday 25 September, 1995. Evidence was taken from the 51 witnesses listed below over the 11 days of 25, 26, 27, 28 September, 2, 3, 4, 9, 10, 12 and 13 October 1995:

Day	Witness	Date
1	Dr Jeremy Christie Brown, Consultant Psychiatrist, Maudsley Hospital	25 Sept.
2	Dr Denise Yeldham, Consultant Psychiatrist, South Devon Healthcare NHS Trust, formerly Jason Mitchell's RMO.	26 Sept.
	Mr Jonathon Eckersley, Social Worker, Suffolk	
	Mr Robert Buxton, Social Worker, Suffolk	
3	Her Honour Judge Shirley Anwyl QC (previously Shirley Ritchie QC), President of the Mental Health Review Tribunal, September 1991	27 Sept.
	Dr N Rathod, Medical Member, Mental Health Review Tribunal 1991	
	Mr B, fellow resident, MIND Hostel, Felixstowe	
	Mr D, fellow resident, MIND Hostel, Felixstowe	
	Mrs A, mother of Mr B	
	Mr A, step-father of Mr B	

Day	Witness	Date
4	Judge Uziell-Hamilton, President of the Mental Health Review Tribunal, April 1993	28 Sept.
	Dr David Duncan, Medical Member, Mental Health Review Tribunal, April 1993	
	Mrs Sandra Fox, Lay Member, Mental Health Review Tribunal, April 1993	
	Mr Jonathan Potts, C3 Division, The Home Office	
	Mr Nigel Shackleford, C3 Division, The Home Office	
5	Miss Jane Barnett, Social Worker, Suffolk	2 Oct.
	Mr John Gillett, Staff Nurse, Easton House, St Clement's Hospital	
	Mrs Joan Rapaport, Social Worker, Surrey – previously West Park Hospital	
6	Mr Ken Dunnett, Mental Health Act Administrator, St Clement's Hospital	3 Oct.
	Mr Ray Sheppard, Health Care Assistant, Easton House, St Clement's Hospital	
	Dr Ashraf Hanna, Senior House Officer, St Clement's Hospital	
	Dr Achmed Mahmoud, Senior House Officer, St Clement's Hospital	
	Dr Najy Hanna, Senior Clinical Medical Officer, St Clement's Hospital	
	Mr Graham Stannard, Enrolled Nurse, Easton House, St Clement's Hospital	
7	Dr Mark Ward, Consultant Forensic Psychiatrist, The Norvic Clinic	4 Oct.
	Mrs Jean Mason, Staff Nurse, Norwich Prison Hospital	
	Mr Andrew Palmer, Staff Nurse, Easton House, St Clement's Hospital	
	Mrs Yvonne Hines, Assistant Ward Manager Easton House, St Clements Hospital	
	Mr Ian Hartley, General Manager, East Suffolk MIND	
	Ms Fiona Gilmour, formerly Project Manager, East Suffolk MIND	
	Ms Tina Graves, Housing Services Manager, East Suffolk MIND	
	Ms Sally Harrington, Project Manager, East Suffolk MIND	
8	Dr Hadrian Ball, Consultant Forensic Psychiatrist, The Norvic Clinic	9 Oct.
	Mr Brian Davis, Primary Nurse, Easton House, St Clement's Hospital	
	Dr M Mohammed, Senior House Officer, St Clement's Hospital	

Day	Witness	Date
8	Mr Vincent Lightbody, former Ward Manager, Easton House, St Clement's Hospital	9 Oct.
	Det. Supt. Peter Worobec, Suffolk Constabulary	
	Det. Const. Paul Royal, Suffolk Constabulary	
	Mrs Jackie Leaver, Technical Instructor, OT Dept., West Park Hospital	
	Dr Koye Odutoye, former Senior House Officer, St Clement's Hospital	
9	Mrs Jane Rutherford, Director of Strategy, Suffolk Health	10 Oct.
	Mrs Janet Dillaway, Assistant Director, Suffolk Social Services	
	Mr David Long, Chief Executive, East Suffolk Local Health Services NHS Trust	
	His Honour Judge Henry Palmer, Regional Chairman, South Thames Mental Health Review Tribunal	
	Mr Craig Marchant, Solicitor	
	Ms Erica Smiter, former Head Occupational Therapist, St Clement's Hospital	
	Miss Jane Barnett, Social Worker, Suffolk	
	Ms Penny Healey, Art Therapist, St Clement's Hospital	
10	Dr Ian Wilson, Consultant Forensic Psychiatrist, Rampton Special Hospital	12 Oct.
	Miss Christine Turnbull, Probation Officer, Suffolk	
	Dr Ray Goddard, Consultant Psychiatrist, St Clement's Hospital, East Suffolk Local Health Services NHS Trust,	
11	Mr Christopher Wilson, son of Arthur and Shirley Wilson (deceased)	13 Oct.
12	Dr Ray Goddard, Consultant Psychiatrist, St Clement's Hospital	16 Nov.
	Dr Mohamed Latif, Visiting Consultant Psychiatrist, Feltham YOI	
	Mr Nigel Warren, former Senior Medical Officer, Feltham YOI	
	Mr Michael Clarke, Governor, Hollesley Bay YOI	
	Dr K Yates, Medical Officer (part time), Hollesley Bay YOI	
13	Miss Jane Barnett, Social Worker, Suffolk	17 Nov.
	Dr Rosemary Wool, Director, Prison Health Care for Prisoners	
	Dr Paul Bowden, Consultant Forensic Psychiatrist, Maudsley Hospital	
	Miss Christine Turnbull, Probation Officer, Suffolk	

Day	*Witness*	*Date*
13	Mr Martin Garside, Assistant Chief Probation Officer, Suffolk	17 Nov.
	Mr Arthur de Frisching, former Governor, Feltham YOI	
	Mr Derek Strong, former Health Care Manager, Feltham YOI	

Evidence was given in public, with the exception of seven witnesses. Mrs Jackie Leaver, a Technical Instructor (Occupational Therapy Dept.) at West Park Hospital in 1991, when Jason Mitchell was a patient, gave her evidence in a private session on the 9 October 1995. The Panel decided that she should be allowed to give evidence in private because earlier in the hearings, a headline in the *East Anglian Daily Times* on Wednesday 27 September had proclaimed: 'Killer's liaison with therapist.' The innuendo of an improper and unprofessional relationship with Jason Mitchell proved to be inaccurate.

On Wednesday 27 September 1995, the Panel journeyed to Felixstowe to hear evidence in a private from Mr B and Mr D, two former residents at the East Suffolk MIND Hostel in Larkhill Way, and Mr B's mother and stepfather. The Panel decided that, to have requested any of them to attend the oral hearings at Bury St Edmunds and given evidence in public, would have been unreasonable and inappropriate in the circumstances.

Penelope Healey, Art Therapist, St Clement's Hospital, requested, with the support of her managers, that she be allowed to present, in camera, Jason Mitchell's collection of drawings and paintings which he had done attending art therapy sessions while at St Clement's Hospital. The Panel agreed that it would be inappropriate to deny this request, given the nature of the material and the need for it to be regarded strictly in context; the viewing took place on Tuesday 10 October 1995.

The only other evidence that the Panel was requested to take in private session, and agreed to do so for reasons for sensitivity, came from Christopher Wilson, son of the deceased, who addressed the Panel on behalf of himself and his sisters Kathryn Clemence and Jill Benson on Friday 13 October 1995.

The privilege of giving evidence in person accorded to these witnesses was not accompanied by any appearance of anonymity in the report, although it was agreed that the art therapy material would not appear in the report per se. The witnesses' evidence (including a note of unscripted interventions) were available on transcript for the parties.

During the course of the Inquiry, in excess of 180 witness statements were obtained, some directly, some indirectly and considered in addition to the documentation assembled from all the relevant organisations and agencies.

The planned procedure of the oral hearings was unexpectedly and abruptly interrupted on Thursday 12 October 1995 for reasons explained below. When Jason Mitchell was held on remand at Feltham YOI in February and March 1990, he was assessed for suitability as a patient at

West Park Hospital under an Interim Hospital Order. To that end, Dr Penrose visited Feltham, in the course of which he asked to see any medical records pertaining to the period 1988/89 when Jason Mitchell had been in Feltham YOI. He was told that none was extant. Subsequently, Dr Pugh wrote seeking any medical records in July 1990 with a view to composing a psychiatric report for the impending proceedings at the Central Criminal court. The Hospital Principal Officer replied that 'after a thorough search, I have been unable to locate any case notes for the years 87-89'. There the matter rested. No medical records were forthcoming at any time from then onwards, and no one involved in the discharge process of 1991 to 1994 had any sight of the records.

The Inquiry Secretariat, being aware of this, nevertheless wrote to the Governor at Feltham YOI and duly received a written response in a similar vein. It was decided to ask the same question of the Governor of Hollesley Bay YOI, where Jason Mitchell had also been detained during the period in question. The initial response was a negative one, with the promise of a more extensive search. During the morning of Thursday 12 October 1995, the Secretariat was advised that the records had been located and all that was required in order to obtain them was Jason Mitchell's consent to their disclosure. The miracles of modern technology, plus the goodwill and continuing help of Dr Wilson's secretary at Rampton Special Hospital, resulted in the documents being despatched by road and delivered to the Secretary in the early evening. The Panel examined the records and deliberated late into the night.

The official transcript for 13 October 1995 records the Chairman's explanation to all present of the circumstances that had arisen and the Panel's decision, subject to taking the evidence of Christopher Wilson in private session, to conclude the hearings for that day and to adjourn the oral hearings until a date to be fixed, probably some time in November.

The Chairman further explained that the Panel believed there to be a great deal of material that required a very thorough investigation and almost certainly the calling of fresh witnesses who were responsible for the care and treatment of Jason Mitchell during that period. Also, there were a number of witnesses who had given evidence in ignorance of the documentation now uncovered. Such witnesses would be supplied with the material to enable them to consider what further evidence they would wish to give to the Panel of Inquiry.

The Panel resumed its oral hearings on Thursday 16 and Friday 17 November 1995, this time in Ipswich; by which time responses had been received from those who had been made aware of additional evidence.

The fresh witnesses who agreed to attend and to give oral evidence on 16 and 17 November 1995 and those recalled to give additional evidence are listed earlier. Dr Goddard also completed giving his evidence on 16 November and the oral hearings were concluded the following day, as planned.

2. Statement of Christopher Wilson, Kathryn Clemence and Jill Benson

My name is Christopher Edward Wilson. I am the son of Arthur and Shirley Wilson who were killed on 12 December 1994 by Jason Mitchell.

First of all, I would like to thank the Panel for the opportunity to make this statement. At an early stage, probably as early as January 1995, we, as a family, discussed whether a Public Inquiry should be held and we all agreed that there should be an Inquiry, mainly for two reasons; first, to publicise any deficiency in the care and community programme and, secondly, and probably more important from our point of view, to find out more about the person that killed our parents and the reasons why.

Unfortunately, there are still many questions that need to be answered. I am not much further forward in understanding fully Jason Mitchell's state of mind but I have learned a great deal about the care and community programme and the way various agencies work. I attended most of the Inquiry and on those days that I was unable to attend, my sister Kathryn attended. As a result, there are some matters which I feel I would like to address.

I have not had the opportunity to see the reports and statements supplied. I have not seen the reports and statements supplied to the Panel and also seen by the various agencies. Having said that, I probably know as much as anybody and more than most, of events that occurred during the period 10 December until the following week.

Certain information has been made available to me by the Police from evidence and from statements made by third parties, and also from statements made by Jason Mitchell. I have no reason to doubt the accuracy of the information that has been supplied to me.

During the Inquiry, it has been suggested on at least four occasions that the deaths of my parents may have been the result of a burglary that went wrong. I do not agree with that view, and neither do the Police.

It may be a convenient explanation for some people if it can be shown that the murder of my parents was a criminal act rather than due to a psychotic illness. It was briefly mentioned by Dr Wilson and he said that it was feasible, but on cross-examination by Mr Thorold, he said that it was unlikely to be the ultimate explanation.

Every time I heard this suggestion it annoyed me and I would therefore suggest an alternative scenario to try to illustrate, in my view, that was not the case. It may also go some way to explaining the mental instability of the person that killed my parents.

On the night of Saturday 10 December, someone attempted to break into my parents' bungalow. There is no question about that. During interviews with the Police, Jason Mitchell said it was him. He suggested to them, and this was mentioned in the prosecution statement at the trial: 'I knew the Wilsons and intended to kill them.'

He also suggested that he was intending to kill on each Sunday leading up to Christmas and then on the 12 days of Christmas. May I remind you this was a Saturday night/early Sunday morning. He was, however, unable to access the premises as it was very secure.

On Monday 12 December, my mother left the house during the morning. She travelled into Ipswich to have Christmas lunch with some friends. My father was at home busying himself. During the early afternoon, he was seen at the front of the house washing his car. The back door was left open and Jason Mitchell has admitted to the Police that he accessed the premises through that door. He went through the conservatory and picked up some tree ties that were in the conservatory, as was mentioned by Mr Thorold, and hid in the back bedroom. Jason Mitchell was in the house from early afternoon.

My father came back into the house and, shortly after, left the premises in the car. We suspect he went to fill the car up with petrol, perhaps did some shopping, we do not know. Jason Mitchell was in the house at this time. He had the opportunity to leave. There was money in the house, in excess of £300, not hidden but clearly visible. A burglar could have taken that money and left. My father came back home and my mother returned some time later on the bus with a friend. Jason Mitchell was still in the house. My mother changed and she telephoned my wife at 4.30 pm. Soon after that, Jason Mitchell was either discovered or he revealed himself and killed my parents. He was hiding in the house for over two hours.

I would like to present some further facts which, in my mind, are inconsistent with a burglary that went wrong. Jason Mitchell did not panic. He shut all the curtains and the blinds. He had a cigarette, a Red Band, which was extinguished into an ornament in the hall. He went into the kitchen and we have on good authority that he ate some of my parents' tea. He took £25 from my father's wallet – only £25 although there was considerably more money in the house. He left the house, locked it and, according to the prosecution statement at the trial, dropped a knife in the garden and then went to a bed and breakfast. In my view, that is not a burglary that has gone wrong.

If I could go on to other matters: Jackie Leaver's long report of early 1991, which includes details of the fantasies that Jason Mitchell told her, has been disregarded by some. According to Dr Goddard, because it was prepared by an untrained person, it was weighted accordingly. There are, however, some interesting points, to my mind, that come out of that report. Jason Mitchell mentioned to Jackie Leaver the purchase of knives. I have noted five occasions where knives have been a relevant factor: At the index offence, Jason Mitchell attacked the church warden with a baseball bat and was also alleged to have been in possession of two knives. Miss Turnbull mentioned the use of a knife at the Richmond Fellowship hostel. At Larkhill, there was some reference to a knife when he attacked one of the other patients with a hammer. I have seen it reported that he threatened an off-licence member of staff with a knife. At Bramford he disposed of a knife in the garden.

In the fantasies, he also mentioned killing a vicar at Bramford. My father was not a vicar but they lived next door to the church. During the weekend that Jason Mitchell absconded, my father was in and out of the church on many occasions, taking items for a jumble sale in and out. There may be some relevance there.

The other point that I found interesting was that in the fantasies, Jason Mitchell said that he would visit a bed and breakfast after the event. That is precisely what he did on 12 December. He did not go home although he lived around the corner. Was he possibly living out his fantasy? Were there warning signs that should have been identified by others?

If I could now briefly mention the evidence that has been presented during the Inquiry. I suspect from the outset that there was going to possibly a 'them and us' situation; it was natural. Witnesses are obviously going to be careful about what they say.

That is my observation and the Panel may feel that I have the picture wrong. However, it was interesting to note that when Mr Weston and Mr Taylor questioned certain witnesses, they had remarkable recall, but on cross-examination by Mr Thorold, they seemed to have extraordinary difficulty in remembering basic facts.

The Panel have investigated thoroughly the passing of previous records, information and details of previous history and I feel it is a very important aspect of the Inquiry. After three weeks further information came to light which, in my view, clearly gave indications of a psychotic illness prior to the index offence. If this information had been made available, different opinions may have been reached.

A further point, before I conclude, relates to the drug-induced psychosis. Great play has been made by certain witnesses of the possibility of drug abuse. I have not heard a scrap of evidence to support this view. It has all been hearsay possibility. I accept that there is a possibility that Jason Mitchell *may* have been a drug user, but no one has convinced me of that. If there was this great concern, why were greater efforts not made to test for drug abuse?

Dr Goddard mentioned the trip to Amsterdam and his explanation for the purpose of that trip. Did Jason Mitchell even go to Amsterdam? We have heard witnesses say that Jason Mitchell lies and fabricates. There is no doubt that he ended up at Epsom. However, he seems to have made this journey from England to Amsterdam and back to England and then ends up in Epsom, of all places, possibly accidentally, I agree, but we do not know the circumstances surrounding that trip.

My family accepts that there is no place in society today for the old style asylums but there must be adequate facilities to replace those types of institutions.

There has been a lot said during the Inquiry about integrating Jason Mitchell into the community. Words used by various witnesses have, however, described him as intimidating; manipulative; dangerous; potentially violent; becomes agitated; is difficult; is disruptive; hostile; fakes and mimics; he lies; winds people up; absconds; his appearance is threatening; he hears voices; he mutters and talks gibberish; is possibly psychotic and warped. One nurse described him as a 'model patient'. I question whether he was suitable to be integrated into the community at all and this view has also been expressed by some witnesses, including Dr Bowden.

Every agency has gone into great detail to explain their role of the care and control of Jason Mitchell and their aspirations for him. We must not forget that he is now locked away for a long, long time. He is also a victim; and I say to those agencies, you have all failed him.

3. International Instruments on Mental Health

The European Convention on Human Rights

The provisions of the European Convention for the Protection of Human Rights (195) which are of relevance to patients with mental disorder are as follows:

Article 3: 'No one shall be subjected to torture or to inhuman or degrading treatment or punishment.'

Article 5.1: This Article guarantees the 'right to liberty and security of the person' but defines a certain number of exceptions 'in accordance with a procedure defined by law' of which Article 5.1(e) includes the lawful detention of 'persons of unsound mind'.

Article 5.2: 'Everyone who is arrested shall be informed promptly, in a language which he understands, of the reasons for his arrest and any charges against him.' This is interpreted to cover detained psychiatric patients as well as accused persons.

Article 5.4: 'Everyone who is deprived of his liberty by arrest or detention shall be entitled to take proceedings by which the lawfulness of his detention shall be decided speedily by a court and his release ordered if the detention is now lawful.'

To date the law, developed by the Commission and Court of Human Rights, has dealt with procedural safeguards. It may well be that the next area of attention for these bodies will be the conditions of confinement and the right to treatment and therapeutic standards. This may be done in the context of Article 3.

In this context the provisions of the European Convention for the Prevention of Torture and Inhuman or Degrading Treatment Punishment (1987) should be noted. This is a Council of Europe Convention establishing a Committee which may visit places of detention to investigate the treatment of detainees. The Committee reports to the Council's Committee of Ministers. The Convention came into force in 1989, and the State is now obliged to provide facilities and information to the visiting Committee in relation to all places of detention, including psychiatric hospitals.

United Nations Convenant

The UN Covenant on Civil and Political Rights provides at Article 9 that:

(i) Everyone has the right to liberty and security of person. No one shall be deprived of his liberty except on such grounds and in accordance with such procedures as are established by law.

(ii) Anyone who is arrested shall be informed, at the time of arrest, of the reasons for his arrest and shall be promptly informed of any charges against him ....

(iii) Anyone who is deprived of his liberty by arrest or detention shall be entitled to take proceedings before a court, in order that the court may decide without delay on the lawfulness of his detention and order his release if the detention is not lawful.

These rights are almost coterminous with those under the European Convention, except that the right to information is 'at the time of arrest'.

Article 7 of the Convenant provides that 'no one shall be subjected to torture or to cruel, inhuman or degrading treatment or punishment. In particular, no one shall be subjected without his free consent to medical or scientific experimentation.'

Article 10.1 provides that 'all persons deprived of their liberty shall be treated with humanity and with respect for the inherent dignity of the human person'.

The Human Rights Committee set up under this Covenant has been very active in protecting the rights of mentally ill patients internationally, and has made it clear that Articles 7 and 10.1 apply to them.

UN Principles for the Protection or Persons with Mental Illness and the Improvement of Mental Health Care

(Adopted by the General Assembly 17 December 1991)

Application

These Principles shall be applied without discrimination of any kind, such as on grounds of disability, race, colour, sex, language, religion, political or other opinion, national, ethnic or social origin, legal or social status, age.

Definitions

In these Principles:

'Counsel' means a legal or other qualified representative;

'Independent authority' means a competent and independent authority prescribed by domestic law;

'Mental healthcare' includes analysis and diagnosis of a person's mental condition and treatment, care and rehabilitation for a mental illness or suspected mental illness;

'Mental health facility' means any establishment, or any unit of an establishment, which as its primary function provides mental health care;

'Mental health practitioner' means a medical doctor, clinical psychologist, nurses, social worker or other appropriately trained and qualified person with specific skills relevant to mental health care;

'Patient' means a person receiving mental health care and includes all persons who are admitted to a mental health facility;

'Personal representative' means a person charged by law with the duty of representing a patient's interests in any specified respect or of exercising specified rights on the patient's behalf, and includes the parent or legal guardian of a minor unless otherwise provided by domestic law;

'The review body' means the body established in accordance with Principle 17 to review the involuntary admission or retention of a patient in a mental health facility.

Principle 16

2. Involuntary admission [to a mental health facility] or retention shall initially be for a short period as specified by domestic law for observation and preliminary treatment pending review of the admission or retention by the review body. The grounds of the admission shall be communicated to the patient without delay and the fact of the admission and the grounds for it shall also be communicated promptly and in detail to the review body, to the patient's personal representative, if any, and, unless the patient objects, to the patient's family ....

Principle 17

Review Body

1. The review body shall be a judicial or other independent and impartial body established by domestic law and functioning in accordance with procedures laid down by domestic law. It shall, in formulating its decisions, have the assistance of one or more qualified and independent mental health practitioners and take their advice into account.

2. The review body's initial review, as required by paragraph 2 of Principle 16, of a decision to admit or retain a person as an involuntary patient shall take place as soon as possible after that decision and shall be conducted in accordance with simple and expeditious procedures as specified by domestic law.

Glossary of Terms

ASW = Approved Social Worker, appointed by Social Services to discharge certain functions as defined in section 145(1) of the Mental Health Act 1983

CCETSW = Central Council for Education and Training in Social Work

CPA = Care Programme Approach

CPN = Community Psychiatric Nurse

CPS = Crown Prosecution Service

C3 = A division of the Home Office containing a mental health section responsible for restricted patient cases

DLP = Discretionary Lifer Panel, a panel of the Parole Board which can recommmend the release of life sentence prisoners

ECHR = European Convention on Human Rights

ESLHS NHS Trust = East Suffolk Local Health Services NHS Trust, responsible, *inter alia*, for mental health services at Easton House, St Clement's Hospital, Ipswich

GMC = General Medical Council

HMP = Her Majesty's Prison

HMYOI = Her Majesty's Young Offenders Institution (see also YOI)

HO = Hospital Order, an order of a criminal court committing a mentally disordered offender to hospital under section 37, Mental Health Act 1983 – with or without a Restriction Order (see RO)

IMR = Inmate Medical Record, used for recording a prisoner's medical case and treatment while imprisoned

MDO = Mentally Disordered Offender

MHA = Mental Health Act (1983) or its predecessor (1959)

MHAC = Mental Health Act Commission for England and Wales

MHRT = Mental Health Review Tribunals, set up under Part V of the Mental Health Act 1983, to which patients have a right to apply for discharge from detention in hospital

NHS Executive Guidance HSG(94)27 = Guidance from the Department of Health on, *inter alia*, the conduct of public inquiries following a homicide committed by or on a mental health patient

PACE = Police and Criminal Evidence Act 1984

OT = Occupational Therapist

RCN = Royal College of Nursing

RCPsych = Royal College of Psychiatrists

RMO = Responsible Medical Officer, the registered medical practitioner in charge of the treatment of a patient in hospital

RO = Restriction Order, an order of a criminal court adjunct to a Hospital Order, made limited or unlimited in time, under section 41 of the Mental Health Act 1983

RSU = Regional Secure Unit
SAMM = Support after Murder and Manslaughter, a voluntary body giving
    support to families of homicide victims
SHA = Suffolk Health Authority
SHO = Senior Hospital Officer
SHSA = Special Hospitals Service Authority, responsible for the Special
    Hospitals at Ashworth, Broadmoor and Rampton
UKCC = United Kingdom Central Council for Nursing, Midwifery and
    Health Visiting
YC = Youth Custody
YOI = Young Offenders Institution

Index